# IRELAND AND THE KNOWLEDGE ECONOMY

## The New Techno-Academic Paradigm

Raymond P. Kinsella
Vincent J. McBrierty

Oak Tree Press

Dublin

Oak Tree Press
Merrion Building
Lower Merrion Street
Dublin 2, Ireland
www.oaktreepress.com

A catalogue record of this book is
available from the British Library.

ISBN 1 86076 112 7

Printed in the Republic of Ireland
by Colour Books Ltd.

The publisher and authors gratefully acknowledge the support of the
Higher Education Authority in the preparation of this publication.

# CONTENTS

# LIST OF TABLES

# LIST OF FIGURES

# GLOSSARY OF TERMS

| | |
|---|---|
| ARP | Applied Research Programme |
| ASEAN | Association of South East Asian Nations |
| ATS | Advanced Technical Skills Programme |
| BERD | Business Expenditure on Research and Development |
| CAO | Central Applications Office |
| CAS | Central Applications System |
| CEAM | Concerted European Action on Magnets |
| CSF | Community Structural Funds |
| DAE | Developing Asean Economies |
| DCM | Developing Companies Market |
| DIAS | Dublin Institute for Advanced Studies |
| DIS | Director of Innovation Services |
| DIT | Dublin Institute of Technology |
| ETIF | Education Technology Investment Fund |
| EFTA | European Free Trade Association |
| EMU | European Monetary Union |
| EIT | Economies in Transition |
| EPO | European Patent Office |
| ERU | Environmental Research Unit |
| ESRI | Economic and Social Research Institute |
| EU | European Union |
| FDI | Foreign Direct Investment |
| GATT | General Agreement on Tariffs and Trade |

| | |
|---|---|
| GDP | Gross Domestic Product |
| GNP | Gross National Product |
| GERD | Gross Expenditure on Research and Development |
| GOVERD | Government Expenditure on Research and Development |
| HE | Higher Education |
| HEA | Higher Education Authority |
| HERD | Higher Education Research and Development |
| HRB | Health Research Board |
| IDA | Industrial Development Authority |
| IFSC | International Financial Services Centre |
| ILO | Industrial Liaison Officer |
| IMF | International Monetary Fund |
| IP | Intellectual Property |
| IPO | Irish Patents Office |
| IPR | Intellectual Property Rights |
| IRDAC | Industrial Research and Development Advisory Committee of the Commission of the European Communities |
| NAFTA | North Atlantic Free Trade Agreement |
| NARC | National Aeronautical Research Centre |
| NBST | National Board for Science and Technology |
| NESC | National Economic and Social Council |
| NCCA | National Campus Company Association |
| NCCF | National Campus Company Forum |
| NCEA | National Council for Educational Awards |
| NMRC | National Microelectronics Research Centre |
| NIEC | Northern Ireland Economic Council |
| NPV | Net Present Value |
| NRDO | National Research Development Organization |
| NSC | National Science Council |

| | |
|---|---|
| NTMA | National Treasury Management Agency |
| NSI | National System of Innovation |
| NUI | National University of Ireland |
| OECD | Organisation for Economic Co-Operation and Development |
| OPT | Option Price Theory |
| OTA | Office of Technology Assessment |
| PAT | Programme for Advanced Technology |
| PCT | Patent Co-operation Treaty |
| R&D | Research and Development |
| RTC | Regional Technical College |
| SIA | Special Investment Account |
| R&TD | Research and Technological Development |
| RIA | Royal Irish Academy |
| S&T | Science and Technology |
| SMEs | Small-and-Medium-Sized Enterprises |
| STI | Science, Technology and Innovation |
| STIAC | Science, Technology and Innovation Advisory Council |
| TBFs | Technology-based Firms |
| TCD | Trinity College Dublin |
| TRIPs | Trade-Related Aspects of Intellectual Property |
| UCC | University College Cork |
| UCD | University College Dublin |
| UCG | University College Galway |
| UK | United Kingdom |
| USA | United States of America |
| USPTO | United States Patent Office |
| VSEs | Very Small and Micro-Enterprises |
| WTO | World Trade Organisation |

# OVERVIEW AND EXECUTIVE SUMMARY

This book builds upon an earlier study entitled, *Economic Rationale for an Enhanced Science and Technology Capability (Forfás, 1994)* which established the key performance parameters for the HE sector and its interface with the wider economy.

The thrust of the current study is to expand upon the concept of "knowledge equity" and its impact on Ireland's burgeoning economy, with special reference to the contribution of the HE sector. The underlying thesis of our research is predicated on a new 'Techno-Academic Paradigm'. It redefines the pivotal importance of the rapidly evolving interface between the HE sector and knowledge-driven industry as the central dynamic of economic growth.

This new paradigm reflects a convergence of knowledge-intensive industry and the HE sector which is being re-engineered and which, together, impart an unprecedented growth dynamic to the emerging 21st century economy. It provides an explanatory framework for the government's watershed initiative in 1998 to invest, through the establishment of an Education Technology Investment Fund (ETIF), amounting to £250 million, in "the development of scientific and technological education [in order to] meet the needs of a rapidly growing knowledge-based economy".

A number of important issues which are the essential foundation of strategic policy designed to promote sustained growth are addressed. Developments in Ireland, in effect, constitute a model whose success in fostering a growth path based on the technological competencies within the HE sector resonates with the latent potential of other small and emerging economies.

These issues include (a) the relationship between Science and Technology and the global economy, (b) the central role of institutions, including education, embodied in Human Capital in the "New Growth Theories" in which technology is treated as endogenous, (c) the nature and role of Intellectual Property, (d) the rapidly increasing contribution of the HE sector to job creation and retention; (e) the importance of the campus company sector, its governance as well as the need for innovative public and private financing mechanisms to support campus company development and, (f) an assessment of the adequacy of market-based and state financing of science and technology.

The substantive elements generated by the analysis in the book, together with the key recommendations based on this analysis, are presented in the summary Chapter 11.

# ACKNOWLEDGEMENTS

It is a pleasure to acknowledge financial support from the Higher Education Authority. Our research has benefited greatly from the help and advice of numerous colleagues, in particular, S. Brown, T. Cooney, F. Coyle, A. Fitzgerald, C. Keely, E. O'Neill, S. Martin and D. Mulvenna. K. Whitaker, L. Ryan and C. Power provided critical comment on the manuscript.

*Chapter 1*

# SCIENCE &TECHNOLOGY
# AND THE ECONOMY

## 1.1 INTRODUCTION: HISTORICAL CONTEXT

As the 20th century draws to a close, societies throughout the world continue to experience change of unprecedented proportions. This change is driven by an unrelenting growth of new knowledge and the science and technology that flows from it. When Francis Bacon penned his famous remark some 400 years ago, "for even knowledge itself is power", he could scarcely have imagined the enduring relevance of his wisdom.[1] Nor that it would foreshadow the advent of a global economy based on the generation and exploitation of knowledge.

Of course, there have been periods of comparable transition in the past: history is peppered with many examples of technological innovation linked to social innovation: the invention of the alphabet in 1000 BC and the printing press in the 16th century — the forerunners of current developments in information technology — are notable examples. Progress at the end of the 19th century in transportation, communication, and industrial practice, coupled with a renaissance in scientific understanding and burgeoning insights into the very nature of matter itself, have also profoundly altered the face of society.

Does the present scenario fit into Spengler's model of "romantic periods of investigation of nature and the invention of new theories giving way to periods of consolidation in which scientific knowledge ossifies", or is it something fundamentally different?[2,3] Two aspects of current progress would argue that it is. Firstly, as Horgan points out, the modern era of rapid scientific and techno-logical progress, viewed from the historical perspective, appears to be "a product of a singular convergence of economic, political and intellectual factors" which introduces a holistic dimension into the equation.[3] Secondly, the phenomenon is a truly global one for, as Yasuhiro Nakasone, former Prime Minister of Japan per-ceived:

> . . . science and technology have a universality that no political power or ideological creed has even begun to approach. Their relationship with culture and society is all-pervasive in their impact on areas of morality, ethics, religion and even aesthetic sensibility.[4]

Information technology in the form of electronic media has trans-formed the world into a veritable "global village" networked by a web of information super-highways. The impact of these devel-opments on societies continues to be so far reaching that they may well change the nature of the nation state itself and the way in which it is governed.[5,6]

The cumulative international effort in science that is driving the global knowledge economy derives from a mosaic of actions at international, national and regional level. These actions are sometimes initiated for economic reasons by industrialists, for reasons of intellectual curiosity by scientists, or for structural support reasons by the political process. Science is truly eclectic.

The effects of technological change pervade all of society, and not always for the better. As always, the law of unintended con-sequences operates. Myriad examples of the shortcomings as well as the benefits of new discoveries have created public anxiety, mistrust and ambivalence on a par with the technological anxie-ties of the last century. Affronts to moral and ethical standards, unwarranted invasion of privacy through the misuse of information data banks, and environmental pollution such as nuclear fall-out or acid rain are notable examples of deleterious side effects that diminish rather than enhance "quality of life" on a global scale. Takeda labelled the 20th century "the age of chaos".[7]

New knowledge with its attendant complexity and sophistication can either enhance or diminish quality of life depending on the manner of its implementation. It does not automatically bring new wisdom with it. One consequence is that more and more specialists are created with ever increasing information at their disposal. Is this generating a society of individuals who know more and more about less and less; in education, is there too much emphasis on information transfer rather than the ability to learn and to understand?

In formulating policy, the risks as well as the benefits of new technology must be clarified. Science and technology (S&T) policy cannot be divorced from society's perception, informed or otherwise, of the whole process of knowledge generation and its dissemination. For this reason, *quality of life* criteria are, quite rightly, being afforded increasingly higher priority in policy formulation. Rational organisational innovation in the management of new discoveries, based on informed judgement, must replace blind belief.

### 1.1.1 The Nature of Science and Technology

It is useful to distinguish between the terms *science* and *technology*. Whereas technology has been around since time immemorial, the *scientification* of technology has not. Colombo argued that, today, much of technology is born and develops on scientific bases, as a form of scientific knowledge itself.[8] The wheel, the printing press and radio are examples of inventions that predated the underlying theories that fully explained them, whereas the transistor and many biotechnological inventions grew out of established research. That progress can be in either direction is evident in the

innovation cycle, driven by new knowledge (market-push) or
market opportunity (market-pull).

Today, science and technology are converging and the bound-
ary between them is becoming increasingly obscured. The path
from science, through technology, into the market place can be a
tortuous one.[9] It is a complex non-linear process involving a range
of complementary inputs in addition to the R&D component
which accounts for no more than perhaps 60 per cent of the total
investment required to bring a new idea to the market.[10]
Prigogine, among others, recognised the need for a re-
conceptualisation of science and its impact on policy that takes
these more complicated issues into account.[11]

### 1.1.2 The Culture Gap

In light of the complex make-up of science and technology, it is
hardly surprising that difficulties arise in relation to the provision
of S&T advice to governments preoccupied on the one hand with
economic growth and, on the other, constrained by limited resources for investment in S&T and innovation. A key ingredient
in the innovation process is technology transfer between those
with the knowledge and those who seek to exploit it. Technology
transfer can occur within defined sectors (*intra*-sectoral transfer,
say, between different enterprises within the business sector) and
between different sectors (*inter*-sectoral transfer, for example,
between universities and industry).

Discussion focuses principally on *inter*-sectoral interactions
where successful technology transfer is predicated on the establishment of synergistic relationships between the following main
participants in science and technology, always bearing in mind
that society ultimately arbitrates the final outcome:[12]

• The knowledge generators who are an important source of
  skills and new knowledge and who play a key role in the dynamics of "New Growth Theories" (*c.f.* Chapter 2)

- Business and industry, as the end users

- Government as facilitator and significant source of funds

- Private finance equity institutions as catalysts.

If effective and balanced relationships are to be established, it is necessary first to understand the cultural differences and perspectives of the main participants, respect these differences, and then to bridge the barriers of language, attitudes, priorities and perspectives. Any process that attempts to impose one culture on another is ultimately destined to fail.

## 1.2 THE CHANGING FACE OF INDUSTRY*

The ability to harness the technology that flows from science for economic development, within an environmentally sensitive and supportive framework, is the key to national prosperity. The industrial sector has undergone major transformation and is passing through a second industrial revolution into a post-industrial phase. Already a third industrial revolution is signalled by the current unrelenting progress in information technology.

But the fruits of new knowledge can only be harnessed effectively within the global context. In this respect, nations are no longer fully in control of their own destiny. Specifically, technological and organisational innovation now transcend, and are no longer configured to, national or political boundaries.

Indeed, it is worth noting at this stage that the term "global" has to be redefined to take account of the fact that important dimensions of business transcend even the global context: space technology also drives developments in telecommunications, materials technology and, prospectively, natural resource management.

---

* Industry embraces all aspects of enterprise in the manufacturing and services sectors.

From the general perspective, there are a number of contributing factors:

- The emergence of new competitor countries like China, India, Argentina, Brazil, Mexico, South-East Asian nations and Central and Eastern European countries has had a significant impact on the central roles of Europe, the United States and Japan. They operate increasingly within the technology domain and are systematically exerting pressure on the competitive capability of the global triad — the EU, US and Japan. It is not yet clear how far the structural shock — reflected in depreciating currencies and Stock Market upheavals — which undermined the "Asian Tiger" economies in 1998, will impact on this scenario. The inherent resilience of these economies, underpinned by IMF policy conditionality attaching to financial assistance, is likely to contribute to a resumption of their growth trend over the medium term.

- Even within the dominant triad there have been major shifts: in 1981, the US government's non-defense per capita spending on R&D was 141 per cent that of the EU and 155 per cent that of Japan; by 1995, it was 96 per cent and 114 per cent respectively; by 2002 it is forecast to fall to about 50 per cent (Figure 1.1). [13]

- Different regions of the world are being integrated into single economic blocs with the concomitant removal of trade barriers (EFTA, EU, NAFTA, ASEAN, GATT). [14]

- Multinationals have become more decentralised and dispersed: "a world-wide web of added value" has been created whereby an increasing number of high-tech products now use components that are manufactured and assembled in many different countries. [15] This changes the rules for foreign investment into regions that seek to develop the multinational sector of their industrial base. Even a modest shift in the pattern of such investment could have a major effect on local employment. A central issue for policy is the following: will the contribution of local enterprise be high value-added or low value-added, high-tech or low-tech?

FIGURE 1.1: GOVERNMENT NON-DEFENSE R&D PER CAPITA FOR THE US, EU AND JAPAN (CONSTANT 1987 DOLLARS)

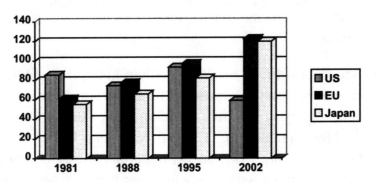

*Source*: Adapted from reference 13.

- Fragmentation and dispersion of the corporate giants has led to reduced employment (down-sizing or right-sizing depending on one's perspective), particularly at middle management level. According to Myers, the corporate workplace will continue to change radically over the next 20 years:

  highly vertical organisations, fully integrated, are going to become networked organisations which are rapidly formed, reformed and re-configured, depending on what is required to do the job.[15]

  In short, human capital has now entered the "disposable age" with enforced early retirements at one end of the scale, and short-term contracts, often without benefits, at the other.[16]

- The corporate giants are also becoming less dependent on in-house research and technological development (R&TD) and, increasingly, are reaping the benefits of access to "global knowledge networks". Permanent graduate recruitment into industry has declined as a result, although the current surge of inward investment into Ireland has reversed the trend in specific, high demand sectors. An OECD review noted that

> although many multinationals still locate their strategic R&D near their corporate headquarters, telemetric networks offer such firms new opportunities for the internationalisation of R&D, as well as for the international sourcing of technological resources.[17]

- Knowledge-driven Small to Medium Enterprises (SMEs) and even Very Small Enterprises of 10 employees or less (VSEs) are now emerging as the significant growth sector of the workforce (Table 1.1).[18] Campus companies linked to Higher Education institutions are an important subset of VSEs and SMEs. Evidence world-wide indicates that they are at the cutting-edge of this sector and are more likely to emerge as Fast Growth Companies.[19] In terms of innovation and the sustainability of the competitive advantage with which they imbue knowledge-driven sectors of industry, campus companies constitute an important new feature of industrial growth.

- The workplace is being transformed by a core of new technologies that have displaced the more traditional ones: they include information and communications technologies, biotechnology, eco-technologies, space technology, energy and new materials.[5] Knowledge, information and associated skills have displaced labour as the primary source of productivity and competitiveness. In short, brains have replaced brawn. On the downside, there is a growing problem of information overload and concomitant stress in the workplace.

TABLE 1.1: SIZE DISTRIBUTION OF ENTERPRISES AND EMPLOYMENT SHARE IN THE EU 12 AND THE US

| | Percentage of Firms | | Percentage of Jobs | |
|---|---|---|---|---|
| | *EUR 12* | *US* | *EUR 12* | *US* |
| Base (millions) | 15,780 | 5,074 | 95,000 | 93,469 |
| Micro-enterprises (0-10 employees) | 93.2 | 78.3 | 31.9 | 12.2 |
| Small enterprises (11-99 employees) | 6.2 | 20.0 | 24.9 | 20.0 |
| Medium enterprises (100-499 employees) | 0.5 | 1.4 | 15.1 | 14.4 |
| Large enterprises (> 500 employees) | 0.1 | 0.3 | 28.1 | 46.4 |
| Total | 100.0 | 100.0 | 100.0 | 100.0 |

*Source:* OECD, 1995; EUR 12 (European Network for SME Research, 1994), 1990; USA, 1990 (US Small Business Administration, 1993).

- The sustained decline in traditional agriculture over the last 100 years has been mirrored by a comparable rise in the information technology sector.[20] Note, however, that certain parts of the agri-sector have been revitalised by current developments in biotechnology. Industries based on design and publishing have also been revolutionised.

- Growth in the services industries has rapidly overtaken manufacturing industry. Successful banking, for example, is now predicated on a facility to effect electronic change of ownership and on timely access to information about money. Such information can be as valuable as money itself. On the down side, instant access to information has created much greater potential for volatility in global financial markets.

- Some commentators are concerned that an approach specifically designed to meet unreasonable profit expectations in the short term through a policy of excessive attrition — with an inevitable erosion of workers' trust, loyalty and commitment — will ultimately jeopardise the future viability of some industries. Stock markets, however, continue to respond positively to a sustained policy of attrition and excessive downsizing and show little sensitivity to the potentially deleterious consequences in the longer term.

### 1.2.1 Barriers to Innovation

The EU Green Paper on Innovation concisely articulates the difficulties experienced by innovators in Europe. Under the caption "Innovation in a Strait-Jacket", the Green Paper states that

> traditional Europe is suspicious and its enterprises tend to shy away from risk. Innovators are seen as a nuisance. Innovators are not only vulnerable at the outset but are faced with an interminable series of obstacles to creativity. Fighting one's way through the existing red tape often feels like running the gauntlet. The main handicaps and obstacles are those affecting the co-ordination of efforts, human resources, private or public financing and the legal and regulatory environment.[21]

The findings of a survey between EU Member States on barriers to innovation during 1990-92 reported in the Green Paper (Table 1.2) concluded that the most important blockages were finance-related followed by the internal competence of the companies and their ability to handle the innovative process.[22]

There are further barriers within the Higher Education (HE) sector itself which, increasingly, is at the cutting edge in terms of delivering the benefits of S&T to industry. The time available for research is dictated by a range of other prescribed duties that include teaching, examination, and administration. In some cases, aberrations in the system which limit the capacity of HE researchers to respond fully to the needs of industry have arisen because of an unprecedented growth in student numbers and chronic structural under-funding.

TABLE 1.2: BARRIERS TO INNOVATION (1990-92). % OF ENTERPRISES INDICATING RELATIVE IMPACT OF EACH BARRIER

| | Firm Size | B | GR | L | DK | D | IRL | I | NL | NO | UK | E |
|---|---|---|---|---|---|---|---|---|---|---|---|---|
| Lack of finance | 1 | 52 | 83 | 43 | 53 | 58 | 60 | 68 | 17 | 56 | 83 | 77 |
| | 2 | 53 | 67 | 22 | 53 | 61 | 50 | 63 | 36 | 50 | 63 | 80 |
| | 3 | 55 | 39 | 30 | 56 | 62 | 63 | 56 | 45 | 41 | 57 | 73 |
| | 4 | 69 | 64 | 21 | 60 | 64 | 60 | 61 | 59 | 45 | 58 | 84 |
| Lack of competence | 1 | 43 | 18 | 27 | 32 | 46 | 52 | 37 | 14 | 41 | 59 | 62 |
| | 2 | 34 | 13 | 7 | 36 | 49 | 34 | 33 | 29 | 54 | 44 | 66 |
| | 3 | 32 | 14 | 17 | 28 | 55 | 55 | 26 | 28 | 48 | 48 | 53 |
| | 4 | 26 | 14 | 11 | 26 | 48 | 35 | 25 | 33 | 36 | 32 | 76 |
| Lack of information | 1 | 26 | 40 | 2 | 23 | 33 | 45 | 33 | 7 | 25 | 37 | 52 |
| | 2 | 32 | 40 | 3 | 22 | 36 | 36 | 29 | 16 | 25 | 27 | 54 |
| | 3 | 24 | 29 | n/a | 17 | 33 | 36 | 24 | 16 | 22 | 43 | 43 |
| | 4 | 23 | 14 | n/a | 16 | 34 | 39 | 20 | 21 | 21 | 21 | 48 |
| Lack of technological opportunities | 1 | 35 | 16 | 16 | 31 | 37 | 38 | 40 | n/a | 31 | 39 | 46 |
| | 2 | 40 | 16 | 28 | 28 | 42 | 28 | 38 | n/a | 30 | 27 | 44 |
| | 3 | 28 | 7 | 17 | 24 | 37 | 41 | 36 | n/a | 26 | 22 | 36 |
| | 4 | 29 | 14 | 30 | 22 | 38 | 36 | 38 | n/a | 28 | 16 | 44 |
| Problems with intellectual property rights | 1 | 29 | 61 | 10 | 27 | 43 | 39 | 38 | n/a | 7 | 34 | 44 |
| | 2 | 28 | 48 | 8 | 19 | 54 | 26 | 32 | n/a | 6 | 23 | 46 |
| | 3 | 23 | 29 | 23 | 15 | 55 | 22 | 27 | n/a | 11 | 35 | 36 |
| | 4 | 24 | 45 | n/a | 16 | 45 | 27 | 28 | n/a | 5 | 16 | 51 |

1 = ≤ 49 employees; 2 = 50–249 employees; 3 = 250–499 employees; 4 = ≥ 500 employees; n/a = not available. Data for Greece and UK are not weighted. B, Belgium; GR, Greece; DK, Denmark; D, Germany; IRL, Ireland; I, Italy; NL, Netherlands; NO, Norway; UK, United Kingdom; E, Spain

The working environment in HE research institutions also exerts a major influence on the pursuit of creative research: an ethos of open, critical inquiry and intellectual curiosity traditionally has been the established benchmark of a first class university.[9] In the drive towards stronger links with industry, great care must be exercised to ensure that the academic ethos of the institution does not become unduly distorted as entrepreneurial and more commercially-driven endeavours are increasingly successful and therefore more visible. Industry too is concerned about possible damage to the central mission of the universities, namely, the production of quality graduates, if trends in this direction go too far.[23]

In addressing these internal concerns, benefits must be seen to outweigh disadvantages in the exercise of the institution's social responsibilities as well as its purely academic role. As in many other instances, balanced judgement is needed to ensure that its central mission is not compromised through the exclusive substitution of *commercial* for *educational* criteria as the dominant operational parameters. A recent critique of Japan's universities restated a number of prerequisites for sustained excellence (Table 1.3).[24]

TABLE 1.3: CONDITIONS FOR EXCELLENCE IN UNIVERSITIES

| |
|---|
| • Excellence should be the primary criterion in decisions on appointments and funding. |
| • Excellence in research is not an excuse for mediocrity in teaching. |
| • Regular and objective assessment of research and teaching is essential. |
| • Flexibility of institutions and departments is essential in responding to changing circumstances and in seizing research opportunities, especially across disciplines. |
| • An institution or department largely relying on internal appointments is unlikely to become or remain a centre of excellence. |
| • Networking internationally is crucial. |
| • Institutions need to be free to decide how the bulk of their income is to be spent on research and teaching, with external funding bodies interfering only to the extent required to ensure that public money is properly spent. |

## 1.3 TECHNOLOGY TRANSFER MODELS

A new Techno-Academic Paradigm has been formulated that encapsulates the key elements for achieving effective technology transfer between the HE sector and industry (Chapter 5).[25-28] Technology transfer is central to any strategy designed to derive commercial benefit from the HE knowledge base. Indeed, efficient technology transfer supports the commercial case for increased investment in S&T within the HE sector since they are, in effect, an important conduit for transforming knowledge into jobs.

Four types of interaction have been identified:[29] research services, consultancy services, training and continuing education services, and research exploitation. Many models or paradigms for technology transfer are described in the literature, some of which are purely analytical, reflecting an academic ethos. Fassin, for example, presented a conservative analysis of the university-industry interaction that articulates the fears and difficulties which many envisage as traps for the pioneer.[30] Others prefer to be guided by hands-on experience and the results of extant technology transfer programmes that have evolved by iterative, experiential steps.

The modes of interaction depend on company size because of significant differences in familiarity with R&D and the ability to absorb it. Thus, the approach adopted with multinationals is quite different to that taken with Small or Micro Enterprises. In such cases, a bimodal strategy is clearly required which reflects the dual nature of Irish industry.

Figure 1.2 sets out a stylised model that captures the main elements of the technology transfer process between universities and the SME sector.[31] This is of particular relevance to a small open economy like Ireland given (a) the strength of the universities, (b) the importance of SMEs to the new industrial strategy and (c) the fact that, increasingly, SMEs are key contributors to the high technology economy.

FIGURE 1.2: STYLISED MODEL FOR TECHNOLOGY TRANSFER

| | Improved Technological Competence<br>Competitiveness of Indigenous Industry/SMEs | | | | |
|---|---|---|---|---|---|
| **Goals** | Improved Access to HE Knowledge/ Information Base | Closer SME/ HE Research Co-operation | Access by SMEs to HE Skills Base | Guidance for High-Tech SME Start-Ups | Provision of "Business Skills Back-Up" for SMEs |
| **University Action Area** | Information Transfer | Technology Transfer | People Transfer | New Start-Ups | Education/ Training Support |
| **Possible Initiatives** | • Science Data base<br>• Internet Access | • Contract Research<br>• Licences and Patents<br>• Technology "Brokerage" | • Teaching Co. Programme<br>• Secondment<br>• Staff Exchane Programmes | • Campus Companies<br>• Science Park/ Precinct<br>• Spin-Out Companies | • Entrepren./ MBA Progs.<br>• Distance Learning<br>• IT In-comp. Progs.<br>• Mgmt/Mkt/ Financial Planning Models |

*Source*: Adapted from Feidler.[31]

At a practical level, the French Innovation Agency, ANVAR, articulated the way in which business in France should prepare for competition throughout the EU in the run up to the next millenium. Its ten-point programme listed in Table 1.4 suggested clear management actions designed to enhance the competitiveness of business in Europe.[32]

The Teaching Company Scheme in the UK provides a comparably good example of a proven technology transfer mechanism.[33]

The rich diversity of the models reported in the literature supports the assertion that there is no unique solution and that each country must find its own procedure for exploiting the central element in all schemes, namely, the knowledge base. The approach of one Irish university, Trinity College Dublin, is predicated on the elements listed in Table 1.5, which both result in a synergistic relationship with industry and which are also perceived as making a useful contribution to the life of the institution.[34]

TABLE 1.4: THE FRENCH INNOVATION MODEL: CHECKLIST OF IMPORTANT INGREDIENTS

| |
|---|
| • Participation in research programmes |
| • Knowledge of the single market |
| • Awareness of technology |
| • Recruitment and training of "Technology Man" |
| • Acquisition of external technology |
| • Identification of scientific and technical partners |
| • Location of industrial and commercial partners |
| • Identification of financial partners |
| • Protection and adaptation of products for different markets |
| • Launch of products into the marketplace |

TABLE 1.5: KEY ELEMENTS IN UNIVERSITY-INDUSTRY INTERACTION

| |
|---|
| • Structures |
| • Symmetry in → Participation ↘ Partnership |
| • Intellectual Property |
| • Speed and Flexibility |

To summarise, the basic ingredients of any meaningful technology transfer mechanism between the academic and industrial sectors invariably include the following points:

- An approach that fully recognises the complementary strengths of each partner.

- Respect for cultural differences and value scales.

- Access to multidisciplinary knowledge that transcends historic academic demarcations.

- Efficient communication, preferably involving a one-to-one relationship between designated individuals in the partner institutions.

### 1.3.1 Industry/HE Sector

Economic growth can be enhanced significantly by developing specific and practical technology transfer mechanisms to exploit the potential synergy between the HE and industry sectors (*c.f.* Section 1.3). But translating aspiration into reality is difficult for a variety of reasons that are rooted in different attitudes and value scales, often involving conflicting issues such as *collaboration* versus *competition* and *public* versus *private* good. A number of specific issues have been identified:[12,35]

- Despite the proactive approach of the state agencies and the HE sector to industry in Europe,[28] there remains a real "information gap". A persuasive body of evidence suggests that individual companies, especially small firms, are still not fully aware of the facilities that are available centrally and how they can add value to their products.

- There are difficulties in collaborating with universities or other outside agencies because of a perceived — and fundamentally misconceived — dilution of competitive advantage.

- Intellectual property rights raise perennial problems that need to be managed in such a way as to be fair to HE institutions while recognising the commercial pressures within which knowledge-driven companies exist and compete. This issue is revisited in Chapters 3 and 4 when the governance of campus companies, including the need for greater standardisation in relation to the management and commercialisation of intellectual property is discussed.

- Industry's desire to keep proprietary information secret conflicts with the normal propensity of academics to publish in scientific journals, the usual outlet for their research.

- Much of industry is preoccupied with short-term survival rather than long-term strategic planning. This short-term operational focus, which eschews a longer term strategic role for science, is due in part to the pressures under which industry typically operates. For example, institutional shareholders often exert pressures that are more dictated by the demand for immediate returns — with a concomitant positive, albeit short-term, effect on share values — than promises of greater breakthroughs at some time in the future (*c.f.* Section 1.2). This "short-termism" is inimical to the development of sustained relationships with the HE sector.

- In the case of subsidiaries of multinational companies, the way in which local R&D is viewed by the company's corporate central research personnel can be a major determinant of local attitudes.

- The level of investment in academic S&T infrastructure often does not reflect the more commercially focused role which it is expected to play or the rapidly increasing numbers seeking entry to higher education which is an emerging feature of the more advanced societies. This reduces the overall capacity to exploit fully the capabilities of the academic knowledge and skills base to the benefit of knowledge-driven industry.

- *Symmetry* between partners, as described by Phillips, circumvents many of the constraints on both HE institutions and companies that wish to participate in this network.[35] Generating such symmetry requires informed managerial skills in industry, in colleges, and in those government departments in charge of S&T resources.

- The industrial base is quite heterogeneous both in the scale and nature of its research needs which range from the definition and precise articulation of problems to the provision of the most sophisticated, multidisciplinary research services. This has bearing on the respective contributions of the different types of institution in the HE sector and the range of services they are best able to provide.

- The fact that the corporate giants are relying to a progressively lesser degree on in-house research in favour of research accessed *via* the strengthening global knowledge network creates an important market niche for the research-based HE sector. But *ex cathedra* pronouncements by industry and policy makers that the primary focus of the universities should be confined to basic research denies the central thrust of our arguments as reflected in the rich entrepreneurial culture that has grown up in the universities in recent decades. As Vest, President of MIT, pointed out, "the institution's ethos is even more important than formal programs in stimulating high-technology entrepreneurs".[36]

At the implementation level, experience shows that the most fruitful interactions tend to be between HE research institutions and those industries that already have a developed research culture, notably subsidiaries of multinationals. This is borne out in the data presented in Table 1.1.

### 1.3.2 Government/HE Sector

Gibbons succinctly identified one of the core problems in achieving effective dialogue between government and the HE sector:

> In any particular situation, there can usually be found a range of scientific opinions. It is this, perhaps more than anything else, which causes confusion and contributes to growing public anxiety that, in some sense, control over the complex technical systems which are the hallmark of our societies has been lost.[37]

Policy-makers are continually and understandably perplexed by the different perspectives and attitudes promulgated by the scientific community. They seldom speak with one voice on issues that ostensibly derive from a precise and verifiable science and which, at first sight, should leave little room for discord. It is not always appreciated by society, and even less by politicians, that science progresses by confrontational debate. Bondi offered some insights into the problem:

> A vital assumption in both science and democracy is that opinions can be altered by discussion, by argument and (above all) by empirical evidence. Indeed, discussion and its necessary precursor, disagreement, are essential for scientific no less than for political progress while recognising the fundamental differences between science (as opposed to science policy) and democratic politics — the élitist, non-authoritarian nature of science where, in contrast to democratic politics, voting and majorities rightly have no place.[38]

In short, the scientific process of decision-making is bound to be *élitist*, while the democratic process of decision-making is *populist*.

Policy-makers who are not scientists also find it difficult to reconcile the notion of intellectual freedom with a focused science policy designed to meet strategic national needs. The situation is further exacerbated when policy is formulated by non-scientists at arm's length from the research community. The 1993 UK White Paper advanced the following viewpoint:

> The decision for government, when it funds science, as it must, is to judge where to place the balance between the freedom for researchers to follow their own instincts and curiosity, and the guidance of large sums of public money towards achieving wider benefits, above all the generation of national prosperity and the improvement of the quality of life. . . . [This] is not a simple task, not least because much basic research will ultimately contribute to wealth creation while some applied research will fail to produce exploitable outcomes. . . . It is not good enough simply to trust the automatic

emergence of applicable results which industry then uses. Nor does government believe that scientists should or could be told, from above, what to work on in order to generate relevant and industrially applicable results.[39]

Partitioning and prioritising funding for different subsets of the research continuum adds to the confusion. As Happer pointed out,

the task is hard enough with strategic research — how do we partition limited funds between research on cancer and development of information highways? The choices are all the harder for basic research, because the payoffs are so unpredictable. . . . [But] a few narrow strategic choices, made by science policy experts, are likely to miss many revolutionary new opportunities.[40]

This supports the viewpoint that investment in S&T should not be based on an either/or policy and that investment in basic and applied research is mutually reinforcing.

### 1.3.3 Industry/Government

The UK White Paper emphasised the need for improved access, particularly by SMEs, to government innovation support programmes.[39] This view was shared by Ireland's Task Force on Small Business, established in 1992 by the then minister Seamus Brennan who subsequently established the Science, Technology and Innovation Advisory Council (STIAC). This made a number of recommendations including *inter alia* rewarding risk, raising finance, reducing administrative burdens on business, providing assistance, and ensuring that the needs of small business will be an identifiable element of future policy.[41]

Two practical policy implications follow. Firstly, companies should be encouraged to build up an R&D culture and capability. This is relatively risky and costly for smaller companies which find it more difficult to absorb the costs and fully capture the benefits of R&D: they need special assistance, for example, through the tax system. Secondly, for many companies, R&D means the application of extant technology for which appropriate technology transfer mechanisms are required. Developments over the last decade or so within the HE sector aimed at servicing the technology needs of smaller companies in particular and increasing their awareness of the availability of such services have made an important start in this direction.

Technology transfer can be costly, and it can only work effectively if there is already a substantial commitment to R&D within the company. By the same token, undue reliance on imported technology leaves a nation's industry over-dependent on technologies already approaching their sell-by date, thus risking the marginalisation of that industry. It is here that a strong basic and applied research capability is important in terms of facilitating the generation, absorption and exploitation of new technologies by companies. It also supports sustained inward investment into Ireland. This is an immediate challenge for governments.

## 1.4 BROADER POLICY ISSUES

The foregoing discussion identified a range of specific issues that impinge on policy development. These and other, more general, perspectives may now be formulated into a number of more generic factors that impact strongly on any developing framework within which policy is shaped.

- *Globalisation:* Societies are now global in the sense that they can no longer operate in isolation. Even within societies themselves, routine access to continuously up-dated global information has empowered populations, thereby creating an information network or "global consciousness" as well as a sense of identity that extends beyond the immediate environment.

- *The Growth of New Knowledge:* The growth of new knowledge has outstripped the procedures required to manage it.

For example, managers and policy-makers often presume to argue in rational scientific terms with the authority of the scientific method, and claiming a precision for the method that science itself no longer claims. As a result, their conclusions are occasionally spurious and potentially damaging to civil human society.

*   *Technocratic Logic:* As Saul argues,[42] blinkered adherence to the so-called "rational approach" stifles both the ability to challenge conventional wisdom and the flexibility to be unconventional in addressing the complex problems of modern society: "Politicians who become devotees of technocratic logic also become prisoners of conventional solutions." He believes also that those who work the system have imposed a virtual dictatorship of vocabulary: to words like "justice", "rationalisation" and "efficiency" one can now add "transparency", "accountability", "performance indicators", "re-engineering", "down-sizing". These terms quickly become clichés that buzz with self-importance but lack the sting of insight. "They come to replace thought . . . they are the modern equivalent of the intellectual void." Furthermore, societies in flux, as history shows, evolve new systems by which those who have the responsibility and power are the ones who, by and large, chart the future progress of society. In short, the management of change is largely in the hands of the policy-makers, technocrats and, more recently, the programme managers. Today, perhaps more than in any other period, power is synonymous with access to knowledge and information, coupled with the ability to use it.[43]

*   *A Holistic Approach:* As indicated in the proposed new Techno-Academic Paradigm (*c.f.* Chapter 5) and reiterated here, the critical role of the non-scientific and technological community in the technology debate can no longer be ignored. If society is to reap the full benefits from today's awesome dis-

coveries, the arts, social sciences and humanities must be involved pro-actively in developing acceptable technology.

- ***Culture of Compliance:*** In higher education, the drive towards (a) increased public intervention and scrutiny, (b) the adoption of a market-oriented ethic, and (c) the consequent dilution of personal and institutional autonomy in countries like Ireland and the UK imposes conformity: public accountability is increasingly interpreted as direct state intervention. It is odd that, in one of the most enlightened eras of civilisation, society is increasingly being subjected to a mandatory culture of compliance.[44,45]

- ***Measurement and Quantification:*** In charting the course of society, policy-makers are concerned with measurement. But is it possible to develop quantitative models to describe adequately the full complexity of society? How can qualities like morality, creativity, scholarship and excellence be measured in financial terms?[46-48] The Nobel economist, Milton Friedman,[49] commenting on higher education policy, argued that "the social benefits are so tenuous and hard to grasp empirically that they ought not to be considered in the economics of education". Herein lies the problem because an approach that measures the quantifiable and ignores what remains distorts the true picture. North[50] warned against neat theories to describe the complexity of real problems, echoing the earlier concerns of Carter and Williams[51] who alluded to analytical oversimplification and the predilection of policy makers for a precision that progressively becomes unreal. This, they argued, "results from the common habit of removing complications for the sake of clarity in analysis. . . . Unfortunately the complications and uncertainties are an essential part of the problem". The inadequacies of this approach are clear in hindsight.

While the mathematical representation of modern societies, in keeping with many other natural phenomena, is a vastly over-simplified abstraction, it nonetheless makes an important contribution to our overall understanding of the way in which they develop, providing, of course, that undue reliance is not placed on the predictions of such analyses in a way that ignores the approximations and limitations of the theories used.[45,52]

The motivation to overcome or to circumvent these difficulties rests on the general acceptance that those nations which have access to new knowledge and have the ability to use it will prosper, others will not. From a policy perspective, "the capacity for innovation can be stimulated or inhibited by the institutional and policy framework within countries".[53]

How then do these observations influence current policy formulation? Sensible and balanced policy requires the harmonisation of inter-connected, disparate and transient inputs into a cohesive strategy. As argued in Section 1.1.2, this can be achieved first by understanding the nature of these inputs and then bridging the cultural differences of the various contributors.

In practice, because of the overriding impact of budgetary matters on policy, governments tend to rely heavily on advisers drawn from the economic and business community. The exclusion of other skills ultimately impoverishes policy-making. What is particularly needed, and often ignored, is the engagement of scientists and technologists who understand the full import of new knowledge, the social scientists and humanists who can interpret the social implications and, of course, society itself. It is then the job of the technocrats to shape these inputs into coherent advice for informed decision by politicians. One of the more important challenges for the policy-maker in this scenario is to account for the changing relationship between science and technology in policy formulation. A central caveat of this thesis is that *feasibility is not synonymous with acceptability.*

## 1.5 IRELAND AS A PROTOTYPE

### 1.5.1 Can Ireland Afford Indigenous R&D?

What are the options for a nation like Ireland whose population is about 5 per cent of the UK, with few world-size indigenous companies and whose Gross National Product (GNP) is relatively small in global terms? Within the following ranking, Ireland — UK — Germany/Japan — US, there is roughly an order of magnitude increase in GNP at each step.[54] This implies that the total amount of direct state support for R&TD in Ireland is proportionately small. Moreover, Ireland's reluctance to devote what resources are available to R&TD has been adversely commented upon by the European Commission whose recent Report on Science and Technology Indicators suggests that "the Irish R&D system seems to rely very much on the presence of multinationals".[55]

#### 1.5.1.1 Two Divergent Perspectives

Regarding industrial research, only the very large companies do research at a significant level and, according to Edwards, "there is a threshold for research and there is little point to undertake research without the resources".[54] Furthermore, Edwards considers expenditure as a proportion of national GDP as irrelevant since, in his view, it is much cheaper to buy the properly researched product than to attempt competition:

> This has been a bitter lesson in the UK where company after company has gone down because they were not big enough to create world class products. When the state has tried to help, the help always seemed to be frittered away in supporting the failing product. I think the government here has learned the lesson and no longer interferes, but the general effect on research has been dire. For example, the electrical companies, once they were privatised, closed *all* their research. A whole row of supporters of university research vanished, and the Research Councils have diverted a large part of their budgets into applied research, often ephemeral, since the organisation

of "programmes" was based on the idea that one supports an
area strongly for five years, then leaves the future support to
"industry", which is usually not there.

SMEs are not a substantial source of revenue for research other
than consultancy service. Edwards's view is that universities in
Ireland must specialise to have world visibility, or alternatively
offer solely good education for their young people with quality,
but small scale, research effort.

Wrixon interprets "world visibility" as a strategic programme
of research in areas identified as critical growth sectors of Ireland's economy to ensure a sustainable economic future:

> The identification of such growth sectors is crucial and, as
> Ireland is an open economy, they are dependent on global
> market opportunities.[56]

He highlights the buoyant manufacturing industry (mainly multinational) as one of the main drivers of economic growth and re-
minds us that there are three additional people employed in the
services industries for every one employed in manufacturing. The
knock-on effects for the educational system are obvious. Though
not large (100,000 people directly employed), the manufacturing
sector is the one with the most value added and with the greatest
multiplier effect in the economy as a whole.

By way of example, Wrixon singles out the electronics/IT sector where over 50,000 people are employed in electronics manufacturing. But the sector is at once dynamic and volatile and is fu-
elled by "constant innovation, new product development and is
characterised by rapid change: 90 per cent of the products of a
modern electronics factory were not even invented three years
ago". He argues for a *National Science and Technology Plan*, first to
develop research in specific areas and, second, to attract inward
research as well as manufacturing investment.

The current situation is the following:

- Ireland's obvious success as the fastest growing economy in the EC — Ireland is currently the biggest percentage exporter of high-tech goods in the EU — cannot be ignored.

- This performance is achieved with no more than 2 per cent direct expenditure by the state on R&D which contrasts with an EU average of 7 per cent and as much as 30 per cent in countries such as the Netherlands and Denmark. Clearly Ireland's exceptional performance in key knowledge-driven sectors is based on major *indirect*, non-state expenditure on R&D, specifically by business which accounts for 69 per cent of the total — the second highest in the EC, next to Sweden — and a further 20 per cent from various EU support schemes.

- The educational system plays an increasingly important part in attracting inward investment by providing strong, specific sector-related, research as well as a continuous supply of highly qualified graduates.

Edwards and Wrixon approach Ireland's position from two different stances that differ essentially in the level of indirect support for R&D by business and the EU. Without such indirect support, the Edwards model prevails; with it, as is currently the case, the Wrixon model is more relevant.

The sustainability of Ireland's economic growth — and its relevance as a template for small economies — requires that Ireland continues with the development and utilisation of R&TD in keeping with the European Commission's reaffirmation that

> access to scientific and technological knowledge and the ability to exploit it are becoming increasingly strategic and decisive for the economic performance of countries and regions in the competitive global economy.[55]

The message is clear: Ireland must ensure that its total research activity continues to grow through increased budgetary provisions in the face of impending cutbacks in support from the EU (post-1999). Ireland's relevance as a role model, emphasising the importance of R&D funding with a demonstrable pay-off in terms of growth and jobs, contrasts with the more pervasive stagnation in European research as a whole.

### 1.5.2 Strategic Policy Development

Driven by this conviction, the rationale behind our approach focuses primarily, though not exclusively, on small open economies. It is predicated on a belief that policy formulation is best approached through an iterative process based on the knowledge gleaned from hands-on experience in industry and the HE sector. Detailed arguments are accordingly developed in the context of experience in Ireland — which is prototypical of many small open economies throughout the world — and then the relevance in the wider context is assessed.

The modernisation of Ireland's industry, away from a dominant traditional agricultural base, has proceeded rapidly over the last three decades and especially so over the last few years. Membership of the European Community since 1971 and concomitant access to its various research programmes, coupled with a more enlightened approach to the value of research and development (R&D), have been largely responsible for the dynamic growth and vitality of research in Ireland in recent times. This has served to obviate the "critical mass" argument invoked by Edwards.

A propensity for imaginative and relevant research, given the right resources and environment, continues a venerable scientific and technological tradition, propagated by such personages as Robert Boyle, the son of the Earl of Cork — often referred to as the "Father of Chemistry" — in the 17th century, Sir William Rowan Hamilton in the 19th century and Ernest Walton in the 20th century. Their formidable and formative scientific achievements have been complemented by others, notably the Earls of Rosse, who transformed the new knowledge of the day into useful technology.[57]

Ireland's recent and highly successful industrial strategy, which is intended to shape the nature and pace of future economic growth, has evolved against this new period of scientific and technological enlightenment. The challenge is to match sustained inward investment with comparable development of Ireland's indigenous industry that is heterogeneous in size, nature of activity and origin.[41]

From a policy perspective, Irish industry has hitherto been subdivided into indigenous, which tend to be low-tech, and foreign-owned (more than 50 per cent of their equity is owned outside the state), which are mainly driven by high-technology. The latter are usually subsidiaries of multinationals which dominate the manufacturing scene. Although representing only 17 per cent of the total number of firms, they generate 45 per cent of employment, 68 per cent of net output and 63 per cent of Business Expenditure on Research and Development (BERD). Even so, only 24 per cent engage in R&D in Ireland and even fewer have a measure of independence from their parents.[58]

Policy must now support the growth potential of small indigenous firms in emerging technologies. The relative cost of generating and/or acquiring and exploiting knowledge is often prohibitive for such firms. Exploitation of the nation's knowledge resources is crucial because small open economies like Ireland can no longer sustain a development strategy based on relative factor costs (wages, labour and so forth), as was the case in the early stages of Ireland's industrial modernisation. In what Lipsey termed the *Techno-Economic Paradigm*,[59] the comparative advantage of small economies in particular must increasingly be in the enhancement and exploitation of the national knowledge base, a thesis which is endorsed and developed further in our analysis.

### 1.5.2.1 Strategic Policy Development: Some Lessons

A number of relevant points emerge in adapting experiences elsewhere to the Irish context:

- Governments routinely use public funding as a policy instrument in prioritising certain broadly defined areas of overriding national interest. It follows that any coherent S&T policy must establish guidelines for prioritising the different fields of research that, in the case of Ireland, have emerged through a consensus among policy-makers, beginning with the seminal OECD analyses[60] through to the Culliton[61], Moriarty[62] and STIAC[13] reports. Most tangibly, perhaps, they are reflected in the prescriptive Programmes for Advanced Technology (PATs).[12] However, this consensus is primarily driven by industry and it does not fully encompass the perspectives of the HE sector where research priorities and funding should better reflect the extent of the HE contribution to the developing national knowledge base which underpins enterprise and jobs. This coincides with Langslet's opinion that the actual fleshing out of research priorities into specific programmes should be left to the scientific community itself, or to private businesses that are willing to provide the necessary finance.[63]

- Scientific creativity is in the domain of the individual. Close dialogue between those directly involved in R&D and those administering and funding it is crucial. As stressed above, scientists should be integrated into the decision-making process so that they can fully appreciate the complex network into which their advice has to fit. Anything that separates those with knowledge of science, technology and industry from the political and decision-making apparatus is counter-productive.[38] This has important implications in shaping the most appropriate policy framework.

- That the needs of industry are short-term, medium-term and long-term is often ignored by policy-makers and industrialists whose time scales for decision making more often than not are short-term. Policy should be based on more realistic time scales for changing a nation's industrial culture.

While the concept of the "Knowledge Economy" is now well-established in the economic and organisation literature — and, equally importantly, in the minds of policy makers — analysis of the economic rationale for increased expenditure still requires a much more developed perspective of the nature and genesis of S&T and its systematic effects on the economy and society.

In Ireland, the advent of the "Knowledge Economy" has placed a particular responsibility on the Higher Education sector where much, but by no means all, of Ireland's R&D capability resides. Ireland still has (a) relatively few large companies with sufficient resources to invest in R&D, (b) few stand-alone, dedicated research institutions and (c) no military or defense research programmes. In fact, Ireland accounts for only 0.3 per cent of the world's research activity.[64]

It is inevitable that the HE institutions continue to train scientists and technologists, support industry and create and interpret new knowledge for commercial exploitation, as well as advancing the frontiers of new knowledge which is the seed corn of future technology.

In short, the HE sector in Ireland is now a major player in policy formulation within an overall framework that embraces the following components:

- The extant infrastructure which supports S&T

- The knowledge and skills base

- The industrial sector and its needs

- Technology transfer between the HE sector and industry

- Private venture capital support for knowledge-based companies

- Areas of future growth and related policy.

Therefore, in developing a comprehensive policy strategy, attention focuses primarily on (a) research and technological development (R&TD), (b) mechanisms that facilitate the commercial exploitation of technology and its transfer to the real economy and (c) an assessment of the economic benefits that flow from increased investment in this S&T base.

## OBSERVATIONS AND RECOMMENDATIONS

- *There is no unique model for exploiting the benefits of new technology: each country must find its own methodology for exploiting the central element in all schemes, namely, the national knowledge base.*

- *The capacity for innovation can be stimulated or inhibited by the institutional and policy framework within nations.*

- *Innovative, pro-active management of new discoveries based on informed judgement must replace effete policies and blind belief in the importance of science and technology.*

- *Policy formulation is best approached through an iterative process based on the knowledge gleaned from hands-on experience.*

- *Scientists should be integrated into the decision making process so that they can fully appreciate the complex network into which their advice has to fit. Procedures that separate those with knowledge of science, technology and industry from the political and decision making apparatus is counterproductive in regard to fostering sustainable economic growth.*

- *If effective and balanced relationships are to be established between the main participants in the generation and use of new technology, it is necessary first to understand their cultural differences and perspectives, respect these differences, and then bridge the barriers of language, attitudes, priorities and perspectives. Any process that attempts to impose one culture on another is destined to fail.*

- *A strong basic as well as applied research capability is important in terms of facilitating the generation, absorption and exploitation of new technologies by companies. It is also necessarily at the heart of any effective strategy aimed at promoting sustained inward investment into Ireland.*

- *Continuing efforts to attract inward investment must be matched with comparable development of Ireland's indigenous industry that is heterogeneous in size, nature of activity and origin. This will lessen both its cyclical and structural vulnerability to change.*

- *A bimodal strategy that reflects the dual nature of the industrial base in Ireland (research-based large multinational versus developing small (SME) or very small (VSE) indigenous enterprises) is required to achieve effective technology transfer between the HE sector and industry. Policy formulation must therefore reflect the business sector profile and take into account, for example, the relative cost of generating and/or acquiring and exploiting knowledge which is often prohibitive for the small firm.*

- *Building up an R&D culture and capability is relatively more risky and costly for smaller companies which find it more difficult to absorb the costs, and fully capture the benefits, of R&D: they need special assistance, for example, through the tax system which is one of the very few policy instruments available to Ireland.*

- *Investment in S&T should not be based on an either/or policy (either applied or basic research): they are mutually reinforcing.*

- *Undue reliance on imported technology leaves a nation's industry over-dependent on technologies already approaching their sell-by date, thus risking the marginalisation of that industry.*

- *An effective national S&T policy must establish guidelines for prioritising the different fields of research but the actual fleshing out of research priorities into specific programmes should be left to the scientific community itself, or to private businesses that are willing to provide the necessary finance.*

- *The HE sector must continue to address the servicing and technology needs of smaller companies in particular and increase their awareness of the availability of such services.*

- *In the drive towards stronger links with industry, care must be exercised to ensure that the academic ethos of the institution does not become unduly distorted as entrepreneurial and more commercially-driven endeavours are increasingly successful and therefore more visible.*

- *Technology transfer depends as much on an academic institution's ethos as on formal technology transfer programmes.*

## References and Notes: Chapter 1

1.   Francis Bacon, Nam et ipsa scientia potestas est (for even knowledge itself is power) in Meditationes Sacrae: De Heresibus, 1597.

2.   O. Spengler, *The Decline of the West*, Authorised translation with notes by C.F.Atkinson, George Allen and Unwin, London, 1926.

3.   J. Horgan, *The End of Science: Facing the Limits of Knowledge in the Twilight of the Scientific Age*, Addison-Wesley, New York, 1996. See also, *London Times Higher Education Supplement* (THES), August 2, 1996, p. 19.

4.   Y. Nakasone, Prime Ministerial Address, in *Europe/Japan: Futures in Science, Technology and Democracy*, V. J. McBrierty (ed.). Butterworths, London, 1986, pp. 5-8.

5.   P. Walley, *Ireland in the 21st Century*, O. Donoghue (ed.), Mercier Press, Dublin, 1995.

6.   W. Frühwald, Science and Technology: on Research and the Universities in Europe, in "The Dancer not the Dance", E. Sagarra and M. Sagarra (eds.), Trinity Jameson Quatercentenary Symposium, Trinity College Dublin, May, 1992, p.2.

7.   Y. Takeda, Synergistic Research and Development for Innovation Towards the Twenty-first Century, in "The Dancer not the Dance", E. Sagarra and M. Sagarra (eds.), Trinity Jameson Quatercentenary Symposium, Trinity College Dublin, May, 1992, pp. 66-74.

8.  U. Colombo, "Technological Innovation: New Forms and Dimensions, New Geographical Balances", in *Europe/Japan: Futures in Science, Technology and Democracy*, V. J. McBrierty (ed.). Butterworths, London, 1986, p. 25.

9.  V.J. McBrierty, "Higher Education into the 21st Century: Science, Technology and the Universities", R.M. Jones Public Lecture, 10 October, 1995. Published by the Queen's University of Belfast in 1997.

10. *The European Report on Science and Technology Indicators*. EUR 15897 EN. European Commission, Luxembourg, 1994, p. 49.

11. I. Prigogine, "Science, Civilisation and Democracy", in *Europe/Japan: Futures in Science, Technology and Democracy*, V.J. Mc Brierty (ed.), Butterworths, London, 1986, pp. 17-24.

12. V.J. McBrierty, "The University/Industry Interface: From the Lab to the Market", *Higher Education Management* 5, 75-94, 1993.

13. *Making Knowledge Work for Us*, Report of the Science, Technology and Innovation Advisory Council, D. Tierney, Chairman, Stationery Office, Dublin 2, Ireland, 1995, Vol. 1, p.6.

14. EFTA (1960), European Free Trade Association: EU (1957), European Union: NAFTA (1991), North Atlantic Free Trade Association: ASEAN (1967), Association of South East Asian Nations GATT, General Agreement on Tariffs and Trade.

15. M.B. Myers, in "Reinventing Our Future, Physics Round Table", *Physics Today*, March, 1994, pp. 34-39.

16. Higher Education Statistics Agency, Preliminary Report, THES, August 2, 1996, p. 3.

17. *Technology and the Economy: The Key relationships*, OECD, Paris, 1992.

18. *Green Paper on Innovation*, Bulletin of the EU, Supplement 5/95. 1995. p.77.

19. R.P. Kinsella, D. J. Storey, W. Clarke and D. Mulvenna, *Irish Fast Growth Firms*, Irish Management Institute, Dublin, 1994.

20. M.U. Porat, *The Information Economy: Definition and Measurement*. Vol. 1, Washington D.C.: US Government Printing Office, 1977.

21. Ref. 18, p. 34.

22. ibid. p. 94.

23. P. H. Abelson, "Evolution of Industrial Research", *Science*, 265, July, 1994, p. 299.

24. J. Maddox, "How to Pursue Academic Excellence", *Nature*, 372, December 1994, pp. 721-3.

25. V.J. McBrierty (ed), *Strategy for Industrial Innovation: The Role of the Third Level Institutions*, Confederation of Irish Industry (now IBEC), Business Study Series, No. 8, March 1981.

26. *Innovation Report 1981*, Confederation of Irish Industry, Business Study Series, No. 10, January 1982.

27. R.P. Kinsella and V.J. McBrierty, "Campus Companies and the Emerging Techno-academic Paradigm: the Irish Experience", *Technovation*, 17(5), 245-251 (1997).

28. *Growth, Competitiveness, Employment: the Challenges and Ways Forward into the 21st Century*, EU Commission White Paper, Bulletin of the European Communities, Supplement 6/93, 1993.

29. *Technology Transfer Between Higher Education and Industry in Europe*, TII Publication, Luxembourg, 1990.

30. Y. Fassin, "Academic Ethos versus Business Ethics", in "University/Industry/Government Relations", V.J. McBrierty and E.P. O'Neill (eds), *Intnl. Jnl. of Technology Management*, 6, 533-46 (1991).

31. H. Feidler, "Establishing a Technology Park as an Example for University-Industry Collaboration", in *Cooperation between Higher Education and Industry*, A. Klingstrom (ed), Uppsala University, 1987.

32. *L'Europe Technologique: Un Guide Pratique*, Courrier ANVAR, Supplement to No. 74. Paris. April, 1990.

33. *UK Teaching Company Scheme, A Review from the Joint SRC/DoI Management Committee*, SRC Publication, November, 1979.

34. V.J. McBrierty and E.P. O'Neill (eds), "University/Industry/Government Relations", *Intnl. Jnl. of Technology Management*, 6, 557-67 (1991).

35. D.I. Phillips, "New Alliances: for Policy and the Conduct of Research and Education", in "University/Industry/Government Relations", V.J. McBrierty and E.P. O'Neill (eds.), *Intnl. Jnl. of Technology Management*, 6, 1991. pp.478-488: see also, Roundtable Program Encourages Academic/Industrial Alliances, APS News, American Physical Society, 3(8), Aug/Sept, 1994, pp.1-3.

36. Cited in L. Savage, MIT: "Innovation and the Economic Impact of a Research University", *Solid State Technology*, August, 1997. pp. 58,60.

37. M. Gibbons, "Technological Advice and Political Decision", in *Europe/Japan: Futures in Science, Technology and Democracy*, V.J. McBrierty (ed.). Butterworths, London, 1986, pp. 130-136.

38. H. Bondi, "Themes and Orientations: Science and Democracy — Common Values in a Dialogue of Civilisations", in *Europe/Japan: Futures in Science,*

*Technology and Democracy*, V.J. McBrierty (ed.). Butterworths, London, 1986, pp. 9-15.

39. *Realising our Potential: A Strategy for Science, Engineering and Technology*, UK White Paper, Cm 2250, HMSO London, 1993.

40. W. Happer, "Diversity Needed in Federal Support of Basic Science after SSC", *American Physical Society News*, March 1994, p. 12.

41. *Taskforce on Small Business*, Stationery Office, Dublin 2, Ireland. March, 1994.

42. J. R. Saul, *Voltaire's Bastards: The Dictatorship of Reason in the West*, New York, Vintage Books, 1992.

43. V. J. McBrierty (ed.), *Europe/Japan: Futures in Science, Technology and Democracy*, Butterworths, London, 1986.

44. F. Millar, "Master of the Universities", *Times Educational Supplement*, May 20 1994, p. 2.

45. V. J. McBrierty, "Science Policy and Higher Education: the Irish Experience", *Studies*, 84, 187-196, 1995.

46. V. J. McBrierty, "The University at Work", *Industry and Higher Education*, December, 1994, pp. 208-214.

47. R. Florax, *The University: a Regional Booster? Economic Impacts of Academic Knowledge Infrastructure*, Avebury Press, UK, 1992, p. 114.

48. J. E. Midwinter, "A Measure of Excellence: Research Assessment in Universities", *IEE Review*, March, 1993, pp. 75-78.

49. Milton Friedman, cited in H. R. Bowen, *Investment in Learning: the Individual and Social Value of American Higher Education*, Jossey-Bass, San Francisco, 1977; see also Ref. 47, p. 32.

50. D. North, cited in P. Tansey, "Sometimes the West is Best", *Irish Sunday Tribune*, C2, 29 May 1994.

51. C.F. Carter and B.R. Williams, *Investment in Innovation*, Oxford University Press, Oxford, 1958.

52. E.E. Peters, *Fractal Market Analysis: Applying Chaos Theory to Investment and Economics*, John Wiley, New York, 1993.

53. *A Strategy for Competitiveness, Growth and Employment*, NESC Report No. 96. 1993.

54. S.F. Edwards, private communication.

55. *Second European Report on S&T Indicators*, 1997, European Commission, EUR 17639 EN, 1997. DGXIII, L-2920, Luxembourg.

56. G.T. Wrixon, "Harnessing R&D for Industrial Development", Paper presented to the IEI Conference, September, 1997.

57. C. Mollan, *The Irish Innovator*, Sampton Press Ltd., Blackrock, Dublin, Ireland. 1995: see also, G. L. Herries-Davies, "Irish Thought in Science", in *The Irish Mind*, R. Kearney (ed.), Wolfhound Press, Dublin, 1985.

58. M. Breathnach, *Research and Development in the Business Sector*, Forfás, Dublin 2, Ireland, 1996.

59. R.G. Lipsey, *Globalisation, Technological Change and Economic Growth*, Northern Ireland Economic Council, July 1993.

60. *Investment in Education: Ireland*, OECD, Paris, 1966. See also, Educational Change in its Historical Context, Irish Education Decision Maker, No. 7, Spring/Summer, 1993.

61. *A Time for Change: Industrial Policy for the 1990s*, Report of the Industrial Policy Review Group (Culliton Committee), Stationery Office, Dublin 2, Ireland.

62. *Employment through Enterprise: Response of the Government to the Moriarty Taskforce on the Implimentation of the Culliton Report*, (P. Moriarty, Chairman), Stationery Office, Dublin 2, 1993.

63. L. R. Langslet, in *Europe/Japan: Futures in Science, Technology and Democracy*, V. J. McBrierty (ed), Butterworths, 1986, pp. 36-39.

64. T. Higgins, *S&T and Economic Development*, Report of the CIRCA Group Europe Ltd., Roebuck Castle, Dublin 4, 1994.

*Chapter 2*

# S&T AND THE NATIONAL KNOWLEDGE BASE: ECONOMIC AND METHODOLOGICAL ISSUES

## 2.1 INTRODUCTION AND OVERVIEW

This chapter develops a conceptual framework within which to analyse the economic rationale for an increased Science and Technology (S&T) capability. It involves four steps.

First, recent developments in growth theory are reviewed. The "New Growth Theories", in particular, suggest that knowledge, subsumed in Human Capital, is now the key factor in economic growth and in national competitive advantage. S&T is the foundation of the national knowledge base whereas Research and Technological Development (R&TD) is a major element in the generation, application and commercialisation of knowledge. It determines the scope for, status, and the rate of product and process innovation. R&TD contributes directly to wealth and job creation and, in addition, adds to the national knowledge base, thereby increasing the economy's potential for generating future growth.

Second, the insights generated by recent theoretical work and validated by empirical studies are seen against the background of fundamentally important shifts in the structure and organisation of industry. These are, perhaps, best captured in Lipsey's *Techno-Economic Paradigm.*[1] As pointed out in Chapter 1, the global economy is now in a state of transition in terms of competitive advantage. The new paradigm is generated, in particular, by knowledge-based production. Increasingly, the development and enhancement of the knowledge infrastructure is both the *attractor* for mobile international industry and the *generator* of competitive domestic industry. It provides a practical basis for funding decisions based on industrial policy criteria.

Third, at the level of policy, recent studies strongly suggest that there are positive spin-offs or externalities associated with an enhancement of the knowledge base. That these benefits transcend and are not fully captured by individual firms provides the rationale for policy interventions aimed at helping to offset the risks and costs attendant on investing in R&TD at the level of individual firms.

Fourth, these developments need to be placed within the broader context of the size structure and technological competence of indigenous industry. As has been noted, for example in Chapter 1, Irish firms are, in the main, small and are still characterised by a low spend on R&TD, despite national and EU initiatives.

The development of an "R&TD Culture" within these companies should be a major policy objective of post-industrial revolution thinking (*cf.* Section 1.2). It must also be seen in the context of the tendency in advanced economies for innovative companies, large and small, to cluster around research institutes and colleges in the HE sector which both generate ideas and provide a skills base to exploit these ideas.

Ensuing chapters set out a new analytical framework to identify and quantify the important economic elements of the burgeoning knowledge base within the HE institutions and to analyse their economic linkages with the real economy.

## 2.2 ECONOMIC GROWTH AND TECHNICAL PROGRESS

It is logical to assess the economic justification for a substantive national S&T capability, and the concomitant need for a new policy framework against the background of an informed view of how far science and technology — the generation of knowledge embodied in new technologies and in the skills base — contributes to economic growth.

At the national level, the rate and composition of growth will influence wealth generation to support rising living standards and to enhance global competitiveness. Within the wider European Union, relative growth rates will influence progress towards convergence between less developed and more prosperous regions with implications, for example, for the sustainability of Economic and Monetary Union (EMU). Whereas as long ago as 1990 the economic gap between the richest and poorest states was about 4:1, the technology gap was 12:1.[2] The European Commission, in successive Framework Programmes, has developed a number of initiatives aimed at redressing this imbalance using S&T policy as an instrument to promote cohesion within the Community.

There is a key issue: to what extent, if at all, can the enhancement of human capital, encompassed by a substantive S&T policy, assist a small open economy like Ireland to converge with more developed economies within the EU? This issue, upon which there are decidedly differing views (*c.f.* Section 1.5.1), is now explored further.

The development of a robust analytical framework to explain the dynamics of economic growth, including transnational differences, is among the most challenging issues addressed by economists during the post-war period. Of the various approaches considered, the Neoclassical model, with subsequent modifications, remains the most influential.[3,4] In its original form, the Neoclassical model was characterised by two factors, namely, capital and labour, albeit within the constraints of highly restrictive assumptions. These included constant returns to scale and diminishing returns to factors of production. The "steady state" production function generated by the model (productivity) was, however, at variance with the observed long-run rise in *per capita* income.

To resolve this dichotomy, the US economist Robert Solow in a landmark study introduced the concept of "Technical Progress" to which some 90 per cent of US economic growth in the period 1910-1949 was attributed.[5] Though not defined at the outset, this concept was, in effect, a *residual*, randomly and exogenously generated, and therefore not amenable to policy control. While the Solow model could not satisfactorily explain transnational differences in growth, it was, nevertheless, an enormously significant starting point.

Recent work succeeded in re-engineering the Neoclassical model to explain the nature of economic growth and the role of technological change. The "new growth theories" encompass a number of important contributions that are directly relevant to understanding the economic rationale for an increased S&T capability as well as the policy implications that flow from this rationale. They embody two important concepts.

- *Human Capital as a Catalyst for Growth:* A key theme in the New Growth Theories concerns the role of Human Capital. Essentially, according to Lucas,[3] there are positive externalities — that is, spill-over benefits that transcend those captured by the individual firm — associated with public investment in measures to enhance skills which raise both individual and collective productivity.

- *Technology and the Economy's Growth Potential:* Solow's concept of "technical progress" has been radically reworked within the new theories. In particular, by making technology endogenous, the new models, in effect, make the knowledge that generates such technologies a factor of production, alongside capital and labour. This creates increasing rather than constant returns to scale at the level of the economy. It also reinforces the rationale for intervention implicit in the "human capital" approach:

> The central concept is that the larger the stock of knowledge (designs and technologies) available to the workforce, the greater will be their productive potential. However, [because knowledge is, in effect, a public good] . . . in a market setting there will be a tendency to under-invest in the accumulation of knowledge through R&D and this will be exacerbated by poorer basic facilities in less developed regions. On both counts there is a justification for public intervention.[4]

More generally, economists have made significant progress in moving from a situation in which exogenous technical progress was all that determined growth to one where the interaction between R&D, the generation and production of new technologies, human capital formation and economic growth can all be discussed within a Neoclassical framework.

## 2.3 EXTERNALITIES AND MARKET FAILURE

It is clear that human capital formation emerges as a key element within the newer economic growth models. It is driven by the generation, diffusion and commercialisation of knowledge. This knowledge is embodied within new technologies and is dependent on the skills base. These are augmented and enhanced by R&TD that creates jobs and wealth directly as well as indirectly by enlarging the growth potential of the economy.

Importantly, the new growth theories demonstrate that the full benefits of knowledge generation are not fully captured by private firms. The situation is further exacerbated when, as in Ireland, the industrial structure is dominated by small firms for whom significant investment in R&TD is both costly and risky. *This again underlines the role of the HE sector as a central technological node within the economy, readily accessible by industry at large.*

There is, it should be said, an impressive empirical basis for this assertion. In a detailed survey, the US business magazine *Fortune* identified access to research institutions and "knowledge workers" as *the* single most important determinant of industrial locations in the US: such was the case for the "Top Ten" cities in which to locate businesses, as perceived by industry itself.[6] Some insight into the underlying economic rationale for this development is provided by Jacobs:

> If we postulate only the usual list of economic forces, cities should fly apart. The theory of production contains nothing to hold a city together . . . the force we need to postulate to account for the central role of cities is . . . the external human capital.[7]

A similar pattern is evident in Europe where a key determinant is the strong education and research presence that coincides with our characterisation of the national knowledge base as both an attractor and subsequent anchor of newer industries.[8]

There is some indication that the pivotal role of science, which is a major function of the Irish HE sector in Ireland in determining economic performance, is now being acknowledged at a policy level. But it is not yet adequately or systematically resourced or formulated in a manner that is either practical or wholly credible despite the promised injection of £250 million in 1997. More often than not, policy has been characterised by incrementalism. The expansion of the science base has been under-funded and typically managed by successive governments in this reactive rather than a proactive management mode. The EU stated as much in their current report on S&T indicators.[9] In particular, there has been a lack of policy consistency between, on the one hand, the conclusions of the studies by a number of agencies and, on the other hand, the timely implementation of the necessary actions.[10-12]

There is, accordingly, a powerful case for public intervention within the framework of an S&T policy to generate and apply knowledge.[12] By strengthening the infrastructure for S&T and enhancing human capital, policy can offset "market failure" because of the private sector's tendency systematically to under-invest in R&TD and, equally, to fail to exploit the positive externalities associated with the development of the knowledge base. Because the returns accrue mainly to society.

## 2.4 LIPSEY'S INDUSTRIAL PARADIGM

The rate of innovation is largely shaped by technology that is, in effect, an "output" of scientific endeavour. Technology subsumes:[1,13]

- *Products* made within an economy

- *Processes* employed to make such products

- *Organisational structure* used to coordinate economic activity

- *Institutions* that constitute the basic structures within which the economy functions.

There is compelling evidence that the technological paradigm which dominated the post-war period, and, at least in part, generated much of the growth of major multinational companies as well as a pattern of "Foreign Direct Investment" driven by factor costs, is being superseded by a new industrial paradigm. The latter is built around the generation and commercialisation of *knowledge* that is, itself, partly driven by enhanced information, transportation systems and so on.

What all of this means is that:

- Both product and process innovation, which are the major determinants of competitiveness, are becoming increasingly science-based.

- The product cycle, that is, time-to-market, is shortening.

- The relative risk associated with innovation is increasing.

The consequences have major implications for policy. Some idea of what this implies can be inferred from Malecki's argument that

> much of what we call technological change is the process of learning by people and, through them, by organisations and nations. The skills embodied in people result in some companies — and some regions and nations — being more prosperous and successful than others.[14]

This is echoed in the view expressed in Ireland's Culliton Report that, in an increasingly integrated and competitive world, skills and technological competence constitute one of the few areas where an economy can generate a differentiated competitive advantage.[15]

## 2.5 S&T: THE INDUSTRIAL DIMENSION

The economic case for a substantive S&T capability rests, to a large degree, on the extent of its contribution to national economic development. The new growth theories, reviewed above, provide important insights into the nature and dynamics of economic growth within and between countries. They strongly suggest that in the emerging global knowledge-based economy, a strong S&T capability is a necessary condition for sustainable growth and national competitiveness.

The commercialisation of technology is a yet more recent imperative and is highlighted in the EU White Paper, *Growth, Competitiveness and Employment,* as one of the key weaknesses in European economic policy.[16] This goes to the heart of the new growth theories which now address in a substantive way the pivotal role of knowledge — embodied in human capital — in explaining the process of economic growth and development.

These new insights also caution against a simplistic approach towards investment in S&T as an element in economic policy. For example, it is in the nature of science that at least part of public investment in S&T must be directed towards research that does not have a predetermined outcome. Why? Precisely because such investment, which generates positive spill-over effects (external-ities) to the economy as a whole, will not normally be made by the private sector. The significant corpus of basic research carried out in the past by the large multinational laboratories — AT&T Bell Labs (now Lucent Technologies), IBM, GE, Xerox and DuPont — has been severely curtailed in recent years. Industry increasingly expects the universities to carry out the necessary basic research and often expects governments to pay for it.

Science and Technology are developed by creative people op-erating in a favourable environment. The importance of culture in defining that environment can hardly be over-emphasised. Sax-enian, for example, noted that the reason why Boston's Route 128 was emulated by Silicon Valley was substantially to do with the culture and structure of the technology-based firms.[17] In a recent authoritative survey, *The Economist* commented that

> research has increasingly concentrated on clusters — places or communities where there is "something in the air" that en-courages risk-taking. This suggests that culture, irritatingly vague though it may sound, is more important for Silicon Valley's success than economic or technological factors.[18]

Vest, in the same vein, considered the ethos within an institution to be the key driver of technology transfer.[19]

The present demographic structure in Ireland and the techno-logically-driven buoyant economy based on a growing recogni-tion of the importance of science, provides a substantial platform on which to develop and consolidate a proactive entrepreneurial technology-based culture as a major policy goal. This is difficult, not least because of the mind-set of financial institutions (*c.f.* Chapter 8) and the continued under-funding of Science and Tech-nology. Nevertheless, it represents a policy imperative that encap-sulates the Techno-Academic Paradigm described in Chapter 5. In particular, the development of such a culture both within individual companies and in clusters resonates with precisely the entrepreneurial culture that already has, quite autonomously, taken root and borne substantial fruit to date within the Irish HE sector.

### 2.5.1 S&T: The Policy Interface

In analysing the nature of S&T and its impact on policy, a number of general elements have been identified:

- Science and its transformation into technology – and, thereby, jobs – involves a continuum of activities ranging from the initial conceptual idea, which is often perceived to be devoid of any immediate commercial benefit or application, to its most applied commercial form. Therefore policy must be holistic and not based on *ad hoc* interventions that can be counterproductive.

- S&T is not static. The knowledge base which drives S&T must be constantly renewed, recognising basic research as its seed corn: extant knowledge is yesterday's knowledge. By the same token, future markets will not be the same as present markets. And these future markets will be shaped by investment in technology today. Therefore, national competitiveness requires that industrial policy be rooted in the basic research capability of the economy. The implicit need for a balanced approach in funding different types of research is reinforced in the UK White Paper, *Realising Our Potential: a Strategy for Science, Engineering and Technology*, which asserted that "the national effort will be neither over-prescribed nor under-focused".[20]

- All contributors to the policy making process must be involved. Science is a driver of technology and care must be taken not to marginalise scientists in S&T policy formulation. Equally, social, cultural, environmental, commercial and defense considerations also drive technology and must also be integrated into the policy-making process.

- Categorising research into different "types" is often no more than an administrative convenience that belies the non-linear, interactive character and latent synergy of the overall research effort. Ultimately, it makes no economic sense exclusively to focus on one area, for example, applied or developmental research, at the expense of basic research. This is a recurring problem in prioritising research funding.

- The growing number of designations used to describe research — basic, fundamental, open-ended, long-term, short-term, strategic, applied, focused, oriented, commercial, and so on — can mean different things to different people. They are sometimes coined by policy makers to justify preconceived funding priorities or, indeed, used by researchers in a way that anticipates the predilections of funding agencies. Any analysis that addresses the economic rationale for S&T expenditure requires a standard nomenclature typology such as the Frascati definitions which are adopted here (Appendix I). [21]

Three elements are important in the context of a small open economy like Ireland: (a) the size profile of industry, (b) the R&D capability of industry and (c) the nature and scope of policy intervention.

### 2.5.2 Size Profile of Industry and the S&T Base

For a small firm, the costs of generating and/or acquiring and exploiting knowledge are often prohibitive. Scale limits their capacity to absorb costs and capture fully the benefits of R&D. This accentuates the problem, noted earlier, that a science-based pattern of innovation is inherently risky, and therefore costly; hence the need for a substantive S&T policy as an integral element of any industrial strategy to offset these disadvantages. In practice, this means enhancing the knowledge base that exists *outside* the firms and the capacity of the firm to access and exploit this knowledge-base within. This, in turn, enhances the capacity of the firm, in time, to grow and to strengthen its own internal technological competence. Policy should therefore embody the following aims:

- Enhance the capacity of the main development agencies to exploit the national knowledge base. This will involve additional resources, both scientific and financial, as well as more innovative forms of networking with technological nodes, both educational and commercial.

- Strengthen mechanisms for transferring technology to small firms and their capacity to absorb and exploit such technology (capability building).

- Focus policy interventions on sectors and industries with high "spillover" effects thereby enhancing the "learning-by-doing" capacity of industry.

- Enhance incentives for co-funding by government and private financial institutions in priority sectors.

### 2.5.3 The R&D Base

Research and Development encompass the creation, and/or adaptation, of knowledge and its commercialisation. This knowledge is subsumed in Human Capital as well as in new technologies. It interacts with other elements to sustain a complex, non-linear process of innovation, thereby contributing directly to growth, employment and competitiveness. More specifically, it enhances the quality of growth, that is, it reduces the dependence on factor costs (labour, wages and so on), again enhancing national competitiveness.[22]

The importance of R&D is demonstrated in the empirical research into Irish companies by the Northern Ireland Economic

Council (NIEC).[23] The survey found that some 90 per cent of companies with an R&D capability introduced a new product or process in the same year; the corresponding figure for other firms in the survey was 10 per cent. Similarly, research into the characteristics of Irish fast growth firms indicated that one of the attributes that differentiated such firms from their peers was the fact that they had a larger R&D capability.[24]

Recent evidence also suggests that the returns to R&D are high.[25,26] This is reflected in the large R&D budgets of multinational companies that seek to maintain and enhance market share through research-driven product development. But exactly the same argument applies in principle, if not in scale, to smaller companies. It follows that a strong R&D capability and culture is important if a national S&T strategy is to play an effective, catalytic role in sustaining the competitiveness of indigenous industry.

There are a number of other contributary factors apart from small size, notably the relative lack of equity finance available to smaller companies that impacts on their ability to participate in R&D. Banks lend primarily on a medium-term *secured* basis and are not comfortable lending to smaller companies for R&D (*c.f.* Chapter 9). In spite of these clear indicators, the CIRCA report noted:

> In Ireland, there is now a serious risk that unless funding policies in relation to universities' research are actually reversed, the whole credibility of an industrial policy based on knowledge-intensive development will sooner or later be seen for what it is — an aspiration without substance.[27]

What all of this means is that there is a "market failure" in relation to the ability of, and incentive for, smaller companies to invest in R&D on a scale commensurate with the objectives of industrial policy. This is predicted by the theoretical models discussed above. More generally, the "anti-risk bias" in the tax incentive framework which underpins industrial policy constitutes a powerful impediment to the development by smaller industry of an R&D capability as a springboard to future growth. Recent budgetary innovations in Ireland, such as the Special Investment Accounts (SIAs) which were introduced in the Irish Finance Act of 1993 with the view to helping small industry, need to be re-engineered to address this problem.

These and related structural weaknesses concerning the scientific base of indigenous knowledge-driven companies require concerted policy intervention. Such interventions have largely been effected, to date, through the Development Agencies and through the HE sector.

### 2.5.4 Policy Intervention

As outlined in Chapter 1, the central purpose of policy intervention is to develop a vibrant industrial base consistent with "quality of life" criteria. For the smaller economies, this involves measures which (a) encourage and support inward investment (b) provide the necessary infrastructure to support indigenous industry and (c) ensure that the required skills base, encompassing well educated and trained manpower and a high R&D capability, is available. Strengthening the link between the knowledge generators, principally the HE institutions, and the knowledge users, namely industry, is now recognised as one of the most important features of economic development strategies in all OECD countries. It is the means by which other governments seek to create tomorrow's jobs.

A range of initiatives by the HE institutions over the last three decades, have (a) greatly enhanced Ireland's human capital, (b) generated a substantial research infrastructure, and (c) provided essential R&D support for industry. A recent study, commissioned by the Higher Education Authority (the agency responsible for disbursing public funds to the universities in Ireland), has reported favorably on the universities' achievements, despite relatively poor infra-structural support by international standards.[27] The 1987 OECD Report[28] and a more recent review[29] also acknowledged the scope and contribution of the research work being carried out in Irish universities.

## 2.6 EU COHESION POLICY

An objective of the European Union is to

> strengthen the scientific and technological basis of European industry and to foster more effectively the exploitation of the potential for industry and jobs of policies on innovation, research and technological development.[16]

A second objective is also to integrate R&D policy into cohesion policy; that is, policies that aim to reduce differences within countries and to promote the scope for convergence between countries like Ireland and more developed economies. Convergence is strongly and positively correlated to differences in national R&D capability. This reinforces the argument for a much closer level of integration between national and EU S&T programmes and, more specifically, for greater leverage by insuring that private financial institutions are both aware of, and participate in, such programmes. The evidence suggests that this is not the case at present.

The EU Commission's analysis in its White Paper[16] points to the pivotal role of R&D in sustaining competitiveness of small industry and, equally, in promoting cohesion. The different programmes encompassed within the Community's S&T strategy under its Fourth Framework Programme are guided by this objective.

The reality, however, is that Ireland's expenditures on R&D, in relative terms, still fall significantly short of that of most other countries of comparable size within the EU.[9] These are countries that are already more advanced than Ireland in investing in the foundations of their national knowledge economy. The fact that

Structural Fund expenditures are, in effect, replacing rather than augmenting national expenditures suggest that national S&T policy has yet to fully adjust to the vision and rationale of Community policy.[30]

This reaffirms the importance of the R&D capability in the HE sector as a central element in the national S&T infrastructure on which the development of Irish industry substantially rests. Many commentators point to the overriding need for the HE sector to focus on applied research, which, in their view, should be industry led. The data presented in the first systematic survey of the entire HE sector confirms that there already is a strong endogenous applied research culture in place.[31]

### 2.6.1 Enhancing the HE Research Capability

The structural weaknesses in Irish industry, especially SMEs, and the low level of spending by industry, promotes the argument for continued enhancement of the HE sector's applied research capability, supported by a vibrant fundamental research base. The importance of this has been recognised in a number of pioneering initiatives, notably the Programmes of Advanced Technology (PATs).[32] These programmes are prescriptive in the sense that designated researchers in identified strategic applied research areas — virtually all of whom are academic researchers — receive the bulk of the available research funding. Such initiatives flow with the tide of Ireland's developmental needs and match similar initiatives in the national S&T programmes in the more advanced economies.

Enhancement of the applied research capability should, therefore, be seen as an essential concomitant of additional support for — and not in any sense competing with — industry's R&D needs. This will require stronger Industry/HE technology transfer mechanisms and a more effective use of HE resources in order to strengthen the capacity of Irish companies, particularly in the indigenous Very Small Enterprise (VSE) sector, to absorb and manage R&D.

The value of basic research as an essential contributor to the overall research provision must be reaffirmed. There is no dichotomy between basic and applied research: they are elements in a continuum of effort. All of the international evidence suggests that a failure to support a well-focussed basic research capability will, downstream, directly and indirectly reduce the job-creating capability of the economy. The case for basic research support in the context of economic development is cogently argued by Mowery.[33]

In short, a comprehensive national S&T policy, developed and implemented within a commercial ethos, must necessarily recognise that many generic job-creating technologies are, ostensibly, the accidental by-product of fundamental research work. And funding should take account of this reality.

## 2.7 ELEMENTS OF A NATIONAL S&T POLICY

To summarise, a national Science and Technology policy should reflect the following characteristics. It should be:

- *Substantive:* S&T policy must be on a scale which reflects the fundamental importance of knowledge — and the national knowledge base — in generating economic activity and sustaining high quality employment. It is self-evident that current resourcing of S&T by this criterion is inadequate. In an economy bounded by a shortage of resources and competing choices, the reality is that the necessary resources can only be created to meet existing and emerging social needs by harnessing S&T.

- *Informed:* Policy must be informed by an understanding of the nature of scientific and technological processes. Without such an understanding, policy cannot be effective or strategically focused. Policy is most effective when it is generated at the interface between those who comprehend the nature of the processes and those who understand the dynamics of commercialising their latent potential. The marginalisation of scientists and technologists can impoverish policy and runs counter to practice in advanced economies.

- *Coherent*: Nations like Ireland cannot afford the luxury of fragmented S&T programmes and uncoordinated funding arrangements. This is not an argument for centralisation. Rather, it is a recognition that in terms of impact, and of ensuring the best return from scarce national resources, coordination makes more sense than fragmentation. The implications, however, are far-reaching. It means, for example, that S&T ideally should be the responsibility of a single government department with a single focus and with a mandate to empower other departments and agencies to undertake S&T work which contributes directly to an integrated national strategy. The dangers of subsuming S&T policy within a broader remit are that funding will be diluted, with reduced funds being contested among different agencies with different priorities.

- *Linked Closely to Higher Education*: Policy should build on the critical mass of knowledge workers, facilities and networks within the HE sector, while maintaining the primacy of the central education and training role which transcends Science and Technology. Recognition of the linkage between science and education by including science in the education portfolio is a welcome step. In an economy dominated by small industry and in a world in which economic and social progress depends on the generation and exploitation of knowledge, it is clear that education must have a central role. It follows that a national S&T policy should build on existing centres of international excellence and foster the development of those emerging areas that can directly and indirectly enhance national competitiveness.

- *Strategically Focused*: A small country such as Ireland, with limited resources, cannot try to encompass all aspects of scientific development at the highest levels. Priorities should be informed by well developed techniques of technology forecasting. In practice, this should involve foresight programmes at national, sectoral and industry level, building where appropriate on the experience of other nations.

- *Incentivised*: Indigenous industry is often criticised for not playing its proper role within scientific and technological research and development. In the case of small business, the Taskforce on Small Business has articulated the reasons why this is so.[34] In tackling this problem, some useful lessons might be drawn from urban development where attractive tax and other incentives have resulted in a transformation of many areas of decline and decay. Such incentives may be equally effective in generating the type and level of research activity needed to promote sustainable growth in the Irish economy.

- *Supported by Higher Education*: For strong economic development to derive from a coherent national S&T policy, there must be a genuine pooling of the human resources available in the HE sector to support the initiative. The formation of regional Science Research Parks drawing on the combined strengths of HE institutions in those regions is an important step in this direction.

## OBSERVATIONS AND RECOMMENDATIONS

- *Science and its transformation into technology, and thereby jobs, involves a continuum of activities ranging from the initial concep-*

*tual idea to its most applied commercial form. Policy must be holistic and not based on ad hoc interventions.*

- *Enhancement of the applied research capability in the HE sector should be seen in conjunction with additional support for, and not in any sense competing with, industry's R&D needs.*

- *Stronger Industry/HE technology transfer mechanisms and a more effective use of HE resources is required to strengthen the capacity of Irish companies, particularly in the indigenous VSE sector, to absorb and manage R&D.*

- *S&T is not static: the knowledge base which drives S&T must be constantly renewed with basic research as its seed corn. Extant knowledge is yesterday's knowledge; future markets will not be present markets.*

- *All stakeholders must be involved in the policy making process. Science is a driver of technology and care must be taken not to marginalise scientists in S&T policy formulation. Equally, social, cultural, environmental, and commercial considerations also drive technology and must similarly be integrated into the policy making process.*

- *Ireland's expenditures on R&D, in relative terms, fall significantly short of those of most other countries of comparable size within the EU. The fact that EU Structural Fund expenditures are, in effect, replacing rather than augmenting national expenditures suggest that Ireland's S&T policy is informed neither by the vision nor the rationale of Community policy.*

- *S&T expenditure must be on a scale that reflects the fundamental importance of knowledge — and the national knowledge base — in generating economic activity and sustaining high quality employment. It is self-evident that current resourcing of S&T in Ireland by this criterion is wholly inadequate.*

- *Co-ordinated funding arrangements, embracing both the public and private sectors, are a necessary condition for an effective S&T policy.*

- *Policy must be informed by an understanding of the nature of scientific and technological processes and, hence, of the management of process innovation.*

- *Categorising research into different "types" is often no more than an administrative convenience that belies the non-linear, interactive character and latent synergy of the overall research effort.*

- *Any analysis that addresses the economic rationale for S&T expenditure requires a standard research nomenclature such as the Frascati definitions.*

- *Policy should build on the critical mass of knowledge workers, facilities and networks within the HE sector, while maintaining the primacy of the central education and training role.*

- *Mechanisms and procedures are necessary to ensure the genuine pooling of the human resources available in the HE sector as the foundation for a national S&T programme. The development of a proactive entrepreneurial technology-based culture at national level is a major policy goal.*

- *The establishment of a system of regional Science Research Parks drawing on the combined strengths of HE institutions in those regions is one important priority in any national S&T strategy.*

## References and Notes: Chapter 2

1. R. G. Lipsey, *Globalisation, Technological Change and Economic Growth*, Northern Ireland Economic Council, July 1993.

2. D. Murphy (ed.), Proceedings of the European Conference on S&T Policy on Social Cohesion, Waterford, 1989. DGXII/635/89 EN.

3. R. Lucas, "On the Mechanics of Economic Development", *Journal of Monetary Economics*, 22, 3-42, 1988.

4. J. Bradley, N. O'Donnell, N. Sheridan and K. Whelan, "Economic Growth and Convergence: Theory and Evidence", Chapter 5 in *Regional Aid and Convergence*, Averbury, Aldershot, UK, 1995.

5.  R. Solow, "A Contribution to the Theory of Economic Growth", *Quarterly Journal of Economics*, 70, 65-94 (1956).

6.  *Fortune Magazine*, December 1993.

7.  J. Jacobs, *Cities and the Wealth of Nations: Principles of Economic Life*, Pelican, London, 1986.

8.  "Education and Research Bring in the Foreign Investor", *Financial Times*, London. 18 May, 1994.

9.  *The European Report on Science and Technology Indicators*, EUR --- European Commission, Luxembourg, 1998.

10. V.J. McBrierty, *Research in Ireland: a University Perspective*, Proceedings, "Vorsprung durch Forschung: the Management of Scientific Research", The Royal Irish Academy Symposium, 5 March 1996.

11. ESRI, *Medium Term Review, 1997-2003*, which underlines the importance of education in sustainable national economic development. ESRI, Dublin, 1997.

12. V.J. McBrierty and R.P. Kinsella, *Partnership for Progress: Examples of Best Practice in University/Business Collaboration*, ACRI Conference in association with the IBEC-CBI Joint Council, Dublin Castle, 20 June 1997. Proceedings, *in press*. In effect, the theoretical basis for the paper draws on the arguments for public intervention initially developed by K. Arrow, 1962, in "Economic Welfare and the Allocation of Resources for Invention" in N. Rosenberg (ed.) *The Economic of Technological Change*, 1971, Penguin, and elaborated by K. Davitt in "Academic Research, Technical Change and Government Policy in J. Kriage and D. Pestre (eds.) *Science in the 20th Century*, 1995, Harwood Academic Publishers. Also, see Forfás, Basic Research Support in Ireland, 1998, Dublin, for further references and an insightful critique of these points.

13. J. Perez. *cited in* ref. 1.

14. E.J. Malecki, *Technology and Economic Development*, Longman Press, London, 1991, p. xi.

15. *A Time for Change: Industrial Policy for the 1990s*, Report of the Industrial Policy Review Group (Culliton Committee), Stationery Office, Dublin 2, Ireland.

16. *Growth, Competitiveness, Employment: the Challenges and Ways Forward into the 21st Century*, EU Commission White Paper, Bulletin of the European Communities, Supplement 6/93, 1993.

17. A. Saxenian, *Regional Advantage: Culture and Competition in Silicon Valley and Route 128*, Harvard University Press, Cambridge, MA, 1994.

18. *The Economist*, "A Survey of Silicon Valley", March 27, 1997, p. 7.

19. C.M. Vest, *cited in* L. Savage, "MIT: Innovation and the Economic Impact of a Research University", *Solid State Technology*, August, 1997, pp. 58, 60.

20. *Realising Our Potential: a Strategy for Science, Engineering and Technology*, UK White Paper, Cm 2250, HMSO, London, 1993.

21. Frascati Manual, OECD, Paris.

22. M. Porter, *The Competitive Advantage of Nations*, Macmillan, London, 1990.

23. *R&D Activity in Northern Ireland*, Northern Ireland Economic Council, Report No. 101, Belfast, 1993.

24. R.P. Kinsella, D.J. Storey, W. Clarke and D. Mulvenna, *Irish Fast Growth Firms*, Irish Management Institute, Dublin, 1994.

25. *The Returns to R&D*, Committee of Vice Chancellors, UK, 1994.

26. Z. Griliches, "Productivity, R&D and Basic Research at the Firm Level in the 1970s", *American Economic Review*, 76(1), 141-154 (1986); see also "R&D and Productivity: Measurement Issues and Econometric Results", *Science*, 237, 31-35 (1992).

27. *The Organisation, Management and Funding of University Research in Ireland and Europe*, the CIRCA Group Europe Ltd, Roebuck Castle, Dublin 4, Ireland. 1996; see also, *The European Report on Science and Technology Indicators 1994*, European Commission, EUR 15897 EN, 1994.

28. OECD, *Universities under Scrutiny*, Paris, 1987.

29. V. J. McBrierty, "Making Sense of Science Policy", *Administration*, 42(2), 143-158, 1994.

30. The European Commission Report on S&T Indicators (1994) made the following statement about Ireland's commitment to creating a strong S&T infrastructure: "[Allocations] indicate a potentially alarming feature . . . that those regions that most need to develop the competitiveness of their industries are spending the least on R&D related activity in their Structural Fund Programmes."

31. R.P. Kinsella and V.J. McBrierty, *Economic Rationale for an Enhanced Science and technology Capability*, Report to Forfás, Ireland's Science and Technology Agency, 1994.

32. V.J. McBrierty, "The University/Industry Interface: From the Lab to the Market", *Higher Education Management*, 5, 75-94, 1993.

33. D.C. Mowery, *Science and Technology Policy in Interdependent Economies*, Kluwer Academic Publishers, Boston, MA, 1994.

34. *Taskforce on Small Business*, Stationery Office, Dublin 2, March, 1994.

*Chapter 3*

# INTELLECTUAL PROPERTY IN A KNOWLEDGE SOCIETY

## 3.1. INTELLECTUAL PROPERTY AND THE ECONOMY

The technology that flows from new knowledge is a valuable and tradable resource because of its direct link to economic growth.[1] It is a form of equity or intellectual property (IP) that can be defined as the beneficial outflow of an innovation process that creates a new idea and transforms it into a marketable product or service.

The interface between the Higher Education sector and the wider knowledge economy is precisely along the axis of intellectual property. It is this reality that justifies the need for a radical new approach to the resourcing of (a) facilities in the HE sector, (b) human resources in the form of researchers and technologists and (c) efficient technology transfer mechanisms to generate and commercialise the intellectual property. It is worth noting that there are also significant "spill-over" effects arising out of research and technological development (R&TD) carried out in the universities to the benefit of small knowledge-based firms both within their hinterland and further afield (*c.f.* Chapter 5).[2] And it is IP that is at the heart of this process.

IP, an intangible asset, is one of the major determinants of competitiveness in today's knowledge-driven society: it will be the chief source of wealth in the coming decades.[3] Increasingly, the larger companies are systematically managing their IP portfolio within new accounting systems that are relevant to knowledge intensive enterprise in the 21st century.[4] In their recent analysis of global healthcare companies, which are particularly knowledge intensive, Morgan Stanley noted that "profitability is a function of intellectual property . . . [and that] the pharmaceutical industry is the ultimate expression of the power of intellectual property." [5]

In short, trade in IP both enables and parallels current shifts in international trade and investment as evidenced, for example, in the pattern of US foreign investment world-wide (*vide infra*, Section 3.5). This reflects a fundamentally new dimension of knowledge, namely, *knowledge* as *equity*[6] which, coupled with the massive up-front investment in the prerequisite R&TD, reinforces the importance of IP ownership or, in modern parlance, intellectual property rights (IPR).

The management of IPR in a knowledge-driven society, like new technology itself, is rendered more difficult because of a pervasive lack of vision and a general indifference towards intellectual property as discussed in the EU *Green Paper on Innovation*.[7] The Green Paper referred to "innovation in a straitjacket" and the perception that innovators are "a nuisance [who are] not only vulnerable at the outset but are faced with an interminable series of obstacles to creativity".[8] It argued for more enlightened perspectives on IPR in order to cope with the increasingly complex challenges presented by the richness and diversity of new knowledge.

## 3.2 THE INNOVATION PROCESS

The innovation process comprises a set of actions that encompasses scientific, technological, design, engineering and marketing inputs. It was initially viewed as a three-step linear progression from basic research through applied research to a third, developmental stage.[9] Subsequent refinements[10] of the linear model have since been overtaken by more realistic, albeit more complex, models of interlinked inputs and intricate feedback loops.[11-13] Unfortunately, less enlightened policy makers have tended to cling to the earlier linear concept that implicitly partitions research into crude categories of basic and applied research in a way that often denies their mutual synergism.[14] Policy continues to suffer as a result.

The commercialisation of knowledge is central to innovation. But the successful exploitation of new knowledge can be quite tortuous and risky, with three major hurdles to overcome (Figure 3.1):[15] the first concerns the commercial viability of the new idea; the second, its acceptability by society; and the third, the availability of the necessary finance to meet development, production and marketing costs. These criteria, in effect, specify the risks involved for those who wish to invest in the necessary research and technological development.

FIGURE 3.1: WINDOWS OF OPPORTUNITY IN THE COMMERCIAL EXPLOITATION OF A NEW DISCOVERY

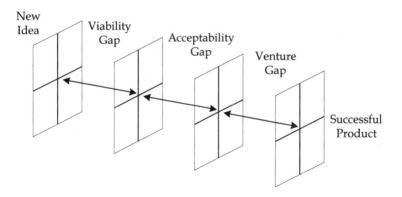

As indicated above, innovation in high technology is expensive and the risks are high — so much so that the scale of investment is often prohibitive for all but the large corporations. Smaller companies, which are at the heart of EU industrial policy, frequently lack the resources — including, crucially, venture capital — and the capability to engage in protracted and, for them, risky investment in R&TD.

Large companies, on the other hand, control a large IP portfolio or a strategic product that may introduce a "public good" dimension into the management of the underlying IP. They also feed off smaller companies. Thus, there is a different but complementary dynamic between the two. Unlike the smaller company, large firms can facilitate the "massification" of technology, establishing new technology "plateaus". Smaller companies, on the other hand, tend to generate "step changes" from these technology plateaus that are, in themselves, crucial to the innovation process when commercialised either by rapid organic growth or through the sale of the underlying IP.

For this reason, the successful exploitation of a new discovery more often than not involves a number of players. A university, for example, carries out the original research; the intellectual property that is generated is then traded to one or more companies — one of which may be a "technology broker"; it is then progressed through the innovation cycle, culminating in the production, marketing and sale of the final product. This is implicit in the screening and filtering process in Figure 3.1.

Estimates of the division of expenditure between the research that creates the original idea and the technological development that exploits it vary widely; a ratio of 60:40 has been authoritatively quoted (Section 1.1.1).[16] The technology development element entails major additional expenditures, principally in capital management and in marketing. These and related investments generate risk, including the risk of technological obsolescence and product liability. There are two consequences. First, inventors including academic researchers do not always appreciate the scale of the additional funding required and, as a result, often have inflated expectations of the worth of their new discovery. This is one of the more difficult barriers to cross in technology transfer negotiations between academic researchers and industry.[17] Secondly, where the research is publicly funded, the contract often stipulates that the results should be in the public domain. Such non-exclusivity clauses constitute a major disincentive to the successful commercialisation of the new idea because companies, understandably, seek exclusive rights to the intellectual property in order to justify the necessary additional post-research expenditure.[18,19] Exclusivity is almost always a *sine qua non* which, incidentally, is an important aspect of the social paradox described in Section 3.8.

## 3.3 THE PATENT SYSTEM

Intellectual property is currently protected in a number of ways: formally, through instruments such as the patent system, copyright, registered designs, trade and service marks, and informally — and inherently more risky — by maintaining trade secrecy and expediting market penetration, thereby gaining time advantage over competitors.

IPR rights, in one form or another, have been recognised for more than fourteen centuries. Irish history recounts the famous judgement by King Diarmaid (*c.* 561 AD) on the copyright infringement by Colmcille (St. Columba) of Finnen's book:[20] "To every cow her young cow, that is, her calf, and to every book its transcript."

The patent system itself is predicated on a philosophy that traces back to its very origins. The word patent derives from the Latin *litterae patentes* which means open letters, as used in medieval times to confer rights and privileges under Royal Seal. The system evolved initially to protect the proprietary knowledge and skills of Venetian glass blowers. The first recorded patent, granted in 1449, gave John of Utynam a 20-year monopoly on the new glass making process that he introduced into England. But there was a price to pay in as much as the full details of the process had to be revealed to the local glass-blowing fraternity.[21]

Such is the case with the current patent system that provides the inventor with legal protection for a fixed period (up to 20 years) in one or more specified countries. Cover is granted for new inventions that meet the principal criteria of novelty, applicability and non-obviousness, *subject to full disclosure of the technical details.*

> The filing of a patent represents an agreement whereby an inventor makes his invention public after an interval that may vary according to the particular system and in return benefits from temporary legal protection from the country in which the patent is filed. The applicant must provide a detailed technical description of his/her invention and set out those aspects which, in his/her opinion, constitute its originality (inventiveness and prior art).[16]

### 3.3.1 Towards Global Harmonisation

The Paris Convention for the protection of intellectual property (1883), along with its subsequent revisions, is the basis of the modern patent system whereby each nation guarantees the same rights of priority as exist within its own borders for all signatory nations — almost 100 in number.

In Europe, negotiations towards a common patent system first began in 1953, leading to the Strasbourg Convention signed in 1963 and, more formally, to the Munich Convention of 1973 under which the European Patent Office (EPO) was established. This created a unified system for granting patents in Europe whereby protection in a number of European countries could be effected by means of a single application to the EPO. EPO patents can only be granted 18 months after initial filing — which involves automatic publication — and patent protection is still governed by the laws of those countries in which the patent is in force. Aside from the practical benefits attaching to a single application for multi-nation protection, the international status of the European patent confers prestige on the patent and obviates any implication of domestic bias or national favouritism.[22]

The General Agreement on Tariffs and Trade (GATT) (1984) required that patents be accessible to any citizen of the World

Trade Organisation (WTO) — the successor to GATT — irrespective of place of invention. Following the Uruguay round of discussions in 1995, the WTO was given responsibility for settling disputes among nations on IP matters. Furthermore, effective January 1, 1996, WTO nations have been granted comparable status to the US when establishing a *Date of Invention* under US Patent Law (Section 8.6).[22,23] The agreement on Trade Related Aspects of Intellectual Property (TRIPs) has also been noteworthy in strengthening patent protection among WTO member nations. More recent developments include passage of the US Trade Law and ratification of the Berne Convention for the Protection of Literary and Artistic Works in 1988.

With the sustained growth in patents — about one million patents are currently processed each year — it is becoming increasingly difficult for IP practitioners to access the burgeoning global information base on intellectual property. Purcell has discussed ways of exploiting the Internet to meet this growing challenge.[24]

The patent system continues to develop, notably in two areas, in order to meet the growing challenges of today's knowledge-driven society: (a) the protection of intellectual property in complex new growth areas such as biotechnology where current European patent law in particular is increasingly inadequate and (b) the harmonisation of national patent systems.

### 3.4 CATEGORIES OF PATENTABLE KNOWLEDGE

There is no inherent difficulty in patenting new machines, products and processes if the invention satisfies established criteria. There are anomalies, however. New computer programs, animals and plant varieties, and methods of therapeutic or surgical treatments can, in principle, be patented in some countries but not in others.[25] Patents are not granted for aesthetic creations, ideas or scientific discoveries that do not have a specified application.

Major problems arise in the biotechnology area which, in fact, is one of the key IP growth areas and which currently attracts the lion's share of public and private research funding.[26] Consider, for example, the invention of a new gene-spliced product that is the same as a naturally occurring protein in nature. Does the intellectual property belong to the researcher who isolated and purified the natural protein or to the one who cloned it? [27]

More fundamentally, the creation of a transgenic non-human animal by transplanting genes from a foreign source into an animal's genome using recombinant DNA techniques has raised profound generic moral, ethical and legal problems.[28] One such transgenic non-human animal — the Harvard Mouse — was patented in the US in 1988.[29] The EPO at first refused to grant a patent on the Mouse, citing Article 53(b) of the European Patent Convention (EPC) which states that

> European patents shall not be granted in respect of . . . plant or animal varieties or essentially biological processes for the production of plants or animals . . . this provision does not apply to micro biological processes or the products thereof.

The Harvard Mouse was first interpreted as an animal variety and therefore not patentable. On appeal, the Examining Division of the EPO allowed the patent but stressed that precedent was not created in the sense that other cases of transgenic animals might well be denied under Article 53(a) as being contrary to public order or morality.[28]

Recurring problems also centre on the term "essentially biological", which is open to interpretation and suffers from the vagaries of translation from one language to another. Difficulties in writing clear patent disclosures on living organisms have been circumvented to some degree by depositing the newly invented micro-organism in an accredited institution. However, the system in practice was difficult to operate and tended to be avoided.[30]

But these are as nothing compared to the prospective technical and moral problems that will arise in relation to IP generated through newly emerging applications in human genetics. Such imponderables illustrate the difficulties in establishing a legal framework for patent protection, particularly in Europe where many of the central issues have yet to be resolved. A recent directive on the legal protection of biotechnological inventions proposed by the European Commission and agreed by the Council of Ministers attempted to improve Europe's legal framework. The European Parliament to date has not ratified the proposals.[31]

### 3.5. IP Ownership and Protection

As pointed out by Alster,[32] and re-echoed by Carroll:[3]

> the concept of intellectual property takes on special urgency in high-technology businesses because invention is the industry's stock and trade. . . . In industries that require heavy investment in research and development, patent enforcement is a matter of survival.

This is the stark reality of IP ownership and protection. Typically, it can take up to twelve years to introduce a new medicine or drug into the American market at a cost that can rise to hundreds of millions of dollars.[33] The creation and development of new software can be comparably expensive. Managing the risk/return trade-off in situations where up-front capital expenditure can be so high is exceedingly problematic.

There are two key aspects of the problem: (a) the worth of IP as a tradable commodity in its own right and (b) patent infringement and the piracy of protected products and processes.

#### 3.5.1. Growth in Trade in IP

The US is a net exporter of IP or technological know-how. In the exchange and use of industrial processes with unaffiliated foreign residents in 1993, for example, the value of exports versus imports was in the ratio of 3:1 which translated into a surplus of $1.7 billion (Table 3.1).[1] This is modest on the overall scale of US trade but it is nonetheless significant and growing. The surplus with Japan ($1,198 million) is consistent with Japan's ability to commercialise non-indigenous scientific discovery to the benefit of its own economy.

TABLE 3.1. US RECEIPTS AND PAYMENTS OF ROYALTIES AND LICENSE FEES ($US MILLION) FOR THE EXCHANGE AND USE OF INDUSTRIAL PROCESSES WITH UNAFFILIATED FOREIGN RESIDENTS (1993) (ADAPTED FROM TABLE 6.3, REF. 1.)

| Country | Receipts | Payment | Balance |
|---|---|---|---|
| All countries | 2,755 | 1,036 | 1,719 |
| Europe | 615 | 801 | (186) |
| EU | 484 | 470 | 14 |
| Germany | 97 | 149 | (52) |
| UK | 113 | 129 | (16) |
| Asia and Pacific | 1,932 | 203 | 1,729 |
| Japan | 1,392 | 194 | 1,198 |

Brackets denote a deficit.

Today more than ever, knowledge is, by its nature, global: it is disseminated through a whole variety of formal and informal mechanisms. There are, therefore, compelling commercial reasons to protect intellectual property as a tradable commodity in its own right. This is particularly so at a time when research and technological development is being internationalised through the formation of strategic alliances at an ever-increasing rate and through the geographical dispersion of a significant element of US R&TD.[34]

### 3.5.2 Patent Infringement, Counterfeiting and Piracy

Infringement of IP by those who do not have ownership rights is a global phenomenon: it is on a scale that is seriously undermining

the profitability and competitiveness of many high-tech companies that trade on world markets.[35] Piracy and patent infringement subvert the incentives that are at the heart of a knowledge-
based economy. In so doing, they erode and distort the basis for
trade both in intellectual property itself and the trade and investment that flow from it.

In 1986, the US International Trade Commission estimated that
losses due to piracy were of the order of $60 billion, principally in
the computer software, pharmaceuticals and entertainment sectors.[36,37] In the packaged software industry, which currently is
worth $77 billion world-wide, US suppliers with 75 per cent of the
global market share lost revenues of the order of $13 billion in
1993.[38] In the pharmaceutical sector, the pirated copy of a new
drug or medicine can often capture as much as 50 per cent of the
world market share and, in some cases, may be launched prior to
the legitimate product. It is also estimated that about one-half of
the computer software in use in Ireland is pirated.[39] Clearly, this is
a problem of major proportions in need of urgent redress but,
again, the issues involved are by no means straightforward.

## 3.6 GLOBAL TRENDS IN PATENTING

Comprehensive and readily accessible patent statistics are compiled by the US (USPTO) and European (EPO) Patent Offices.[40]
The two systems differ in a number of respects that make direct
comparisons difficult:

- The USPTO lists patents granted whereas the EPO lists patents filed.

- In the US patent system — which now extends to procedures in
  other WTO nations — the "date of invention" has legal significance in determining priority of invention. There are three possible Dates of Invention: (a) *conception*, that is when the inventor
  conceived the idea of the complete and operable invention; (b)
  the *actual reduction to practice* whereby the complete and oper-

able invention was actually made; and (c) the *constructive reduction to practice* which is the "effective filing date" of a US patent application.[23] Evidence in the form of notebook records, suitably validated, is crucial in determining the date of conception and of due diligence in reducing the original idea to practice.

• In spite of the savings associated with the single procedure for multiple filings in Europe through the European Patent Office (EPO), overall costs are still comparatively high.[33] US companies which currently file about 30 per cent of all European patents (Table 3.2) and must therefore bear a substantial financial burden have been particularly disadvantaged.[41] The relative cost disadvantage which has militated against the development of a more robust IP capability within the EU has recently been ameliorated with proposed fee reductions of the order of 20 per cent, which took effect from July 1997.

The progress of the top five performers in the EPO league table over the period from 1982 to 1995 (Table 3.2) reveals the spectacular growth in the number of patents filed by the Japanese — typical of the DAEs in general — which is in contrast to the parallel decline in UK patents.

TABLE 3.2: PER CENT SHARE OF PATENTS FILED WITH THE EUROPEAN PATENT OFFICE: TOP FIVE PERFORMERS, 1982–95

| Country | 1982 | 1985 | 1988 | 1991 | 1994 | 1995 |
|---------|------|------|------|------|------|------|
| US | 27.0 | 27.4 | 26.2 | 25.0 | 29.3 | 29.0 |
| Germany | 23.1 | 21.9 | 21.4 | 20.0 | 19.6 | 19.1 |
| Japan | 12.9 | 15.3 | 18.0 | 22.3 | 17.0 | 18.0 |
| France | 9.6 | 8.6 | 8.5 | 8.6 | 7.8 | 7.6 |
| UK | 8.5 | 7.7 | 7.2 | 5.2 | 5.3 | 5.4 |

*Source*: EU Commission.

The reported growth rates furnished in Table 3.3 denote the increase or decrease in the share of total US and European patents in each class of activity, but not the actual increase or decrease in absolute numbers.[42,43] Note the impressive performance of Japan and the Developing Asian Economies (DAEs) relative to the rest of the world. The number of US patents granted to Japan exceeds the combined total for the EU, the European Free Trade Association (EFTA) and Economies in Transition (EIT).[43] It is noteworthy that Japanese researchers, in contrast to their US counterparts, place as much emphasis on *incremental* improvements as on fundamental breakthroughs. Taiwan and South Korea are increasing their portfolio of US patents quite rapidly, particularly in the communications and electronic component sectors. The EU share of US patents, in contrast, has been falling in recent years, largely due to declining German and UK performance.

Overall, the EPO and USPTO patent statistics show comparable trends that resonate with EU innovation and industrial policies. The following general observations can be drawn: [44]

- The EU is the world's leading producer of pharmaceutical products; output in 1993 was one-third larger than the US and twice as large as Japan. Patent profiles also reveal strength in aerospace, non-electrical machinery and motor vehicles.

- Europe's core scientific weaknesses are in the computer, electronic and instruments sectors. Note, however, that Ireland and the Netherlands show evidence of modest technological advantage in electronics, albeit from a very small base, in contrast to the rest of Europe.

TABLE 3.3. AVERAGE ANNUAL GROWTH RATES IN US AND EUROPEAN PATENTING (1981-1993) OF COUNTRY GROUP SHARES BY SECTOR (%)[42]

| | Aerospace | | Electronics | | Pharmacy | | Machinery Equipment | | Transport | | Chemicals | | Other Industries | |
|---|---|---|---|---|---|---|---|---|---|---|---|---|---|---|
| | Europe | US | Europe | US | Europe | US | Europe | US | Europe | US | Europe | US | Europe | US |
| EU | -0.06 | 0.54 | -3.43 | -4.73 | -2.38 | -1.59 | -0.78 | -1.72 | 0.46 | -1.32 | -2.02 | -1.17 | -0.77 | -2.21 |
| EFTA | 9.29 | -5.42 | -2.58 | -4.10 | -3.44 | -3.52 | -0.80 | -2.80 | -2.94 | -5.41 | -4.80 | -2.59 | -2.16 | -3.29 |
| EIT | - | - | -0.69 | -16.48 | 3.86 | -7.95 | -1.17 | -15.23 | -1.52 | -14.55 | 4.62 | -12.35 | -2.76 | -15.97 |
| NAFTA | -1.52 | -0.81 | 0.72 | -0.45 | 2.67 | 0.51 | -0.90 | -0.54 | -2.84 | -0.97 | 1.01 | -0.42 | 0.24 | -0.19 |
| Other America | - | - | -8.58 | 3.72 | 12.92 | -7.80 | 1.59 | 2.59 | -1.77 | -5.65 | 0.13 | 10.17 | -0.43 | 4.19 |
| Japan | 3.89 | 17.78 | 6.16 | 3.37 | 2.37 | 2.08 | 6.36 | 4.27 | 5.34 | 3.38 | 6.19 | 3.87 | 5.85 | 3.65 |
| DAE | - | - | 23.07 | 25.22 | 19.05 | 22.04 | 22.75 | 23.16 | 8.23 | 17.57 | 13.99 | 16.08 | 16.98 | 18.50 |
| Asian | - | - | 5.19 | 15.75 | -19.66 | -1.86 | -3.29 | 4.74 | -9.48 | - | 3.83 | 13.67 | -4.39 | 0.93 |
| Other Asia | - | - | 12.01 | 19.72 | 15.45 | 14.27 | 29.35 | 20.42 | -7.29 | - | 3.22 | 14.40 | 2.36 | 12.88 |
| Oceania | - | 2.58 | -0.81 | -3.99 | 3.31 | 3.23 | -2.03 | -1.91 | -5.14 | -0.30 | 1.24 | -3.48 | -3.79 | -2.20 |
| IL/ZA | 4.65 | - | 12.47 | 2.43 | 31.48 | 4.16 | 1.07 | -0.50 | 4.07 | -0.22 | 8.02 | -0.46 | 2.82 | 0.18 |

- The relative scientific strength of the US in information and computer sciences as well as mechanical and electrical/electronic engineering is broadly the reverse of the EU.

- Although the EU is strong in scientific output performance (as gauged, for example, in world publications) and has broadly maintained its share of total global R&D expenditures, its share of US and European patents has declined substantially during the 1980s. This reflects the lack of an informed and supportive infrastructure and Europe's diminished ability, or desire, to translate new scientific discoveries into useful technology and to take risks.

### 3.6.1 The New Dynamic

In the scenario outlined thus far, it is apparent that patent activity in Europe lags behind the US and lacks the vibrancy and growth of Japan and the developing Asian Economies. Effete policies, a pervasive lack of entrepreneurial and risk-taking culture and shifts in inward investment away from Europe are major contributors. US foreign investment is a case in point where, historically, much of this investment was located in Europe. As recently as 1993, almost 25 per cent was sourced in Germany with an additional 15 per cent in the UK, some 9 per cent in France and as much as 6 per cent in Ireland. In the interim, there was evidence of a progressive shift away from Europe towards the Pacific Basin, reflecting the growing stature of the new Asian economies. This trend has now abated. Against the backdrop of the EU Single Market and, more significantly, a prospective Federal Europe, a re-invigorated US/EU research and development axis is emerging. The commitment within the EU to a competitiveness strategy that is innovation-led is likely to reinforce the importance of intellectual property in trade and investment relations between what are now two of the major global trading blocs. As signalled in the EU *Green Paper on Innovation*,[7] this whole process raises important issues regarding the cultivation, management and protection of intellectual property as the foundation stone of this new axis.

### 3.7 IPR IN IRELAND

Ireland is a convenient template for examining the nature of this process. The macroeconomic performance of the Irish economy in recent years is without precedent within the wider EU. Real growth has averaged 6 per cent, within a context of macroeconomic stability directed towards participation in Economic and Monetary Union (EMU). The extraordinarily strong performance of the Irish economy reflects both a significant strengthening of indigenous industry and the continued attraction of foreign investment on a scale quite beyond that expected in terms of Ireland's size.

The importance of innovation and R&D has been officially recognised, but not adequately acted upon despite the conclusions of the STIAC report that reaffirmed the importance of investment in R&D and the central role of the universities.[45] The pharmaceutical industry, for example, is one of the motors of Ireland's record export-led growth. A recent authoritative analysis of global healthcare industries concluded that "a great pharmaceutical company should have a product portfolio in 2005 which is substantially concentrated in products not yet on the market".[5] Yet, as pointed out by the recent CIRCA report,[46] there has been a systematic under-investment in university R&D, a significant proportion of which underpins developments in the pharmaceutical sector. A similar concern was expressed by the EU in its recent report on science and technology indicators.[47]

The issue is not whether the importance of innovation has been recognised: it has. Rather, the reality is that the central role of intellectual property is not reflected in focused resourcing, notably within the university sector. Given our earlier emphasis on intellectual property management as the basis for global foreign direct investment and, equally, the greatly accelerated product cycle requiring new responses in terms of management, this represents a fatal weakness in industrial strategy.

This weakness expresses itself in a basic failure to provide sufficient incentives to attract and retain researchers in the science-based disciplines within Irish universities. Notwithstanding recent policy interventions, this simple failure not only impedes the ability of the economy to leverage expenditures on infrastructure — and more important, Ireland's success in attracting knowledge-driven foreign direct investment — but also fatally undermines policies aimed at fostering indigenous technology-based industries. Bright science and engineering graduates will no longer be motivated to remain in research at a time when the differential between their paltry stipend as postgraduates and prospective salaries outside the university is becoming greater and greater. The cost of rectifying this deficiency is, we estimate, of the order of £10 million which is small in the context of Ireland's overall budget for training.

More specifically, the extraordinary confluence of factors in Europe arising from the impact of the single market, the single currency, and the reshaping of the entire European continent, represents a unique window of opportunity that will not re-occur. The effective exploitation of this, whether at a national level or at the level of the wider EU, has, at its heart, the issue of intellectual property development.

Two major themes focus on the importance of innovation in knowledge-driven economies and the pivotal role of Ireland's participation within the EU that, specifically, has provided the essential underpinnings of Ireland's R&D programmes. At the same time, both domestic and foreign investment in Ireland is predicated on the 21st century European economy. The challenge for Ireland in this regard mirrors that of the wider EU, namely, rectifying the systematic under-investment in R&D and the failure to align both policy and institutions (including the financial sector) to the central role of intellectual property as the bedrock of economic prosperity. Lacking a substantive identification with, and resourcing of, intellectual property, the platform supporting Ireland's present prosperity is, from a medium-term perspective, both shallow and fragile.

### 3.7.1 Patenting in Ireland

The patent culture in Ireland is grossly under-developed. According to the World Competitiveness Report of 1994, Ireland ranked 25th of 41 countries reviewed.[48] This is confirmed by the data in Table 3.4 which lists the number of US patents granted in selected countries between 1977 and 1996.[49] Successive studies, notably STIAC,[45] recommended urgent remedial action in two main areas, namely (a) the need for less costly and more streamlined procedures for filing, evaluating and granting patents in Ireland and (b) a strengthening of the nation's support structures for promoting the commercialisation of new discoveries. Both of these issues are considered below.

*The Irish Patents Office (IPO):* The stated mission of the IPO is "to provide an efficient and effective system of intellectual property protection that will encourage technological progress and promote enterprise".[31] There has been a welcome decrease in the backlog of patent applications from 18,585 to 13,325 over the calendar year 1995, due principally to the new procedures introduced in the 1992 Patents Act and to Ireland's ratification of the European Patent Convention (EPC) and the Patent Co-operation Treaty (PCT) in the same year. A total of 990 patent applications were received in 1995 of which 840 were from within the state. Of these, 628 were for short-term patents — a new instrument which provides a rapid grant of an unexamined patent for a period of ten years — as specified in the 1992 Act. The number of European patents designating Ireland, that is, having the same legal status as if they were granted by the Irish Patents Office, was 804 compared with 66 in 1994. Over the 10-year period from 1985-95, just under 47 per cent of patent applications filed were successful.

TABLE 3.4: PATENT COUNTS BY COUNTRY AND YEAR[49]

| Country | 1977 | 1980 | 1985 | 1990 | 1995 | 1996 | Total 1977-96 |
|---|---|---|---|---|---|---|---|
| France | 2,195 | 2,150 | 2,516 | 3,093 | 3,010 | 3,016 | 52,749 |
| Germany | 5,653 | 5,895 | 6,906 | 7,861 | 6,874 | 7,125 | 136,169 |
| Greece | 11 | 3 | 12 | 10 | 8 | 18 | 238 |
| Ireland | 18 | 21 | 31 | 61 | 59 | 88 | 830 |
| Japan | 6,500 | 4,401 | 13,351 | 20,743 | 22,871 | 24,059 | 307,609 |
| Norway | 117 | 86 | 106 | 119 | 138 | 150 | 2,275 |
| Portugal | 4 | 2 | 6 | 7 | 3 | 4 | 102 |
| Spain | 101 | 71 | 85 | 148 | 168 | 187 | 2,369 |
| UK | 2,773 | 2,498 | 2,620 | 3,017 | 2,681 | 2,674 | 52,796 |
| USA | 45,047 | 40,769 | 43,393 | 52,976 | 64,510 | 69,419 | 985,317 |

*National Support Structures:* The costs of patenting, developing, licensing and, when necessary, defending intellectual property can be prohibitive, particularly for small firms and entrepreneurs.[50] In Europe, the cost of filing and maintaining a patent can be as much as six times more expensive than in the US (*c.f.* Section 3.6). STIAC proposed a number of innovative steps which, in some instances, have been adopted.[51]

- The introduction of a less costly *short-term patent*, following the spirit of an earlier UK initiative in the form of an *unregistered design right*, which effected automatic protection at much reduced cost, based on the inventor's written specification of what is to be protected in place of registration.

- The issuance of an invention certificate or warrant.

- The promotion of an "Ethical Intellectual Property Charter" whereby Irish firms would be invited to adopt a set of principles to ensure that the intellectual property which rightfully belongs to others is not knowingly infringed.

- The granting of tax relief on the outlay involved in establishing patent rights and on royalties earned on certain patents.

Forbairt (*cf.* Section 6.2) through its Invention Service provides assistance on the development and commercialisation of inventions. The inventor is advised on relevant issues such as the timing of the patent application, the degree of novelty, prototype development, preparation of business plans and interpretation of the current tax legislation relating to patents. In a limited number of cases, 100 per cent funding is advanced to cover patent costs in return for an equity stake in the form of a royalty that is levied on any future income.

Forbairt has also initiated a series of workshops to redress systematically the general lack of readily accessible information on matters relating to intellectual property, in keeping with proposals in the STIAC report. A handbook on IP and its protection has recently been prepared for the HE sector.[52] The UK White Paper had earlier proposed that their Patent Office adopt a more aggressive commercial approach, and, in response, their Patent Office now has a marketing division which exploits a variety of information dissemination mechanisms such as exhibitions, seminars and multimedia packages on patents and licensing.[53]

### 3.8 THE SOCIAL PARADOX

Despite the compelling arguments in support of strong legal protection of IP, there remain conflicting viewpoints on the permissible level of monopoly power that can attach to proprietary new knowledge. On the one hand, inventors see patent protection as the economic incentive to innovate while others argue that patents create monopolies that inhibit competition and maintain high prices to the ultimate detriment of the consumer. The historical ebb and flow of support for IP, as well as divergent national practices, reflects the inherent tension between the two viewpoints. This is clearly illustrated in the way in which the patent system has evolved in the US since the 18th century (Table 3.5).[27]

TABLE 3.5: HISTORICAL EVOLUTION OF PATENT PROTECTION IN THE US

| Year | Action |
|---|---|
| 1787 | Monopoly rights granted to owners of "new and useful ideas" for a limited time under Article I, Section 8 of the Constitution. Thomas Jefferson named first Commissioner of Patents. |
| 1800s | Industrial revolution in US helped by a strengthening of the rights of property owners, patent and copyright laws |
| 1950s | Proliferation of antitrust suits by the Justice Department against companies that enforce their patent rights. |
| 1974 | First manufacturing trade deficit in US focuses attention on intellectual property infringement. No action by Congress. |
| 1976 | Landmark lawsuit by Polaroid against Kodak upheld in Federal Court. |
| 1982 | Court of Appeals for the Federal Circuit created by Congress to deal with all patent appeals generates a swing in favour of patent holders. |
| 1986 | Burgeoning patent litigation following Kodak's enforced exit from the instant camera business. |
| 1988 | Landmark trade bill giving property holders strong leverage in international trade signed into law, bringing the number of intellectual property laws passed by Congress to 14 in the period 1983-89. |
| 1995 | First indications that the pendulum may have swung too far in favour of the patent holder. |

*Source*: Adapted from ref. 27.

Today, in the international arena, legal redress against patent infringement is increasingly effective but the deeper economic and social conflicts continue unabated. The global balance of power is shifting from "technologically disenfranchised imitators to technologically franchised innovators" because of the link between strong foreign competition and weak intellectual property protection.[27]

There is also a sea change within the US itself, notably following the successful outcome of Polaroid's IP infringement lawsuit against Kodak some two decades ago. Up to that time, the relative weakness of IP protection had an increasingly negative impact on investment in R&D and US global competitiveness. Laws enacted to promote healthy domestic competition were, in effect, adversely affecting US global competitiveness.[54] Enactment of the National Co-operative Research Act in 1984 at least partially redressed this difficulty. Strengthening legal protection for IP has instilled greater confidence to invest in the necessary R&TD, notably in the pharmaceutical industry where the inherent risks are high and IP infringement is widespread: spending has increased from $4.1 billion in 1985 to nearly $16 billion in 1996.[26] But the dangers of too great a swing towards IP protection — as is evident at the present time — are very real. At issue here is a resolution of a social paradox which becomes particularly acute in the global economy of the 21st century where intellectual property is the essential foundation for the generation and commercialisation of innovation and growth.

This dichotomy between the requirements of public policy and private incentives needs to be highlighted and resolved and it is further sharpened by the scale of *public* investment in the formation of intellectual property through free access by industry to publicly funded research published in scientific journals. Consider the following three scenarios:

## 1. The creation of untenable monopolies

When Shockley, Brattain and Bardeen of AT&T Bell Telephone Laboratories (now Lucent Technologies) announced the invention of the transistor in June, 1948, the US government in its wisdom decided that the patent conferred too much power and control on one company. In the event, the technology was made freely available to those who wished to exploit it.

This, albeit extreme, case indicates one safeguard in the form of competition policy which has a role to play in preventing large companies internalising the full benefits of IP to the potential disadvantage of society at large.

## 2. The "David and Goliath" scenario

The possibility now exists for large corporations to exploit the legal defense of patents as a means to restrict the development of, or even close down, smaller competitors who may not be in a position to bear the costs of infringement suits, irrespective of the merits or demerits of their case. The cost of legal out-of-court proceedings in defending intellectual property rights in Europe was 1.8 million ECU in 1994.[55] Kingston has proposed a practical approach based on compulsory arbitration by experts to reduce the costs of defending IP.[50]

The problem is all the more pressing since knowledge-driven small-and-medium-sized enterprises (SMEs), and even micro-enterprises, are currently the major job creators. Deficiencies in this area undermine national innovation systems — and hence the basis for participation in international trade — with serious knock-on implications for smaller open economies. Moreover, at the policy level, such weaknesses diminish the potential leverage of tax and structural policies aimed at supporting R&TD. Clearly, procedures at the national level for protecting intellectual property need to be made accessible to, and cost effective for, smaller companies.

Effective technology transfer and diffusion programmes can also help to maximise spill-over effects of R&TD carried out by large companies. Cross-sectoral programmes between firms, large and small, aimed at generating new knowledge are also important in promoting the diffusion of IP right across the economy. These approaches — as the Japanese experience shows — can be effective in fostering knowledge creation and use in the wider population of small firms which tend to be employment intensive.

## 3. Accessibility to new drugs

Patented drugs are expensive because the market price must recoup *all* development, clinical trials, production and marketing costs as well as generating profit. Only a small proportion of potential new drugs reach the marketplace. But the huge investment in those drugs that fail to reach the market must also be recouped. The post-development costs, including manufacturing the drug, are a small fraction of the overall costs. In many cases, the difference between the marginal cost of producing the drug and the market price determined by the company which holds the patent can be so high as to place the drug out of reach of the less well off in society.

Figure 3.2 clarifies the logistics involved in terms of the price-versus-quantity profile and the relationship between the marginal and proprietary costs of a drug.[56,57] $P_C$ is the marginal cost and $Q_C$ is the quantity sold at or near the marginal cost; $Q_M$ denotes the quantity sold at the proprietary cost, $P_M$, set by the company. The profit directly accruing from patent protection is denoted by the area of the rectangle A: this is the so-called monopoly profit. The value to the consumer who pays the marginal cost — the consumer surplus — is represented by the area A+B+C. The much reduced consumer surplus at the higher price, $P_M$, is denoted by the area B.

FIGURE 3.2: SCHEMATIC ILLUSTRATING THE DEMAND PROFILE OF A NEW DRUG[55]

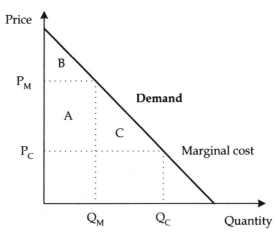

The pharmaceutical sector can rightly claim that it should be appropriately rewarded for the massive high-risk, up-front investment in R&TD that (a) produced the drug or medicine, (b) created jobs and (c) improved the general health and well-being of society. At the same time, society could argue, first, that much of the benefit is eroded if the drug is so expensive as to place it out of reach of the marginalised in society and, second, that the price does not reflect the essential prior knowledge, generated through publicly funded research, which has also contributed to the breakthrough.

Prior knowledge is also at issue in the growing tensions that are currently bedevilling the *Human Genome Project* involving a network of global partners. The aim of the project, which involves massive public investment, is to map out the human genetic codes. However, some participants in the project have claimed individual proprietary rights by patenting key breakthroughs of significant commercial potential to the detriment of other partners, of members of the public at large who have provided critical statistical data on a range of health disorders and, by implication, of the project as a whole.

The net return to society for its public support of research is also compromised by the current tendency of large corporations to dominate the global IP market while downsizing and shedding jobs. They are, in effect, maximising their profits while reducing the tangible returns on public investment in R&TD to society.

How can this dilemma be addressed equitably, particularly in the case of new drugs and medicines? Government, for example, could further subsidise the initial research from the public purse to supplement its indirect contribution to the creation of relevant prior knowledge in the literature. This is generally not the best way to proceed since governments have a poor record in identifying winners. Alternatively, the current widespread practice of introducing a preferential subsidy for the less well-off in society at the point of purchase is a workable solution if the price of the drug or medicine takes into account society's contribution to the development costs. Kremer has mooted an imaginative scheme whereby government purchases the drug against rival companies at auction for subsequent sale to the public at the marginal cost of production.[56] In the absence of detailed further analysis, the scheme, though admirable in its quest for an equitable solution to this paradox, appears to raise as many problems as it solves.[57]

## OBSERVATIONS AND RECOMMENDATIONS

- *The technology that flows from new knowledge is a valuable and tradable resource because of its direct link to economic growth.*

- *Intellectual property is a tradable commodity in its own right.*

- *This reflects a new perspective on knowledge, namely, knowledge as equity which, in turn, reinforces the importance of intellectual prop-*

*erty rights (IPR) whose scale, scope and importance in national economic development and in global trade cannot be over-stressed.*

- *Inventors, including academic researchers, do not always appreciate the scale of the additional funding required and often have inflated expectations of the worth of their new discovery.*

- *Non-exclusivity clauses in publicly-funded research contracts can constitute a major disincentive to the successful commercialisation of the new idea because companies seek exclusive rights to the intellectual property in order to justify the necessary additional post-research expenditure.*

- *Major legal ambiguities in protecting new discoveries in the biotechnology area remain to be solved.*

- *Despite recent EU and WTO initiatives, patent infringement and piracy are rampant.*

- *Patent activity in Europe lags behind the US and it lacks the vibrancy and growth of Japan and the Developing Asian Economies.*

- *The commitment within the EU to a competitiveness strategy that is innovation-led is likely to reinforce the importance of intellectual property in trade and investment.*

- *The patent culture in Ireland is grossly under-developed.*

- *The challenge for Ireland mirrors that of the wider EU, namely, rectifying the systematic under-investment in R&D and aligning both policy and institutions (including the financial sector) to the central role of intellectual property as the bedrock of economic prosperity.*

- *Despite compelling arguments in support of strong legal protection of IP, there remain conflicting viewpoints on the permissible level of monopoly power which should attach to proprietary new knowledge. This has led to a social paradox that is at the heart of issue of intellectual property management.*

- *Initiatives to resolve this paradox that seek to diffuse the economic benefits of IP throughout society at large will, no doubt, act as an effective counterweight against the tendency of the very large corporations to shift the historic and equitable balance between public good and private profit towards the private sector. By the same token, procedures at the national level for protecting intellectual property need to be made accessible to, and cost effective for, smaller companies.*

## References and Notes: Chapter 3

1.  V.J. McBrierty and R.P. Kinsella, *The Role of Intellectual Property in a Knowledge Society: The Social Paradox*, Studies, March, 1998: Note also that US receipts for all trade in intellectual property exceeded $20 billion in 1993 which was a factor of two higher than the 1988 receipts: *Science and Engineering Indicators, 1996.* National Science Board, Washington DC: US Government Printing Office, 1996 (NSB 96-21), p.6.14-15, 267.

2.  J.I. Bernstein and P. Mohnen, *J. Intnl. Economics*, 44, 315-338 (1998).

3.  See, for example, C. Carroll, "R&D-Laying Golden Eggs", *Management*, September, 1996, pp. 36-37.

4.  Ikujiro Nonaka, "The Knowledge Creating Company", *Harvard Business Review*, Nov.-Dec., 1991, pp. 96-104.

5.  Morgan Stanley, *Competitive Analysis*, London, 1997, pp. 85, 86.

6.  V.J. McBrierty, *The University and Research: Aims, Conditions, Resources*, in "The Role of the University in Society", Proceedings of the NUI Conference in Dublin Castle, 20-21 May, 1994, pp. 79-93; see also R.P. Kinsella and V.J. McBrierty, "Campus Companies and the Emerging Techno-academic Paradigm: the Irish Experience", *Technovation*, 17(5), 245-251 (1997).

7.  *Green Paper on Innovation*, Bulletin of the European Union, Supplement 5/95, published by the European Commission, 1996.

8.  *ibid.* p.34.

9.  V. Bush, *Science — The Endless Frontier: A Report to the President for a Program of Postwar Scientific research*, 1945. Reprinted by the National Science Foundation, Washington DC 1980.

10. See, for example, R. Roy, "Applied Research Needs New Funding Scheme", *Chemical and Engineering News*, Aug. 2, 1971, p. 13.

11. D. Stokes, *Pasteur's Quadrant*, Brookings Institution, Washington, DC, 1997.

12. S.J. Klein and N. Rosenberg, "An Overview of Innovation", in *The Positive Sum Strategy: Harnessing Technology for Economic Growth*, R. Landau and N. Rosenberg (eds.), National Academy Press, Washington, DC, 1986, p. 289.

13. OECD, *Proposed Guidelines for Collecting and Interpreting Technological Innovation Data*, Paris, 1982.

14. *Science, Technology and Innovation, The White Paper*, Government Stationery Office, Dublin 2, Oct. 1996.

15. V. J. McBrierty, *Higher Education into the 21st Century: Science, Technology and the Universities*, R.M. Jones Memorial Lecture, The Queen's University of Belfast, 10 October 1995, Published by QUB, Belfast, N. Ireland (1996).

16. *European Report on Science and Technology Indicators, 1994.* European Commission, EUR 15897, 1994. DGXIII, L-2920, Luxembourg, p. 49.

17. V.J. McBrierty and E.P. O'Neill, (eds), "University/Industry/Government Relations", *Intnl. Jnl. Of Technology Management*, 6 (5/6), 557-67 (1991).

18. T. Gering, "University Technology Licensing,: Risks, Technology Sectors, Strategic and Economic Potential", *Industry and Higher Education*, April, 1995, pp. 72-77.

19. T. Gering and H. Schmied, "Intellectual Property Issues: Technology Licensing — Costs versus Benefits", *Higher Education Management*, 5, 100-110, March, 1993.

20. A. O'Kelleher and G. Schoeperle (eds), Betha Colaim Chille, Compiled by Maghnas O'Domhnaill in 1532. University of Illinois, 1918; reprinted by Dundalgan Press Ltd, 1994.

21. *The Derwent Guide to Patents*, Derwent Publications Ltd., Derwent House, 14 Great Queen St., London, WC2B 5DF, England.

22. R. Barre, ref. 15, pp. M-10,11.

23. P. Coyle, private communication. See also, G.J. Mossinghoff, "IP Protection Increases Worldwide", *Les Nouvelles*, Vol. XXXI, No. 4, Dec. 1996, pp. 159-63.

24. A.F. Purcell, "Intellectual Property Resources on the Global Internet", *Patent World*, June/July, 1996, pp. 18-26

25. In India, to take just one example, following relaxation of patent laws in 1970, a patent was available in respect of a manufacturing process but not a product. "This triggered a proliferation of domestic pharmaceutical companies mostly churning out cheap copies of patented drugs". *London Financial Times*, 18 February 1997.

26. *Science and Engineering Indicators, 1996.* National Science Board, Washington DC: US Government Printing Office, 1996. (NSB 96-21). p. 4-24.

27. P. Dwyer, L. Jereski, Z. Schiller and D. Lee, "The Battle Raging over Intellectual Property", *Business Week*, May 1989, pp. 80-87.

28. R.K. Seide and A. Giaccio, "Patenting Animals", *Chemistry and Industry*, 21, August, 1995, p .656.

29. P. Leder and T. Steward, US Patent No. 4,736,866. (1988).

30. U. Schmoch, H. Grupp, T. Reiss and E. Strauss, *Monitoring Science-based Biotechnology by Means of Patent Indicators*, Research Evaluation, 1(2), August 1991, Beech Tree Publishing, Guilford, Surrey, England, pp. 61-68.

31. *Sixty-eighth Annual Report of the Controller of Patents, Designs and Trademarks, 1995*, Government Stationery Office, Dublin 2, Ireland.

32. N. Alster, "New Profits from Patents", *Fortune*, April 25, 1988, pp. 69-72.

33. AIPLA Report, "The Costs of European Patent Protection", *Managing Intellectual Property*, Issue 57, March 1996, pp. 19-27.

34. *Direct Investment Abroad: Operations of US Parent Companies and their Parent Affiliates*, Bureau of Economic Analysis, US Department of Commerce, Washington DC: GPO. 1993; see also "IBM's $350m Factory Will be Record Irish Inward Investment", *London Financial Times*, Friday, Dec. 13, 1996.

35. J. Nurton, "Catching up with the Counterfeiters", *Managing Intellectual Property*, Issue 57, March 1996, pp. 28-32.

36. F. Rice, "How Copycats Steal Billions", *Fortune*, April 22, 1991, pp. 85-88.

37. A. Rawsthorn, "Report on International Intellectual Property Alliance data", *London Financial Times*, February 10, 1997, p.6.

38. M.L. Good, "Globalisation of Technology Poses Challenges for Policymakers", *American Physical Society News*, July, 1996, p. 12.

39. *Foresight*, The IP Bulletin, Summer Edition, 1996. F R Kelly and Co., 27 Clyde Road, Dublin 4, Ireland.

40. The global statistical data on patents has been concisely reviewed in the reports on science, engineering and technology indicators published annually by The National Science Board, National Science Foundation in Washington and by The Office for Official Publications, European Commission, Luxembourg.

41. OECD, *Using Patent Data as S&T Indicators*, Patent Manual, Table 6, Paris, 1994; see also, I. Taylor, "Patents are a Virtue", *Times Higher Education Supplement*, May 10, 1996, p. 10.

42. Ref. 156, pp. 43, 47.

43. Economies in Transition (EITs): Bulgaria, Czech Republic, Hungary, Poland, Rumania, Slovak Republic, Ukraine, Russia (excluding other CIS countries).

44. Ref. 16, pp. 58, 83, 103.

45. *Making Knowledge Work for Us*, Report of the Science, Technology and Innovation Advisory Council, D. Tierney, Chairman, Stationery Office, Dublin 2, Ireland. 1995

46. *A Comparative International Assessment of the Organisation, Management and Funding of University Research in Ireland and Europe*, The CIRCA Group Europe Ltd., Roebuck Castle, Belfield, Dublin 4, Ireland. Report commissioned by the Higher Education Authority.

47. *Second European Report on S&T Indicators, 1997*, European Commission, EUR 17639 EN DGXIII, L-2920, Luxembourg.

48. *World Competitiveness Report, 1997*.

49. Statistics prepared by the US Patent and Trademark Office, Washington, DC, March, 1997.

50. W. Kingston, "Reducing the Cost of Resolving Intellectual Property Disputes", *European Jnl. of Law and Economics*, 1995, 2, 85-92.

51. Ref. 45, pp. E1-8.

52. *Intellectual Property and Licensing for Third Level Colleges*, Forbairt, 1997.

53. *Realising Our Potential: A Strategy for Science, Engineering and Technology*, UK White Paper, Cm 2250, HMSO, London, 1993.

54. Ref. 26, p. 4.16.

55. Ref. 7, p. 43.

56. M. Kremer, *A Mechanism for Encouraging Innovation*, HIID Discussion Paper, No. 533, May 1996.

57. *The Economist*, June 15, 1996, p. 93.

*Chapter 4*

# INTELLECTUAL PROPERTY RIGHTS IN THE HIGHER EDUCATION SECTOR

## 4.1 ACADEMIC RESEARCH AND INNOVATION

It has been argued in earlier chapters that the HE sector is a rich and diverse source of new knowledge underpinning the nation's overall innovation culture. This is a general feature right across Europe, as recently confirmed, for example, in a recent evaluation of the situation in Germany where the role of the HE sector as generators of intellectual and human capital and the subsequent transfer of these outputs to industry were clearly evident.[1] The views of the German *Transferstellen* responsible for the management of academic IP, indicated that

> German academics have a low awareness of IP matters, that current legal aspects of academic ownership of IP are considered by *Transferstellen* to be a hindrance to the effective transfer of technology between HE Institutions and industry and that despite institutional differences between Germany and the UK, the issues of *Transferstellen* resource and intellectual constraintsand inadequate incentive structures are a common theme between the two countries.[1]

As pointed out in the foregoing chapter, the extent to which new knowledge can be exploited to the benefit of society is intimately linked to the level of protection afforded to the intellectual property that derives from it. The contribution of academic research is becoming ever more important with the move away from in-house basic and applied research by industry towards a policy of out-sourcing that exploits the research capabilities of academic institutions in perceived priority areas. Parenthetically, these developments have turned out to be a double-edged sword for the universities in the following respect. On the one hand, refocusing attention on basic research — perceived historically to be the key strength of universities — is intrinsically to be welcomed. But the worrying corollary — and one that determines an adequate payback to society — is a policy that implicitly tries to exclude the universities from the more applied areas of innovative research and the intellectual property that flows from it.[2] This is advocated, for example, in the Irish White Paper on Science, Technology and Innovation in stating that "innovation is ultimately a matter for the business sector"[3] and often by industry itself which, additionally, expects government to pay for much of the basic research. In such circumstances, the price exacted from the academic institutions — and the concomitant diminished returns to society — for increased spending on basic research is too high.

Advocating this rather limited role for the universities runs counter to the growth of a strong and vibrant innovative culture in the Irish HE sector over the past three decades.[4] Prior to these developments, the translation of basic and applied research into new technology — and the concomitant creation of intellectual property rights (IPR) — was, in the main, a matter for industry. This is no longer the case for two main reasons: First, as explained in Section 1.1.1, the link between science and technology is now much more intimate in the sense that exploitable technology tends to develop conjointly with scientific discovery: they are more often than not twinned at birth.[5] Second, the level of state funding for many European universities, as the OECD has pointed out, has not kept pace with the demand for higher education which itself has created the current phenomenon of "mass education". This has placed ever-increasing strain on the public purse.[6-8]

These trends, notably the almost exponential increase in the numbers seeking admission to higher education, have compelled the university sector in Ireland to develop new sources of income to counter inadequate public funding. The need to ensure that the autonomy of the university is not subverted in the process by an over-dependence on the state is an important additional factor. A similar course of action has been advocated for universities in the UK in the face of current major shortfalls in funding.[4]

## 4.2 EXPLOITATION OF ACADEMIC INTELLECTUAL PROPERTY

As indicated in Section 3.2, the full exploitation of academic IP inevitably involves partnership between the university and one or more industrial, financial, or broker agencies. Establishing such partnerships is not routine because of fundamental cultural differences between the main players, particularly in the area of intellectual property rights (IPR):

- Conflict can arise between publication as the ultimate goal of academics and industry's need to maintain total secrecy, at least until IP rights are fully protected.

- The diversity of views on ownership and shared benefits of IPR in joint venture arrangements between the universities and their partners is a perennial problem.

- There is a pervasive lack of awareness as to the value of "knowledge equity" relative to "finance equity".[8]

Comerford has summed up the contrasting approaches to the development of IP in the universities and in industry in Table 4.1.[10]

With the growth in innovation in the universities and other HE research institutions, it is essential that intellectual property generated by academics is properly protected and exploited to the benefit of the institution and the community. To this end, the extent to which new knowledge is translated into intellectual property within the HE research institutions is explored from the perspectives and predilections of (a) the research practitioners themselves and (b) the policy makers within and without the academic

research institutions who are responsible for establishing and
maintaining a favourable operational environment to promote
such entrepreneurial activities.

TABLE 4.1: COMERFORD'S COMPARISON OF IP SOURCES:
UNIVERSITIES AND INDUSTRY[10]

| University | Industry |
|---|---|
| More R : Less D | Less R : More D |
| Technology Push | Market Pull |
| Prototype | Market ready |
| High Technical and Commercial Risks | Lower Technical and Commercial Risks |
| More innovative | Less innovative |
| World-wide license | Limited territory |
| IP at early stage | IP developed |

A prerequisite examination of developments in US universities
and colleges whose innovation culture is at a significantly more
advanced stage serves to clarify the issues involved.

## 4.3. INTELLECTUAL PROPERTY IN US ACADEMIC RESEARCH INSTITUTIONS

In the science and technology area, IP licensing in universities in
the United States has developed exponentially since the passage
of the Bayh-Dole Act in 1980. This legislation for the first time
gave the universities (and small businesses) the title to all IP created in research sponsored by government and the right to license
it freely to industry. If Europe were to follow suit, the development of an entrepreneurial culture would be greatly enhanced
and impediments such as the non-exclusivity clauses in some
government research contracts, discussed in Section 4.2, would
disappear.[2,11]

A number of additional factors influence the development of IP in US academic research institutions. On the positive side there is, by extension of Colombo's ideas,[5] a close relationship between patenting and the R&D that created the new idea: US patent culture generally tends to focus more on original breakthroughs than on the incremental improvements of existing know-how in the later developmental phase of the innovation cycle. In support of this observation, academic papers account for about 50 per cent of scientific papers cited in US patent applications; in the biomedical and clinical sectors, the proportion is 65 per cent.[12]

Nonetheless, links with industry remain strong: typically, in 1993, 38 per cent of publications from industry involved collaboration with academic researchers which represented a significant increase on the 1981 figure of 22 per cent.[13]

On the downside, good ideas find practical expression in precise and imaginative experimentation. There is evidence that this essential base for IP development is being eroded by a creeping obsolescence of research facilities in US universities (*c.f.* Section 6.4).[14] Further issues include the excessive shift of academic duties towards formal teaching to cope with the increasing demand for university education and the inordinately high investment in time devoted to the negotiation and management of successful research contracts which is a further drain on the time available for hands-on research. This feature of the US higher education sector is similar to trends within the EU.

Innovative companies such as 3M, in contrast, see the value of nurturing IP by facilitating and funding new ideas generated by their staff. In effect, this pro-active approach is leveraging the inbuilt knowledge equity of the company.[2,9]

More fundamentally, the sustained development of a balanced patent culture in the university sector requires a change in traditional attitudes. The 1996 report on *Science and Engineering Indicators* cited the views of engineers in the US who considered that:

traditional outputs such as papers for presentations, theses, and conference papers continued to be of much greater importance to faculty than commercial processes and products, patents, or invention disclosures.[15]

These prevailing attitudes reflect the more trenchant, traditional performance indicators for promotion within academic research institutions. Such attitudes can and must be revised and updated to reflect the role of the university in modern society, but in a way that does not create a culture of compliance or compromise the universities' academic standards and their ethos of freedom of expression and fundamental inquiry.

In spite of such difficulties, overall statistics reveal the sustained development of a patent culture in the US academic sector that parallels the growth in the overall contribution of academic researchers to the total US R&D effort: support for academic research increased from 10 per cent in 1980 to 13 per cent in 1995 and the academic sector continues to be the largest source of basic research in the US. The life sciences received the lion's share of funding and, more significantly, applied research carried out in the universities and colleges attracted funds that increased from $4.3 billion in 1990 to $5.5 billion in 1995.[16]

Figure 4.1 portrays the impressive growth in the number of US academic institutions, both public and private, in receipt of patents. The number more than doubled, from 80 in 1980 to 165 in 1994.[17] Of these, the share of the 100 largest research universities, based on the size of their research funding, increased from 75 per cent to 85 per cent of all newly issued academic patents over this period. The number of patents awarded to universities increased seven-fold in two decades compared with an overall two-fold increase in patents as a whole: university patents now represent about 3 per cent of all US patents awarded in 1994 compared with 1 per cent in 1980.

FIGURE 4.1: NUMBER OF PATENTS GRANTED TO US ACADEMIC
INSTITUTIONS AND NUMBER OF INSTITUTIONS GRANTED PATENTS[17]

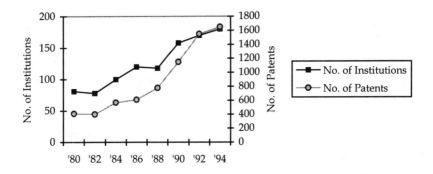

Intellectual property generated in the universities is also becoming more focused with time. Table 4.2 lists the 13 most active
classes in order of importance.[17] The number in the first three
utility categories — defined in terms of their likely area of application — grew from 8 per cent in the early 1970s to 25 per cent of
the total in the 1990s.[18-20]

Gross earnings from IP received by the US universities
amounted to $172 million in 1992 and $242 million in 1993. As
pointed out by Gering, this not only demonstrates an increasing
awareness by academic institutions of the value of intellectual
property but also the propensity of companies and investors to
exploit its market potential. The knock-on effects of technology
licensing in the US universities for the economy as a whole in
1992 are shown in Table 4.3.[11]

Using the example of the US universities, Gering assessed the
risks involved in protecting and licensing new technology in
terms of a number of pertinent indicators.[11] Only 10-20 per cent of
licensing agreements yielded substantial revenue; annual income
per license ranged between $18,000 and 28,000 depending on the
maturity of the technology licensing programme; income was
about 0.5-1 per cent of the university's investment in research,
rising to nearly 2 per cent in 1993; and legal fees typically

amounted to 0.24 per cent of research expenditures. Furthermore, it took between three and fifteen years for a typical programme to reach maturity, that is, to generate income in excess of expenses on a regular basis: *in short, technology licensing strategies are long-term.*

TABLE 4.2. TOTAL NUMBER OF PATENTS GRANTED TO US ACADEMIC INSTITUTIONS AND PATENTS ISSUED IN THE FIRST 13 UTILITY CLASSES, IN ORDER OF IMPORTANCE[18]

| Class | Title | 69–73 | 74–78 | 79–83 | 84–88 | 89–94 |
|---|---|---|---|---|---|---|
| 435 | Chemistry: molecular biology and microbiology | 31 | 77 | 149 | 312 | 63 |
| 514 | Drug, bio-effecting and body-treating compositions | 27 | 87 | 171 | 353 | 789 |
| 424 | " | 31 | 66 | 102 | 183 | 518 |
| 128 | Surgery | 32 | 49 | 67 | 125 | 306 |
| 250 | Radiant energy | 22 | 54 | 36 | 71 | 241 |
| 530 | Chemistry: natural resins or derivatives; peptides or proteins | 0 | 0 | 41 | 111 | 229 |
| 324 | Electricity: measuring and testing | 23 | 19 | 27 | 80 | 192 |
| 204 | Chemistry: electrical and wave energy | 28 | 33 | 47 | 62 | 188 |
| 364 | Electrical computers and data processing systems | 0 | 17 | 0 | 49 | 178 |
| 73 | Measuring and testing | 56 | 49 | 55 | 89 | 171 |
| 359 | Optics: systems (including communication) and elements | 19 | 32 | 30 | 50 | 158 |
| 536 | Organic compounds — part 532-570 classes | 11 | 26 | 30 | 43 | 147 |
| 427 | Coating processes | 0 | 0 | 0 | 0 | 137 |
| Total number of patents in all classes | | 1,125 | 1,658 | 1,982 | 3,441 | 8,630 |

TABLE 4.3: MINIMUM BENEFITS TO THE ECONOMY OF LICENSING
ACTIVITIES IN US UNIVERSITIES (1992)[11]

| Direct sale by licensees of products | $9 billion |
|---|---|
| Direct job retention/creation | 53,000 |
| Indirect job retention/creation* | 250,000 |
| Direct federal, state and local sales taxes | $1.8 billion |

\* Using standard economic multipliers

## 4.4 EUROPEAN ACADEMIC RESEARCH INSTITUTIONS

The European Higher Education sector has yet to develop a patent culture comparable to that in the US. In many institutions, hurdles of a more philosophical and attitudinal nature have yet to be surmounted. In the past many university administrations considered the exploitation of intellectual property to be inherently risky and at odds with the university's traditional mission. More fundamentally, it has been observed that

> university technology licensing is an ineffective technology transfer mechanism that [for philosophical reasons] may not even be adaptable to existing legal requirements in some European countries.[11]

This is one reason why the formal administration and management of intellectual property in many European universities is either lax or non-existent. By the same token, collated statistical data on the patent performance of European academic institutions is sparse and fragmented.

Despite these historical impediments, there is a growing appreciation of the worth of new technology and the value of patents as "performance indicators". Emerging policy reflects this new perception.

The legal position on ownership of IPR arising out of university research has been discussed in a number of studies of which the UK Report on *Intellectual Property in the Public Sector Research Base* is a notable example.[22] The university or other research institution is entitled to ownership of a patent resulting from an invention or discovery made by a member of staff. This is the norm in industry. The distribution of royalties that may accrue is a separate issue. Copyright, on the other hand, belongs to the author except, perhaps, in the area of computer software development.

Packer reviewed the whole question of IPR in UK academic institutions and drew a number of conclusions:[23]

- Institutions differ widely in their approach to IP.

- The area is rapidly developing.

- The level of patenting is linked to the number of Industrial Liaison Officers (ILOs) and level of support funding.

- There is a long delay between the creation of patents and the flow of benefits, in agreement with the views of Gering.

- The official view that modest changes in current practice will lead to major improvements is refuted: it "understates the cultural and organisational resources and competencies that are needed to translate scientific findings into patentable claims".

A more recent report from the Parliamentary Office of Science and Technology in the UK argued that

> the success of the policy to encourage commercialisation of public sector research-based work could be evaluated by examining data on trends in the numbers and commercial value of patents granted to government research establishments, research council institutes and universities.[24]

The then UK Minister for Science and Technology further urged the universities to exploit their innovative ideas in science and technology to the fullest in order to secure wealth for the nation.

In reviewing the collated data for a number of academic institutions in the US, the UK and Germany, Gering identified a direct relationship between the number of employees in a technology licensing programme, the number of invention disclosures annually and the number of new contracts per annum, while also highlighting a number of beneficial side-effects of licensing programmes.[11] Apart from short-term income that can be substantial, a portfolio of patents adds considerable weight to the university's negotiating position when setting up research contracts and joint ventures with industry. Experience in Trinity College Dublin confirms these findings (*c.f.* Section 4.6).[4]

In summary, technology licensing programmes clearly make an important and growing contribution to the strategic development of the HE sector in today's more enlightened knowledge-driven society. Despite the burden of traditional conservatism, European universities are becoming increasingly more aggressive in capturing the commercial benefits of their knowledge and skills base without in any way threatening their central pedagogical mission.

## 4.5 THE IRISH HIGHER EDUCATION SECTOR

The creation and management of intellectual property in Irish HE research institutions has been sporadic and unstructured. The infrastructure has many weaknesses of both an attitudinal and a practical nature; research equipment is wholly inadequate with minimal public resources devoted to its improvement. The obsolescence level is high (*c.f.* Section 6.4). From a policy perspective, this is puzzling in light of the importance of academic research in attracting inward investment.

A 1994 survey revealed that many of the institutions were only now putting patent policies in place.[25] Improved procedures and support structures to ensure IP protection has given an important boost to the creation of a patent culture within the Irish academic community. The STIAC report in particular discussed a number of joint HE/Industry partnership mechanisms to deal with the thorny question of IPR.[26] Four scenarios are summarised in Table 4.5.

TABLE 4.4: IPR IN JOINT HE/INDUSTRY PARTNERSHIPS.[26]

| Scenario | Source of Idea | Source of Funding | Ownership of IPR HE/Ind. |
|----------|----------------|-------------------|--------------------------|
| 1 | HE | HE | 100 : 0 |
| 2 | HE | Ind. | 70 : 30 |
| 3 | Ind. | Ind. | 0 : 100 |
| 4 | Joint | Ind. | 50 : 50 |

The report also recommended that the following guidelines be drawn up to facilitate the efficient exploitation of IP arising out of academic/industry linkages:

- Academics and industrialists involved in R&D projects should be trained in all aspects of intellectual property and the realities of commercial exploitation.

- The source of the new ideas should be established and the originator's ownership of those ideas respected.

- All projects should be covered by a contract at the outset.

- Confidentiality agreements should be signed before any prior disclosures.

- The legal position regarding ownership of, and benefits from, any new intellectual property that might arise directly out of the project must be fully understood by both parties at the outset.

- Licensing should take place according to normal commercial, arm's length, criteria, in accord with current commercial licensing practice.

- Academic staff should be motivated and rewarded. As an initial guideline, it is proposed that the reward for an academic inventor should be 25 per cent of the institution's share or a smaller share in the case of a large commercial success, wherever possible through a tax free royalty mechanism.

- Commercial and industrial partners involved in legal contracts with the HE sector should recognise the predilection of academic researchers to publish in learned journals, provided this does not involve sensitive information or compromise the patent protection process through premature publication.

Comerford identified twelve items in a "Heads of Agreement" between a university and its contracting partner, usually industry (Table 4.5).

TABLE 4.5: ELEMENTS IN A "HEAD OF AGREEMENT" BETWEEN A UNIVERSITY AND A CONTRACTING PARTNER[10]

| Heads of Agreement |
| --- |
| 1. Licensing parties |
| 2. Technology/IP |
| 3. Territories |
| 4. Exclusivity |
| 5. Down payments and royalties |
| 6. Minimum royalties |
| 7. Improvement |
| 8. Infringements |
| 9. Warranties |
| 10. Accounts |
| 11. Termination, duration |
| 12. Law of which country |

## 4.6 IPR POLICY AT TRINITY COLLEGE DUBLIN

It is informative to examine the experience of one Irish university, Trinity College Dublin, which has displayed a progressive attitude towards IP and its protection. The College's informed vision of the benefits and rewards attaching to IPR is, more or less, typical of the Irish HE sector as a whole.

In the past, researchers tended to squander their intellectual property rights because of inexperience, perceived legal difficulties, unease with confidentiality agreements, filing costs, drafting difficulties, low success rates and diversion of management time and resources.[27] This either prevented any useful application of their work, since no one would invest in it without appropriate IP protection, or the benefits were automatically handed over to more venturous individuals who were enriched as a result of the intellectual endeavours of others.

Established procedures in TCD, by and large, follow the guidelines articulated above although differing in points of detail. In exploiting IPR, generally through agreements with industry, the College places a premium on its reputation as a trustworthy institution and its ability to do business on a basis of trust. This underpins TCD's approach to confidentiality agreements and research contracts. Within its policy framework, academic staff assign ownership of new inventions to the College and, for their part, they receive (a) the right to spend up to 20 per cent of their time as paid consultants in approved areas of activity, (b) professional liability insurance for approved activities and (c) a share of royalties. In this way, the College recognises that the creation of intellectual property involves personal, institutional and external investment, all of which must be exceptionally acknowledged and rewarded.

Royalties are shared with College inventors, net of legal costs, according to a system that has been in operation for several years. If earnings are small, then up to 90 per cent is apportioned to the inventors. If earnings are large, 80 per cent goes to the College. Intermediate cases are on a sliding scale. Authors of software receive a minimum of two-thirds of royalty earnings. In a more recent modification of the system, the inventors' share has been increased in the case of multiple inventors.

Research funded directly by government under the Programmes for Advanced Technology (PATs) initially presented special problems (*c.f.* Section 6.3.3).[28] Royalty earnings are now treated under the general College system described above rather than a system imposed by government. This approach is more compatible with the general wishes of industry. As the Director of Innovation Services in TCD pointed out,

> we know of no IP from our College which survived the attention of government or its agencies and led to success: one reason is that most companies' interest in IP dies away if there are multiple owners. The prospect of having to refer matters to a government department kills commercial prospects in a large number of cases.[27]

Experience in TCD can be summarised as follows:

- Disagreements with industrial partners are costly and cannot be afforded.

- Issues of principle should be avoided.

- Major companies are easiest to deal with: they value their reputation in their dealings with universities.

- The optimum interaction is between a designated individual in the university and one in the partner company.

- Researchers should be trained to understand the full range of issues involved.

- Inventors must have realistic expectations: many inventions, however clever, are not marketable.

- Successful inventors should be rewarded.

- The institution must have a declared policy on IPR.

- Clear IPR clauses in contracts that are well understood by both parties are essential.

- The College's royalty income should benefit all sectors of the College.

- If a business benefits from academic IP, ensure that the transaction is valued.

Although the number of patents granted to academic researchers in Ireland is small by international standards, some are of high international standing as is evident in Appendix II which describes four examples of IP developed by scientists in TCD and its research partners in recent times.

In summary, the role of the university has changed radically in the new innovation age because of the heightened strategic importance of education in a society that is now truly knowledge-driven. The HE sector is all the more important in Ireland, a small open economy, because it houses a significant proportion of the nation's knowledge generators.

In recent decades a burgeoning innovation culture has developed in Irish universities in response to the challenges of this new age. Paradoxically, these developments have been driven by a spirit of "self-help" in the face of wholly inadequate state funding. Irish universities have had to develop a culture of self-sufficiency in order to survive sustained cuts in public support at a time when the demand for higher education was rampantly increasing. Returns on IPR are an important source of direct and indirect revenue. At the national level, the demonstrated prowess of the universities as innovators has supported the current unprecedented growth of inward investment and economic prosperity in Ireland.

## OBSERVATIONS AND RECOMMENDATIONS

- *The role of the university has changed radically in the new innovation age because of the heightened strategic importance of education in a society which is now truly knowledge-driven.*

- *The HE sector is a rich and diverse source of new knowledge that underpins the nation's overall innovation culture.*

- *With the growth in innovation in the universities and other HE research institutions, it is essential that the intellectual property generated by academics is properly protected and exploited to the benefit of the institution and the community at large.*

- *The creation and management of intellectual property in Irish HE research institutions has been sporadic and unstructured. Institutions differ widely in their approach to IP.*

- *The sustained development of a balanced patent culture in the university sector requires a change in traditional attitudes coupled with measurement of performance.*

- *There is a growing appreciation of the worth of new technology and the value of patents as "performance indicators" in the HE sector.*

- *Limiting the universities' role to basic research alone runs counter to the growth of a strong and vibrant innovation culture in the Irish HE sector over the past three decades.*

- *The essential base for academic IP development is being eroded by a obsolescence of research facilities in universities. Initiatives such as the Education Technology Investment Fund (ETIF) are critical.*

- *Equally, the excessive shift of academic workloads towards formal teaching in meeting the increasing demand for university education, and the inordinate time required to successfully negotiate and manage research grants, erode research time.*

- *Intellectual property generated in the universities is becoming more focused with time.*

- *Ireland like most of Europe lags well behind the US in the area of academic intellectual property protection.*

- *Innovative companies should be encouraged to see the value of nurturing IP by facilitating and funding new ideas generated by their staff. This pro-active approach can leverage the in-built knowledge equity of the company.*

- *There is an increasing awareness by academic institutions of the value of intellectual property and a growing propensity of companies and investors to exploit its market potential. The knock-on effects of technology licensing for the economy as a whole are considerable.*

- *Only 10-20 per cent of licensing agreements yielded substantial revenue and it takes between three and fifteen years for a typical programme to reach maturity, that is, to generate income in excess of expenses on a regular basis: technology licensing strategies are long-term.*

- *A portfolio of patents adds considerable weight to the university's negotiating position when setting up research contracts and joint ventures with industry.*

- *Academics and industrialists involved in R&D projects should be formally trained in all aspects of managing intellectual property and the realities of its commercial exploitation.*

- *The proposals of the Science, Technology and Innovation Advisory Council (STIAC) to draw up and adhere to a Charter defining the key parameters in university/industry interactions should be implemented.*

- *The establishment of mutual trust is a key factor in joint university/industry collaboration.*

- *The creation of intellectual property involves personal, institutional and external investment, all of which must be recognised and also rewarded.*

- *Although the number of patents granted to academic researchers in Ireland is small by global standards, some are of high international standing.*

- *The almost exponential increase in the numbers seeking admission to higher education has compelled the Irish university sector to develop new sources of income to counter inadequate public funding. It is important that initiatives such as these are not penalised by a concomitant reduction in state funding.*

- *At the national level, the demonstrated prowess of the universities as innovators continues to support the current unprecedented growth of inward investment and economic prosperity in Ireland. The scale and importance of this support should be explicitly recognised.*

## Chapter 4: References and Notes

1. A.R. Gourlay and K.E. Hargreaves, "Technology Transfer and Intellectual property Management in German HEIs: Current Themes and Perspectives", Economic Research Paper No. 98/1, Dept. of Economics, Loughborough University, February, 1998.

2. V.J. McBrierty and R.P. Kinsella, "Intellectual Property in a Knowledge: The Role of the Universities", *Industry and Higher Education*, December 1997, pp. 341-348.

3. *Science, Technology and Innovation, The White Paper*, Stationery Office, Dublin 2. October 1996.

4. V.J. McBrierty, "The Changing Face of Universities in the Innovation Age", *Physics World*, January, 1997, pp. 15-17.

5. U. Colombo, "Technological Innovation: New Forms and Dimensions, New Geographical Balances", in *Europe/Japan: Futures in Science, Technology and Democracy*, V.J. McBrierty (ed.), Butterworths, London, 1986, p. 25.

6. OECD, *Problems and Prospects of Research Training in the 1990s*, Paris, 1993, p. 5.

7. M. Skilbeck, "The Role of the Humanities", Trinity Jameson Quatercentenary Symposium, E. Sagarra and M. Sagarra (eds.), Trinity College Dublin, 1993, pp. 88-97.

8.   V.J. McBrierty, "Science Policy and Higher Education: the Irish Experience", *Studies*, 1995, 84, 187- 196.

9.   V.J. McBrierty and R.P. Kinsella, "Universities and Industrial Spin-Outs", Proc. 9th European Seed Capital Fund Network Conference, Dublin 25-26 April, 1994, pp. 49-53.

10.  K.A. Comerford, "Licensing University Technology", in University/ Industry Seminar, December, 1994, University College, Dublin, Belfield, Dublin 4.

11.  T. Gering, "University Technology Licensing,: Risks, Technology Sectors, Strategic and Economic Potential", *Industry and Higher Education*, April, 1995, pp. 72-77.

12.  *Science and Engineering Indicators, 1996*, National Science Board, Washington DC: US Government Printing Office, 1996 (NSB 96-21), pp. 5-5.

13.  *ibid.* p. 5-38.

14.  *ibid.* p. 5-19.

15.  "The Nature of Engineering Research in US Universities" in *Science and Engineering Indicators, 1996*, National Science Board, Washington DC: US Government Printing Office, 1996 (NSB 96-21), p. 5-13.

16.  Ref. 12, pp. 4-12, 13.

17.  Compiled from Figures 5.28 and 5.29, ref. 11, p. 5-42.

18.  Ref. 12, pp. 252-3.

19.  R. Henderson, A. Jaffe and M. Trajtenberg, "Universities as a Source of Commercial Technology: a Detailed Analysis of University Patenting", 1965-88, NBER Working Paper, No. 5068, March, 1995.

20.  Association of University Technology Managers Inc., *Licensing Survey*, 1993, Norwalk, CT.

21.  L.K. Rosenthal and C. Fung, "Technology Survey of 20 Universities", in *Les Nouvelles, Journal of the Licensing Executive Society*, Vol. XXV, No. 3, Sept. 1990.

22.  *Intellectual Property in the Public Sector Research Base*, Cabinet Office, Office of Science and Technology, HMSO, London, 1992.

23.  K. Packer, "Patenting Activity in UK Universities", *Industry and Higher Education*, 8(4), 243, December 1994.

24.  I. Taylor, the then UK Minister for Science and Technology, "Patents is a Virtue", *Times Higher Education Supplement*, May 10, 1996, p. 10.

25. R.P. Kinsella and V.J. McBrierty, *Economic Rationale for an Enhanced Science and Technology Capability*, Report to Forfás, Ireland's Science Policy Agency. 1994.

26. *Making Knowledge Work for Us*, Report of the Science, Technology and Innovation Advisory Council (STIAC), (D. Tierney, Chairman), Stationery Office, Dublin 2, Ireland, 1995.

27. E.P. O'Neill, Director of Innovation Services, TCD, "College Policy on Intellectual Property", in University/Industry Seminar, University College, Dublin, Belfield, Dublin 4, December, 1994.

28. The Programmes for Advanced Technology (PATS) are specially funded programmes in designated strategic areas of research. They are prescriptive in the sense that participation is not routinely accessible by the research community at large.

*Chapter 5*

# UNIVERSITIES AND ECONOMIC GROWTH: THE EMERGING TECHNO-ACADEMIC PARADIGM

## 5.1 BACKGROUND

A paradigm shift is a singularly rare event. The industrial revolution of the 19th century, to take one example, shifted the trajectory of economic history. In terms of organisational structure, the introduction of limited liability was an event of similar significance. A paradigm shift of comparable magnitude is now in progress whose genesis lies in the process of continual innovation, driven by technology. The key word is *continual*; the key resource is *knowledge*. And it is around this resource — the generation, diffusion and commercialisation of knowledge — that the institutional bases of the post-industrial economy and society are being reconfigured (*c.f.* Section 1.1).

The wellsprings of this new era of economic history lie in the science base which is defined, in essence, as the generation of knowledge through the systematic investigation of our world and the diffusion and application of this knowledge. The universities give tangible expression to this science base. What all this means is that the HE sector is now central to the process of growth and of consequential societal change because of its important contribution to knowledge generation.

Consequently, it is more and more the case that the universities are catalysts for research-driven economic growth: universities in the US are leaders in this regard. But developments in information technology (IT), and more especially the Internet, now presage a truly borderless knowledge base. It no longer makes sense to see the university — and particularly the knowledge base that it encompasses — as a regional or national resource. Rather, the university is a node in an increasingly seamless global knowledge base, one that has a progressively larger interface with the knowledge-driven economy. This enormously increases the critical mass of its economic impact and also increases the leverage that a single university or a national system of universities has within its economic hinterland.

We are still only at the beginning of this paradigm shift, but its importance is increasingly evident. And already a cultural transformation, which is central to the argument developed herein, is equally evident with truly systemic effects for the national economy. In broad terms, this is what is inferred by the emerging Techno-Academic Paradigm.

The industrial revolution provides a useful touchstone in assessing the true nature and long-term effects of this shift. The technological bases of the industrial revolution — the spinning jenny and the development of the steam engine are examples — rapidly diffused through the economy, generating, in economic parlance, enormously powerful externalities. This led to a process of technological innovation and stepped increases in productivity that, once begun, were cumulative. The brute strength of technology had an extraordinary effect on productivity, permanently shifting the trajectory of growth not only in the UK but, by diffusion, within the rapidly widening global trading economy. Knowledge, or intellectual capital, is what drove this change process. But it was episodic and fortuitous with the universities playing a marginal role at that time.

This time it is different. The knowledge base is now extensive, it is embedded in societal institutions and attitudes, and it is developing endogenously. The network of universities is central to the generation, interpretation (through teaching and enhancement of the skills base) and commercialisation of knowledge. The direct and dynamic interface between the universities as academic institutions and continually emergent technological innovation is evident, in the growth corridors in the US (for example, Silicon Valley and Route 128 in Boston) and in the rapid proliferation of science parks. In a more immediate sense, it is evident in evolving systems of technology transfer and in the blurring of any distinction between the hitherto compartmentalised science base, on the one hand, and the strategic activities of the multinational companies and the rapidly growing knowledge-intensive small industry sector on the other.

This does not mean that the universities have a monopoly of intellectual capital: manifestly they do not. But the strengthening linkage between the two cultures points to the significance of this new paradigm for national and global patterns of economic growth.

## 5.2 THE INNOVATION FRAMEWORK

The European White Paper on *Growth, Competitiveness and Employment* succinctly summed up the importance of entrepreneurship and innovation in today's society:

> This decade is witnessing a forging of a link of unprecedented magnitude and significance between the technological and innovation process and economic and social organisation.[1]

The European Commission, through its various financing initiatives and policy interventions, continues to play a central role in developing an innovation framework. This includes, in particular, the Commission's first action plan for innovation and the ongoing Framework Programme, encompassing a range of initiatives bearing, in part, on the need to stimulate innovation and to protect the special needs of Small-and-Medium-Sized Enterprises (SMEs). What is especially important is a new emphasis on education and also on the legal and proprietary aspects of new knowledge.[2] These are, we believe, central to the development of any national innovation system.

The framework within which the innovation process operates is shaped, in turn, by new developments in information and communications technology. As pointed out in Section 1.2, the nature and *modus operandi* of industry has also changed in a way that exploits the fruits of new discoveries across the board. Change driven by innovation is now systemic and is transforming industry. New organisational structures are emerging which reflect a culture of continual change and continual innovation. To summarise:

- Current developments fall into four broad categories: globalisation, networking, management of change and the need for a holistic approach in managing innovation.

- The global economy now operates *via* information superhighways and networks whereby industry's research needs and product development can be sourced globally. This "virtual organisation" is now a reality. Walley's view of "a global web of added value" captures the way in which the manufacture and assembly of many high-tech products are sourced and distributed around the world.[3]

- Most of all new industry is knowledge-driven, it is born out of new knowledge and it requires access to the sources of new knowledge to ensure its continued growth. It is precisely this fact that gives the HE knowledge base a pivotal role within the emerging knowledge industries.

It is important to place this initiative in its wider context. To begin with, it paralleled similar initiatives in other OECD countries, all of which sought to facilitate product and process innovation in what is an increasingly "borderless" economy. Secondly, and importantly, the STIAC initiative reinforced a central feature of Ireland's emerging industrial policy, namely, the direct and immediate linkage between, on the one hand, industrial policy including, in particular, the development of small-and-medium-sized enterprises and, on the other, S&T policy.[4] In Ireland, these functions are now encompassed within a single development agency, Enterprise Ireland, operating in conjuction with Forfás, a body with special responsibility for policy and foresight review (*c.f.* Table 6.4).

The size structure of Irish industry also bears heavily on industrial policy.[5] Innovative capability has a direct and immediate relevance to industrial policy. In 1994, for example, 83 per cent of firms had no more than 10 employees and, understandably, did not at their present level of development have an adequate R&D capability.[6] In consequence, the HE institutions which house much of the national research effort, especially in Ireland, have acquired an enhanced strategic dimension in the sense that academic entrepreneurship can no longer be viewed as a mere cosmetic appendage to the central teaching function of those institutions. Since access to the national and international knowledge base by emergent industrial technologies is the main driver of national competitive advantage, the accessibility of the HE knowledge base by industry at large is all the more important. This contrasts with the research base in industry itself which is company-specific. *In short, the systematic development and use of the academic knowledge resource is now an imperative, especially for smaller countries like Ireland and for less developed regions within the European Union (EU).*

All of this can be embodied within a new Techno-Academic Paradigm in which the academic knowledge base is, for the first time, centre stage as one of the key determinants of industrial change.[7] It builds upon a number of earlier reports, two of which specifically anticipated the importance of the HE institutions and defined the basic requirements for HE/Industry interactions.[8,9] The paradigm, which is now at the heart of national competitive

strategies, sets out a new conceptual approach to academic entrepreneurship that stems from a number of sources: [5,7,10,11]

- The perception that knowledge is a form of equity.

- The empirical results of a systematic analysis of entrepreneurial achievement in the HE sector.

- The developing role of universities in risk-sharing in enterprise development.

- The realisation that the human dimension is critically important in the commercialisation of technology and its subsequent
  diffusion throughout society.


### 5.3 KNOWLEDGE EQUITY

As pointed out in Chapter 1, knowledge is now a tradable commodity. This is seldom recognised when new ideas are advanced
as security for venture capital to exploit new knowledge in the
market place. Financial institutions in Ireland, as in most European countries, are averse to risk, in contrast, for example, to the
situation in North America (*c.f.* Chapter 9). The banks and investment institutions which, paradoxically, exploit new technology to the full in their own day-to-day dealings are reticent about
committing significant sums of money to new, potentially high-
growth, knowledge-based companies.

This reflects a simple but profoundly important reality, namely,
an inability to price technological risk and to adjust to a knowledge-driven market place in which financial needs must be secured, not on physical assets, but rather on the inherent commercial potential of intellectual property as discussed in the preceding
two chapters.

The mechanisms by which knowledge equity is created and
subsequently exploited to the benefit of the community are illustrated in Figure 5.1.

FIGURE 5.1: THE INPUTS INTO THE NATION'S KNOWLEDGE AND THE BENEFICIAL OUTPUTS THAT FLOW FROM IT[10]

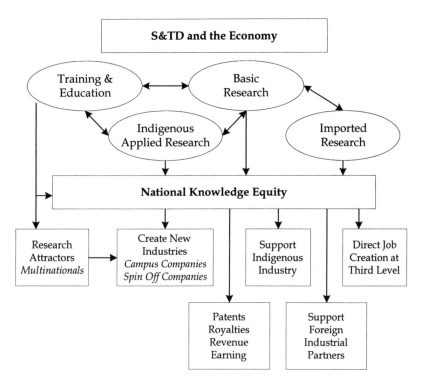

Basic, applied and imported research, along with the education and training of graduates, constitute the academic contribution to the "national knowledge equity" base. The beneficial outputs include the following:[10,12]

- The availability of highly trained graduates and a readily accessible R&D capability for potential inward investors, usually subsidiaries of multinationals which support and sometimes spawn subsidiary service industries.

- The creation of new indigenous enterprise, of which campus companies are an example.

- The provision of R&D support for extant foreign and indigenous firms.

- Direct job creation within the academic institutions in fulfilling contract research obligations.

- Tangible evidence of a vibrant national technology profile through participation in EU research and international publications in the scientific and patent literature.

- Patents and royalty earnings arising from the growing corpus of protected intellectual property.

## 5.4 EMPIRICAL PERFORMANCE DATA FOR THE HE SECTOR

In an earlier report,[5] the performance of the HE sector was evaluated under a number of headings: contract research, patents, campus company formation and jobs created. Impressive evidence was presented of the developing knowledge base in the HE sector that supports significant new job creation and retention both within and without Irish academic institutions. The data compiled in 1994 are updated and reviewed in subsequent chapters. These activities do not subvert but, rather, parallel the HE sector's central function of teaching and research.

## 5.5 RISK-SHARING

The notion of knowledge as a form of equity, especially for high-tech SMEs, has direct bearing on job creation as illustrated in Figure 5.2 which indicates the route from new ideas to the market place. Using the correct "systems engineering", *knowledge* and *finance* equity can be transformed into new enterprise and job creation. In this regard, campus companies are one of the most visible manifestations of the new academic entrepreneurship. These are companies run by academics who wish to commercialise their research within the infrastructure of the college itself (*c.f.* Chapter 7). They are rapidly becoming a significant component of the nation's SME sector.

FIGURE 5.2: THE ROUTE FROM KNOWLEDGE AND FINANCE EQUITY TO JOB CREATION[7]

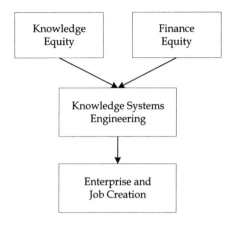

Their growth is predicated on access to venture capital. As discussed more fully in Chapters 7-9, the availability and cost of venture capital should be informed by the fact that campus companies carry significantly less risk than SMEs in general because of risk-sharing by the host institution — in this case the university (Figure 5.3). The lower level of risk reflects a number of factors:

- An exhaustive evaluation is carried out by the institution on the potential long-term viability of the venture prior to granting campus company status.

- When established, the company carries the imprimatur of the university.

- Academics retain their full salary during the difficult start-up period.

- The campus company has access to an established network of contacts and expertise, not only within the institution but throughout the EU and beyond.

FIGURE 5.3: CAMPUS VENTURE CAPITAL MODEL EMBODYING THE
NOTION OF RISK-SHARING[7]

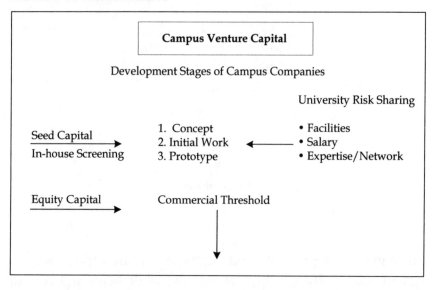

It is in this sense that the institution shares the risk. From the
venture capital perspective, the management costs are significantly less that would otherwise be the case, for the following reasons:

- The rigorous screening process required by the host institution greatly reduces the risks involved.

- Campus companies in Ireland form a ring-fenced sector of industrial growth that can be treated as an integrated unit. It is
  therefore possible to devise a single, cost-effective management scheme for the sector as a whole.

- The use of universities as an intrinsic source of objective technological evaluation in venture capital decision-taking is becoming more prevalent in the venture capital world. It is all
  the more effective in the case of campus companies about
  which the universities have intimate knowledge. Evaluation
  costs are therefore significantly reduced.

## 5.6 A HOLISTIC APPROACH: THE HUMAN DIMENSION

In developing and supporting national enterprise, attention thus far has focused predominantly on the science and technology-based disciplines. However, many attempts to commercialise the fruits of research fail because the human dimension of technological development has been ignored. Social, ethical, and moral considerations, for example, can be as important as technological criteria in the overall acceptability, or otherwise, of new technology. To date, the views of the arts, humanities and social sciences have largely been ignored. The picture phone developed by Bell Laboratories in the early 1970s is an example of a technological triumph and a market failure because the human dimension was ignored; at that stage, society had not been ready for the new technology.

Industry is leading the way in responding to this weakness. Lucent Technologies in the United States, for example, established a "Human Centered Engineering Research Laboratory" in which about 100 cognitive psychologists, physicists, mathematicians and computer scientists work together to probe psyches as well as physics. Early conclusions of the group indicated, for example, that tele-conferencing would not have the impact anticipated by many simply because of the human dimension. The transmission of video images over telephone wires conventionally uses coding algorithms at the transmission and receiving ends that eliminate important detail from the transmitted images by compressing them into fewer bytes of data in order to reduce transmission costs. The over-riding fact is that human beings are very perceptive in interpreting facial expressions and body language that impact in a subtle and important way on decision-making, and those subtle expressions are exactly what the coder removes in compressing the image data.[10]

The message is simple: the successful development and diffusion of science and technology, commensurate with "quality-of-life" ideals, requires a holistic approach involving both scientific and humanistic inputs.

Although the universities are, in principle, the institutions best suited to the development of a coordinated approach to the creation and use of science and technology, they have not shown the necessary leadership. They must follow industry's lead by establishing operational networks between the pertinent science, engineering, business, economic, social science, arts and humanities disciplines, thereby creating a more holistic and cohesive strategy in addressing the developing needs of the community.

## 5.7 A NEW TECHNO-ACADEMIC PARADIGM

It is clear from the foregoing that the universities and other research-oriented institutions in the Irish HE sector have a central role to play in the 21st century and in the knowledge-based society in which it will be located. This will require a sustained development of entrepreneurial thinking, innovation and professionalism if the fruits of their research — independently assessed as being of high international calibre[11] — are to bring maximum benefit to society. Our experience in this area, which has been iterative in nature and predicated on a "learning by doing" philosophy, points to the emergence of a new Techno-Academic Paradigm, the elements of which are the following:

- An integrated approach to the creation of a "national knowledge equity" base.

- The utilisation of this equity base *via* an ever-strengthening HE/industry interface and effective technology transfer.

- A more enlightened approach to intellectual property.

- The need to address the human side of technological development by adopting a more holistic approach incorporating the arts and humanities into the strategy for exploiting science and technology.

## 5.8 POLICY CONSTRAINTS

The new Techno-Academic Paradigm has also grown out of perceived deficiencies in national policy and the way it affects key aspects of innovation. Two areas are particularly affected: inadequate infra-structural state support and the way in which Irish universities are funded.

### 5.8.1 Infrastructural Support

The economic resources invested by Ireland in research and technological development are 1.2 per cent of gross domestic product (GDP) compared with 3 per cent by Japan, 2.5 per cent by the US, an EU average of 2 per cent and an OECD average of 2.22 per cent. Ireland is hovering at the bottom of the European league table. Funding devoted to academic R&D divides broadly into two categories: the first includes applied research within the Programmes for Advanced Technology (PATs) which attracts about £15 million (*c.f.* Section 6.4). These prescriptive programmes are at the cutting edge of current research in designated areas and are concerned with bridging the gap between emerging technologies and extant capabilities. The second category is concerned with funding for non-prescriptive, competitive research (currently £8 million) which is wholly inadequate: it is of the order of 1 per cent of the total S&T budget.

### 5.8.2 University Funding and the Unit Cost Mechanism

A unit cost model, based on contact hours, is used to distribute the budget throughout the university sector. Designed to achieve the laudable goal of greater transparency and equity, it is, nonetheless, deficient in a number of important respects. The model specifically excludes the contribution of university academic staff in the following areas (Figure 5.4):

- Service to the community

- Personal research

- Participation in national policy development

- Participation/organisation of network

- National representation in Europe and elsewhere

- Conference attendance/organisation

- Service to semi-state agencies (for example, Forfás, Forbairt, IDA Ireland)

- Service to industry

- Job creation.

FIGURE 5.4: THE FORGOTTEN FACTORS IN THE UNIT COST MECHANISM FOR UNIVERSITIES

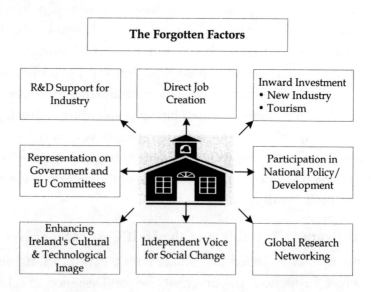

Note, in particular, that the time spent by academics in providing service to industry and in creating jobs is not taken into account in determining the state grant to individual Irish universities. This is a major disincentive, at odds with other branches of government which, in principle if not always in practice, place a high priority on such developments.

Attempts by the Higher Education Authority to validate time spent in serving the community above and beyond the core provision — as currently specified in the unit cost model — were rejected by the University Heads. They argued in terms of an *increased* budgetary allocation for such activities rather than creating an additional category for the distribution of the extant grant. The argument that all universities proportionately contribute to the community as an implicit rather than explicit feature of the unit cost model is flawed: those universities with a highly developed contribution to research and technology transfer are at an obvious disadvantage.

Improvements in policy formulation are part of an ongoing process in determining the most effective manner for translating aspiration into practice. Figure 5.5 illustrates the factors that will beneficially lead to a widening of the Techno-Academic *Corridor of Opportunity*. Research in three main areas is suggested to facilitate the practical implementation of these determinants:

- Further examination of the nature of academic entrepreneurship.

- Development of a policy strategy for fostering cohesive entrepreneurship in the HE sector across the relevant disciplines.

- An ongoing systematic survey of progress and performance in the HE sector, based upon the work carried out in 1994.[5]

FIGURE 5.5: FACTORS WHICH WILL LEAD TO WIDENING THE
TECHNO-ACADEMIC CORRIDOR OF OPPORTUNITY

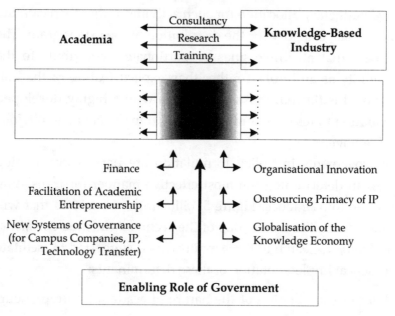

## OBSERVATIONS AND RECOMMENDATIONS

- *A new Techno-Academic Paradigm is proposed to account for current trends in S&T and the pivotal role of the HE institutions in S&T-based economic growth.*

- *Current developments in S&T fall into a number of categories, namely, invention, commercialisation, dissemination, globalisation and leveraging (upgrading to maximise the life cycle). These, in turn, require networking, flexible processes to manage change, innovation and a holistic approach to technology change through agreement.*

- *The human capital dimension of technology development and diffusion throughout society requires considerably enhanced emphasis*

- *The global economy now operates via information superhighways and networks whereby industry's research needs and product development can be sourced globally. This "virtual organisation" is now a reality.*

- *Innovation now occurs in what is an increasingly "borderless" economy.*

- *Most of all new industry is knowledge-driven, it is born out of new knowledge and it requires access to the sources of new knowledge to ensure its continued growth. It is precisely this fact that gives the HE knowledge base a pivotal role within the emerging knowledge industries.*

- *The direct and dynamic interface between the universities as academic institutions, and continually emergent technological innovation is evident in the growth corridors in the US and in the rapid proliferation of science parks throughout developed and developing nations.*

- *The HE sector is now central to the process of economic growth and of consequential societal change because of its important contribution to knowledge generation: the universities are catalysts for research-driven economic growth.*

- *The university is a node in an increasingly seamless global knowledge base, one which has a progressively larger interface with the knowledge-driven economy.*

- *Academic entrepreneurship can no longer be viewed as a mere cosmetic appendage to the central teaching function of the higher education research institutions.*

- *The importance of "national knowledge equity" in achieving economic prosperity is central. It has direct bearing on job creation.*

- *Financial institutions in Ireland, as in most European countries, are averse to risk, in contrast, for example, to the situation in North America.*

- *This reflects a simple but profoundly important reality, namely, an inability to price technological risk and to adjust to a knowledge-driven market place in which financial needs must be secured, not alone on physical assets, but on knowledge as equity.*

- *Campus companies form a growing sector of Ireland's indigenous industry.*

- *The universities participate in financial risk-sharing in the establishment and promotion of campus companies.*

- *Management costs of providing and monitoring venture capital are significantly lower for campus companies compared with other SMEs. The risks are also significantly lower.*

- *The main policy constraints include a paucity of funding for R&D and inadequate funding for the universities and other HE institutions. The Unit Cost Mechanism for distributing funds between Irish universities is, albeit unintentionally, impeding effective technology transfer between the universities and society at large.*

- *The diminishing supply of research students undercuts the capacity of universities to foster knowledge-driven growth. The economic consequences are potentially damaging.*

- *Policy research directions for the future include further examination of the nature of academic entrepreneurship; ongoing development of policy strategies for fostering cohesive entrepreneurship in the HE sector across the relevant disciplines; and continuous and systematic surveys of progress and performance in the HE sector.*

## Chapter 5: References and Notes

1.  *Growth, Competitiveness, Employment: the Challenges and Ways Forward into the 21st Century.* EU Commission White Paper, Bulletin of the European Communities, Supplement 6/93, 1993.

2.  European Commission Background Report, *Innovation for Growth and Development in Europe*, B7/97, April, 1997.

3.  P. Walley, in *Ireland into the 21st Century*, O. Donoghue, (ed.), Mercier, Dublin, 1995.

4.  *Making Knowledge Work for Us*, Report of the Science, Technology and Innovation Advisory Council (STIAC), D. Tierney (Chairman), Stationery Office, Dublin 2, Ireland, 1995.

5.  R.P. Kinsella and V.J. McBrierty, *Economic Rationale for an Enhanced National Science and Technological Capability.* Report prepared for Forfás, the Irish Science Policy Agency, 1994.

6.  *Taskforce on Small Business*, Stationery Office, Dublin 2, March, 1994.

7.  R.P. Kinsella and V.J. McBrierty, "Campus Companies and the Emerging Techno-Academic Paradigm: the Irish Experience", *Technovation*, 1997, 17,. 245-251.

8.  V.J. McBrierty, *Strategy for Innovation: the Role of the Third Level Institutions*, Confederation of Irish Industry (now IBEC), Business Study Series, No. 8, 1981.

9.  V.J. McBrierty, *Strategy for Forging Links between Academics and Industry*, Confederation of Irish Industry (now IBEC), Business Study Series, No. 10, 12, 1982.

10. V.J. McBrierty, *The University and Research: Aims, Conditions, Resources.* In "The Role of the University in Society", Proceedings of the NUI Conference in Dublin Castle, Ireland, 20-21 May 1994, pp. 79-93.

11. V.J. McBrierty, "Science Policy and Higher Education: the Irish Experience", *Studies*, 1995, 84, 187-196.

12. *A Comparative International Assessment of the Organisation, Management and Funding of University Research in Ireland and Europe.*, Report commissioned by the HEA , CIRCA Group Europe Ltd., Roebuck Castle, Dublin 4, Ireland, 1995.

*Chapter 6*

# DEVELOPING STRATEGIES FOR S&T

## 6.1 INTRODUCTION

The EU White paper on *Growth, Competitiveness and Employment* addressed the challenges of the new knowledge and information era.[1] The *Green Paper on Innovation* further clarified the central role of education in the innovation process and noted that "separations between research, university and industry, education and the business world are still too strong".[2]

Current perspectives on the strategic role of Science and Technology (S&T) in Ireland's economic development mirror these concerns and, in response, wide-ranging initiatives were undertaken:

- The semi-state agency structure for developing and delivering S&T programmes was reorganised.[3]

- A comprehensive examination of all aspects of S&T policy by the Science, Technology and Innovation Advisory Council (STIAC)[4] served as the precursor to the White Paper on Science, Technology and Innovation published in 1996.[5]

- An exhaustive review of the education sector resulted in (a) a National Education Convention which made far-reaching proposals,[6] (b) legislation which, for the first time, formally acknowledged a research role for the non-university HE sector, (c) a White Paper on Education[7] and (d) new university legislation.[8]

Of course, developments in education *per se* are only of direct concern in so far as they influence the link between education and S&T as encapsulated in the Techno-Academic Paradigm (Chapter 5).[9]

## 6.2 EXISTING POLICY FRAMEWORK

Policy is shaped in the first instance by a clear visualisation of the way in which S&T impacts on a nation's future growth and prosperity, having due respect for its cultural and aesthetic traditions. The practical implementation of the ideal is then subject to various constraints on available human and fiscal resources. For example, the ability to carry out leading edge research is predicated on adequate funding, modern equipment and well-trained research personnel. National policies are also dependent on international developments since nations are no longer fully in control of their own destiny.

Returns on available and often inadequate funding can only be maximised with vision and imaginative management. In such circumstances, a philosophy of *investment* in the future must replace the more established notion of *expenditure* in the areas of education and R&D. But this approach, as in all areas of public expenditure, can only be justified in the context of transparency and accountability which is based on measurable returns on the investments made.

The following discussion describes the iterative development of S&T policy in Ireland in the context of pervasive global influences. A number of practical issues that highlight inherent difficulties in meeting the strict norms of transparency and accountability in the area of S&T are addressed in Section 6.2.2.

### 6.2.1 Strategic S&T Framework and Objectives

Ireland's future S&T strategy is comprehensively articulated in the STIAC Report.[4] The flow chart in Figure 6.1 indicates the key inputs which shaped STIAC's deliberations. The main findings, clarified in a subsequent Forfás Report,[10] were subsumed into the STI White Paper which must, in turn, be considered in parallel with the White Paper on Education and the new legislation on the management of universities.

FIGURE 6.1: KEY INPUTS THAT SHAPED CURRENT POLICY ON STI

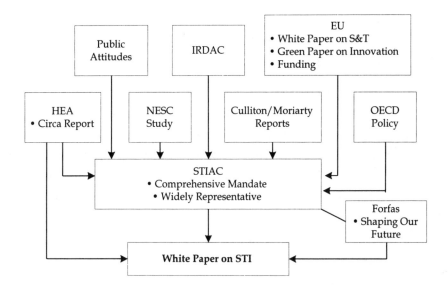

Scrutiny of the policy documentation as a whole reveals a number of paradoxes regarding the contribution of the HE sector.

- The White Paper on STI is internally inconsistent in proposing, on the one hand, that the universities should confine their attention to "basic research and the development of high levels of knowledge and skills" while, on the other, recognising that basic research "represents only one-third of the total research carried out in the colleges [and that] over the past decade, college research activity has become more oriented towards applied and developmental research, as academic researchers generate funds through external contracts".[5] The White Paper also asserts that "innovation is ultimately a matter for the business sector".

It has rightly been argued by many that basic research, training and education are core responsibilities of a university,[11] but not exclusively so. Intellectual curiosity finds expression in all forms of research and development. To imply that the universities have no role in the commercialisation of research is at odds with the innovation culture that has grown up in the universities and the increasing number of campus companies and additional job creation which that culture has produced (*c.f.* Chapter 7).

- The STI White Paper and the new legislation on the management of universities are predicated on radically conflicting approaches: the university legislation is largely interventionist whereas the STI White Paper promotes a new, non-interventionist "contractarian" relationship between government and the universities. It is recalled that funding is a major policy instrument which, understandably, is used to tailor the output of the HE sector to the perceived needs of government as guardian of the public purse. But, as in the UK, this promotes a "culture of compliance" which is anathema to the ethos of university education and research (*c.f.* Section 1.4).

Note, however, that a comprehensive R&D role for the universities is implicit in other, more specific, recommendations. The White Paper on Education states that

> each institution will develop and publish an explicit policy statement on its approach to its research activities [Research Charter], including the broad balance between research and teaching commitments within disciplines [and that] the Department of Enterprise and Employment and the Department of Education will be involved in the discussions on the Research Charter with the Colleges. . . . The policy will also set out the key aims of research activity and the principal criteria for evaluating the effectiveness of research within institutions.[7]

This theme is also promoted in the CIRCA Report on university research which argues that

> the HEA and the universities [should] produce a formal pol-
> icy for research in the university sector [and that] each insti-
> tution should establish its own flexible framework and struc-
> ture for strategic research planning and policy.[12]

Universities are in transition and no doubt their role will be clari-fied in time. In any event, an enhanced R&D contribution from the universities will impact in a major way on (a) the division of academic time between research and lecturing, (b) the choice of appropriate areas of research in each institution to ensure "critical mass", (c) the development of essential support services, and (d) the identification of acceptable performance indicators for re-search evaluation. This latter issue in particular tends to be fore-most in the minds of policy makers who seek quantitative models, often oblivious of the attendant dangers outlined in Section 1.4.

The proposed Research Charter for the HE sector[4] must inevi-tably include two key elements in the contractual arrangements and incentives structures if distortions and tensions across the HE sector as a whole are to be avoided.

- Best practice procedures for managing and, where appropri-ate, commercialising research are required through robust contractual arrangements as between the institution, the end user and the knowledge generators, particularly when dealing with protected intellectual property.

- A rigorous appraisal of an institution's potential downstream liability is also a priority. There is little extant guidance in terms of international "best practice" in this regard and the implications of a transposition into Ireland of the litigious culture which has already established itself, for example, in the US, raises important issues of professional liability for the state, research institutions and individual researchers.

The discussion that follows highlights the difficulties in arriving at reasonable input/output measures in funding R&D.

## 6.2.2 Economic Returns on R&D Spending

There are formidable difficulties — as, indeed, Forfás (1998) have recently noted — in extracting unambiguous measures of public expenditure on R&D and, accordingly, strictly quantitative estimates of returns are difficult to make.[13,14] The absence of such rigorous cost-benefit analysis impoverishes policy-making and inevitably introduces tensions and ambiguities in the ongoing debate on S&T policy. While this problem is virtually intractable, at a minimum, the level of approximation inherent in any empirical approach must be defined.

Paul argued that, even if such data were available,

> typical cost benefit analyses can, at best, be indicative and, at worst, spurious . . . [and therefore] attempts to evaluate the work purely on *ex-post* financial criteria may not only be inaccurate but also misleading.[14]

He proposed the additional use of non-financial allocation criteria that are reasonably systematic. These include scoring models, reliable private sector market data and research effectiveness indicators.

Similar problems in estimating the outputs of R&D were experienced in the past by the now defunct Office of Technology Assessment (OTA) in the US which identified the major difficulties as (a) the pursuit of socially desirable, high risk investment, (b) problems of benefit measurement and (c) the availability of many outputs at zero marginal cost and zero price where the cost of collecting revenues outweigh the cost of production.

According to the OTA, government cannot carry over private sector methodology to assess monetary returns to publicly funded R&D except, perhaps, in areas like health and aviation.[15] Walshe and co-workers viewed R&D as a knowledge multiplier when considered in terms of

> a flow of spending or a stock of accumulated knowledge from R&D expenditures which depreciates as new products or processes are introduced. The R&D conducted in one sector can have productivity-enhancing effects in the sector which performs the R&D either through cost reduction (process innovations) or market expansion (product innovation).[13]

This captures the dynamics of positive externalities or spin-offs embodied in the generation and commercialisation of knowledge. R&D returns are complemented by outputs that spill over into other areas because of (a) downstream benefits to users who do not pay for the original research, (b) inspiration generated in other areas or, in some cases, direct copying or adapting the new technology and (c) the mobility of knowledge which accompanies the mobility of research staff. A distinction is therefore drawn between "[private] economic returns that are appropriated by the R&D performer and [social] returns which cannot be appropriated by the R&D performer but by society at large".[14] The complementarity of R&D with other inputs is also emphasised:

- *R&D and capital*: Concerns the relationship between knowledge and finance equity.

- *In-house R&D and R&D performed elsewhere*: Stresses the dual role of R&D as the capacity to learn and to "absorb" and that knowledge cannot be absorbed without cost.

- *The relationship between R&D and productivity growth*: Influences supply and demand: as demand and output expand, productivity will be increased if there are increasing returns to scale.

Further complexities are introduced in estimating returns on R&D in addition to these readily identifiable spill-over effects. First, it is difficult to assess the contribution of R&D in product and process development since it is only one of several inputs into the innovation process. The estimated contribution of R&D as a percentage of total expenditure on innovation of 60 per cent reported in Section 1.1.1[16] is refined in the more detailed data that take firm size into account (Table 6.1). From an econometric perspective, Griliches drew the following conclusions:[18]

- The stock of R&D capital contributes significantly to differences in productivity between sectors.

- The effects of basic research in the private sector are positive and significant.

- Privately financed research has slightly higher returns than publicly funded research in the US.

TABLE 6.1: THE SHARE (%) OF R&D IN THE TOTAL INNOVATION EXPENDITURE AVERAGED OVER NINE COUNTRIES IN 1992[17]

| Firm Size | Range (Min-Max) (%) | Average (%) | Ireland (%) |
|-----------|--------------------|-------------|-------------|
| 1-49      | 7-45               | 28          | 34          |
| 50-249    | 17-69              | 39          | 27          |
| 250-499   | 34-57              | 45          | 45          |
| >500      | 16-71              | 49          | 16          |

Within widely varying limits in the literature, 10-40 per cent (net of depreciation) is considered to be a reasonable estimate of *private* rates of return; *social* rates can be 50-100 per cent higher. The uncertainty is due to many factors including the type and mix of R&D.

Social rates of return on public R&D spending connected with patented new technology are also increasingly important. In the case of new drug development, for example, the question of public good versus private gain is particularly relevant when the cost of the drug or medicine is priced out of the reach of the less well-off in society in order to recoup the company's development costs. As discussed in Section 3.8, little or no account is taken of prior knowledge as a significant element in the development of the intellectual property, a large part of which was funded from public sources.[19]

Overall, the study by Walshe and co-workers concluded that

> based on the available evidence, technological change seems to have been a very important factor, perhaps the most important factor, underlying long-term economic growth in the United States and elsewhere.[13]

### 6.2.3 Sourcing Innovation and Technology Transfer

Policy designed to maximise the benefits of the nation's R&D capabilities must ensure effective technology transfer from the knowledge generators to the knowledge users. Where, in fact, does industry source its innovation? A survey of European industry identified the most important sources under three headings:[20]

- *Internal Sources*, including sources within the enterprise and within the group of enterprises

- *External Sources*, including suppliers of materials, components, equipment, customers, competitors and consultancy firms

- *Research Establishments*, including universities, HE institutions, government laboratories and technical institutions.

As shown in Table 6.2, industry is less inclined to use the HE sector compared with other sources. This is due, in part, to the cultural problems discussed in Section 1.4.1 and to the general misconception that the universities' strength lies exclusively in *basic* as opposed to *applied* research, a view that is often promoted by industry itself and by some policy makers.[21] As stressed above, this perception denies the dynamic entrepreneurial culture that has grown up in the Irish universities and, to a lesser extent, the non-university institutions in recent decades.[22] The fact that the level of involvement with universities increases with the size of the company concerned is no doubt due to the level of R&D activity in the company and its ability to absorb the latest leading-edge technologies. Very small companies tend not to have developed an in-house R&D culture, creating, in turn, a communications gap that fuels their reticence in approaching universities in the first place.

TABLE 6.2: THE IMPORTANCE TO INDUSTRY OF VARIOUS SOURCES OF INNOVATION: THE PERCENTAGE OF FIRMS THAT HAVE RATED THE STATED SOURCE AS "VERY IMPORTANT"[20]

| Firm Size | 1-49 | 50-249 | 250-499 | >500 |
|---|---|---|---|---|
| Internal sources and capabilities | 51% | 58% | 62% | 72% |
| External sources | 85% | 83% | 82% | 85% |
| Universities and research establishments | 21% | 21% | 27% | 32% |

These general observations are borne out in Ireland where, it is recalled, the bulk of Irish indigenous industry tends to be low-tech, comprising micro-enterprises of 10 employees or less. Subsidiaries of multinationals are generally high-tech, larger, and therefore more amenable to partnership arrangements with HE institutions. This argues for a twin track approach involving more imaginative innovation transfer mechanisms specifically tailored to micro-enterprises and large multinationals, respectively.

Clearly, there is still some way to go in breaking down the cultural barriers between the HE sector and industry, particularly small industry. Until these issues are properly addressed, industry will continue to meet the greater part of its innovation needs from sources other than the universities and research establishments, which is unfortunate in light of the relevant, growing and accessible R&D resource in the HE sector.

### 6.2.4 Policy Agencies

A number of agencies in the public sector are directly or indirectly concerned with policy formulation and its implementation (Table

6.3). These semi-state agencies, operating under the aegis of their respective government departments, have recently been assigned more focused responsibilities in order to deliver an improved service to industry. The majority of them impact in one way or another on the HE sector.

TABLE 6.3: MAIN GOVERNMENT AGENCIES/DEPARTMENTS* WITH A LEGISLATIVE MANDATE TO SUPPORT AND/OR PERFORM R&D (1997)[27]

| Department/Agency | Amount** | Description |
|---|---|---|
| HEA | £39.7 m | R&D in Third Level Colleges |
| IDA Ireland | £ 7.1 m | Grant-aid for R&D projects in MNEs |
| Forbairt (Enterprise Ireland) | £43.7 m | R&D for companies and funding of PATs and other in-house R&D |
| Teagasc | £22.7 m | R&D for food and agriculture sectors |
| Marine Institute | £ 5.9 m | R&D in marine related areas |
| Shannon Development | £ 8.3 m | Grant-aid for R&D projects in companies |
| Department of Social Welfare | £ 2.2 m | Social research, including the Combat Poverty Agency |
| HRB | £ 4.7 m | Medical and health research |
| ESRI | £ 2.9 m | Economic and social research |
| Dept of Agriculture, Food & Forestry | £ 7.3 m | Developmental work in crop and livestock areas |
| NMRC | £ 8.5 m | R&D in microelectronics |
| Údarás na Gaeltachta | £ 2.0 m | Grant-aid for R&D projects in companies |
| Others | £11.9 m | R&D work of 20 other agencies |
| Total | £164.9 m | |

* where there are transfers of funds from one institution to another the funds are accounted for in the performing agency/department.

** includes earned income.

### 6.2.4.1 *The Semi-state Agencies*

The first coherent elements of an indigenous technological capability in Ireland surfaced in the early 1960s. The creation of the National Science Council (NSC) in 1967, a quasi-executive division of the Department of Finance, followed a comprehensive joint Irish-OECD survey in the preceding year.[23] A further OECD Review in 1974 identified the need to

> foster the emergence and subsequent establishment of co-ordinated Science, Technology and Innovation (STI) policy, as well as the build-up of state research institutes, universities, related public services including technical consultancy, testing, formation of standards, and also environmental, economic and social research/activities throughout the 1970s and 1980s.[24]

The National Board for Science and Technology (NBST), the first semi-state body responsible for S&T, was set up in 1978. EOLAS, established in 1987, was an important precedent in persuading the (then) Department of Industry and Commerce that support for Science and Technology was a valid diversion of industrial development funds away from what would then have been seen as conventional industrial development activity, principally by the Industrial Development Authority (IDA). EOLAS was also responsible for establishing the Programmes for Advanced Technology (PATs) into which government invested major funding since 1990.

Overall responsibility for S&T policy is now subsumed within Forfás following the restructuring exercise in 1994 which retained the principle, but changed the form, of intervention to offset market failure within Irish industry. Forbairt was allocated the dual responsibility for indigenous industry and the management of public research funding programmes; IDA Ireland is concerned with job creation through inward investment; and Forfás retains overall responsibility for policy development. In addition, in 1998 Forbairt and the Irish Trade Board were subsumed within a single development agency: Enterprise Ireland (see Table 6.4).

TABLE 6.4: EVOLUTION OF SEMI-STATE S&T AGENCIES IN IRELAND[3]

| Era | Agency | Function | Growth Pattern | Perceived Output | Function then Transferred |
|---|---|---|---|---|---|
| 1960s | IIRS | Advice to Government on S&T | Developed reporting mechanisms | Functional | to NBST |
| 1960s | National Science Council | Industrial research and standards | Rapid growth to 1980 | Inadequately resourced vis a vis its mission | to Eolas |
| 1979 | National Board for S&T | Statutory mandate for advice and analysis | Rapid growth | • Technically sound<br>• Supportive for researchers<br>• Failed to acquire administration legitimacy | to Eolas |
| 1987 | Eolas | National S&T Agency – adviser, analyser, performer | Initial decline followed by growth with Community Structural Funds | • Managed many national efforts in S&T<br>• Bridge between academia and industry: support for basic and applied research | to Forbairt |
| 1994 | Forbairt | Support for indigenous industry, R&D grant mgmt. | Decline anticipated in S&T focus | Less technology – more support to business and SME but not clear | partly to Forfás |
| 1994 | Forfás | State S&T policy | None anticipated | Policy status and advice to government | to Forbairt and Forfás |
| 1998 | Enterprise Ireland (replaces Forbairt) | Single agency for indigenous industry, includes former Trade Board | Not yet clear. | One stop shop for indigenous industry, including technology support. | |

The STIAC report which made far-reaching recommendations on the development of, and support for, a cohesive *National System of Innovation* (NSI) (Figure 6.2), prompted a rapid response in a number of key areas. The White Paper was published in 1996;[5] a Minister of State with special responsibility for Science and Technology attended Cabinet meetings for the first time, albeit in a non-voting capacity; a special committee was given the dual mandate of evaluating the STIAC Council's recommendations and advising on how best to implement them; and two widely representative bodies with responsibility for policy (Science, Technology and Innovation Council) and the evaluation of research proposals and administration of public research funds (the National Research Support Fund Board) were established.

FIGURE 6.2: CONTRIBUTION FROM THE HE SECTOR AND RELATED INSTITUTIONS TO THE NATIONAL SYSTEM OF INNOVATION

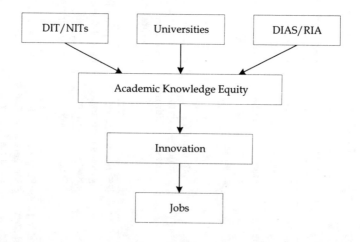

The publicly funded agencies listed in Table 6.3 collectively represent a comprehensive range of bodies within the S&T system. This approach has both advantages and disadvantages (Table 6.5).

TABLE 6.5: ADVANTAGES AND DISADVANTAGES OF THE WIDE
RANGE OF IRISH INSTITUTIONS CONCERNED WITH S&T

| Advantages | Disadvantages |
|---|---|
| • Diversity<br><br>• Flexibility<br><br>• Multi-functional: delivery/<br>policy/monitoring roles | • Fragmentation<br><br>• Lack of transparency<br><br>• Lack of "critical mass" when<br>major EU funding expires<br><br>• Anti-strategic<br><br>• Lack of coherent policy |

### 6.2.4.2 Ireland's Higher Education Sector

The Techno-Academic Paradigm described in Chapter 5 high-lights the central role of higher education in exploiting S&T to achieve economic prosperity.[9,22] Ireland's HE sector is based on a binary system that provides professional (university) and voca-tional (non-university) education and training. The Higher Edu-cation Authority (HEA) and the National Council for Educational Awards (NCEA) have respective responsibility for the university and non-university sectors which include the following:

• Seven university colleges — Trinity College Dublin (the Univer-sity of Dublin), founded in 1591; St. Patrick's College, Maynooth (1795); the National University of Ireland (NUI) with constituent colleges in Cork, Galway, and Dublin (1845); and the two more recently established universities — the University of Limerick (1970) and Dublin City University (1975). The Universities Act (1997) encompassed a number of far-reaching changes in univer-sity management, including autonomous status for the constitu-ent colleges of the NUI.[8] It is also anticipated that the HEA would assume overall responsibility for the HE sector as a whole.

- The Dublin Institute of Technology (DIT) which, in 1979, became the parent body of six constituent colleges in the Dublin area, some of which date back to the 1890s.

  Eleven Regional Technical Colleges (RTCs) (1970s) strategically located around the country provide complementary technical and vocational education and training. They have recently been re-designated National Institutes of Technology. Prior to 1992, both the DIT and the RTCs operated under common legislation. Since that time, the Dublin Institute of Technology Act (1992) and the Regional Colleges Act (1992), effected separate status and redefined responsibilities. The new legislation legally empowered the non-university colleges to pursue R&D; prior to 1992, they were, *de jure*, precluded from carrying out research although, *de facto*, research was undertaken in the DIT and a number of the RTCs. The DIT has since been granted degree-awarding powers.

- While not formally part of the HE sector as such, the Dublin Institute for Advanced Studies (DIAS) (1940) and the Royal Irish Academy (RIA) (1776), a designated body under the HEA Act, contribute in an important way to the nation's educational, scientific and literary achievements.

### 6.3 NATIONAL EXPENDITURE ON S&T

S&T expenditure is made up of four components: higher education, business, government and private non-profit. Table 6.6 indicates the source and distribution of the S&T funds among the participating sectors in 1995.[25] Note that the total expenditure on S&T of IR£1,146 million in 1995 included £581 million on R&D, 66 per cent of which was carried out in the business sector. Government sources account for about £586 million of the total spend on S&T which increased to £693 million in 1997. EU Community Framework funding continued to be a major source of revenue, accounting for about 7 per cent of the total in 1995.

TABLE 6.6: DISTRIBUTION OF FUNDS FOR SCIENCE AND TECHNOLOGY IN 1995 (£M)[25]

| Source of Funds | Research & Development | | | | | | S&T Info. | Tech. Services | Tech. Transfer | S&T Ed* & Training | Other* | Total |
|---|---|---|---|---|---|---|---|---|---|---|---|---|
| | Business | Third level | PATS** | Gov't | Private | Total | | | | | | |
| Exchequer Direct | | 7.2 | 3.1 | 41.8 | | 52.1 | 22.1 | 146.2 | 1.1 | 200.9 | 39.3 | 461.7 |
| Exchequer Indirect | | 43.8 | | | | 43.8 | | | | | | 43.8 |
| CSF Funds | 18.0 | 3.7 | 6.6 | 14.2 | | 42.5 | 6.2 | 9.0 | 2.5 | 9.4 | 11.0 | 80.6 |
| EU Contracts | 8.8 | 18.4 | 4.1 | 5.8 | | 37.1 | 0.8 | 1.8 | | | 0.6 | 40.3 |
| Business | 359.2 | 4.9 | 3.8 | 6.2 | 1.0 | 375.1 | 7.5 | 12.3 | | | 1.2 | 396.1 |
| Other Income | 10.9 | 10.0 | 2.6 | 3.9 | 3.0 | 30.4 | 6.1 | 14.7 | * | 70.0 | 2.2 | 123.4 |
| Total | 396.9 | 88 | 20.2 | 71.9 | 4.0 | 581 | 42.7 | 184.0 | 3.6 | 280.3 | 54.3 | 1145.9 |
| | BERD | HERD | GOVERD | | PNP | GERD | | | | | | |

* Programmes in government agencies only

** AMT Ireland is classified under S&T information and technical services.

Table 6.7 compares government funding on S&T in 1997 with funding for 1986 and 1996. The data highlight the important impact of EU funding of S&T. Table 6.8 shows the 1997 allocation to the major departments, whereas Table 6.9 lists the Gross Expenditure on R&D (GERD) and the expenditure on R&D in the HE sector (HERD) as a percentage of Gross Domestic Product (GDP) over the 1993-95 period.[26] The total spend on R&D (GERD) in Ireland is below the OECD and EU averages of 2.22 per cent and 1.97 per cent: Ireland still continues to hover near the bottom of the OECD and EU league tables. Nevertheless, GERD has increased steadily over the period 1988–95 (Figure 6.3). Data for selected countries are furnished in Table 6.10.

The provision of significant R&D funding earmarked to industry from the then EU Measure 6 Programme, amounting to £23 million in 1993 and £16 million in 1994, was a substantial initiative in policy terms. The greater awareness of the contribution of R&D in national strategies that prompted this scale of funding markedly improved the entrepreneurial climate of the country.

FIGURE 6.3: GROSS EXPENDITURE ON R&D AS % OF GDP, 1988 AND 1995

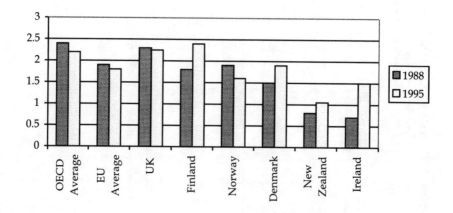

TABLE 6.7: SOURCE OF GOVERNMENT FUNDING OF SCIENCE AND TECHNOLOGY 1986, 1996 AND 1997[27]

|  | 1986 | | 1996 | | 1997 | |
|---|---|---|---|---|---|---|
|  | £m | % | £m | % | £m | % |
| Exchequer Funds | 316 | 81 | 539 | 69 | 559 | 68 |
| CSF Funds | 2 | .6 | 106 | 14 | 133 | 16 |
| Total Public Funds | 318 | 82 | 645 | 83 | 692 | 84 |
| Earned Income | 69 | 18 | 130 | 17 | 127 | 16 |
| TOTAL | 388 | 100 | 776 | 100 | 819 | 100 |

TABLE 6.8: FUNDING ALLOCATIONS TO THE MAJOR DEPARTMENTS[27]

| S&T: Major Depts: | Exchequer | CSF | Income | Total | % |
|---|---|---|---|---|---|
| Education/Manpower | 264,430 (69.5%) | 70,868 (18.6%) | 45,349 (11.9%) | 380,647 (100%) | 46.44 |
| Health | 136,871 (94%) | | 8,716 (6%) | 145,587 (100%) | 17.76 |
| Industry | 33,740 (29.5%) | 44,846 (39.2%) | 35,770 (31.3%) | 114,356 (100%) | 13.95 |
| Total All Departments | 559,040 | 133,311 | 127,235 | 819,586 | |

TABLE 6.9: GROSS EXPENDITURE ON R&D (GERD) AND EXPENDITURE IN THE HE SECTOR (HERD) IN IRELAND[26]

|  | 1993 | 1994 | 1995 |
|---|---|---|---|
| HERD | £84 m | £95 m | £108 m |
| % GDP | 0.26 | 0.27 | 0.28 |
| GERD | £404 m | £491 m | £584 m |
| % GDP | 1.24 | 1.41 | 1.54 |
| EU Average % | 1.95 | 1.90 | 1.84 |
| OECD Average % | 2.22 | 2.14 | 2.16 |

TABLE 6.10: GROSS EXPENDITURE ON R&D (GERD) AS PER CENT
GDP TOTAL EXPENDITURE

|              | Total Expenditure (% GDP) |
|--------------|:-------------------------:|
| Finland      | 2.32                      |
| OECD Average | 2.16                      |
| Netherlands  | 2.14                      |
| EU Average   | 1.84                      |
| Denmark      | 1.82                      |
| Norway       | 1.65                      |
| Ireland      | 1.40                      |
| New Zealand  | 1.03                      |
| Portugal     | 0.60                      |

## 6.3.1 Business Expenditure on R&D (BERD)

The steady increase in BERD from 0.47 per cent GDP in 1982 to
1.02 per cent GDP in 1995 continues to bring Ireland in line with
comparable small economies (Figure 6.4). While the sustained
growth of 17 per cent real annual increase in business-performed
R&D between 1988 and 1995 is one of the most impressive of all
OECD countries, current expenditure still lags behind the OECD
(1.5 per cent GDP) and EU (1.2 per cent GDP) averages. It is significant that multinationals, mostly in the electronics, computers,
chemicals, pharmaceutical and healthcare fields, account for two-
thirds of the overall expenditure.[26]

Table 6.11 compares the business *vs.* public expenditure on
R&D in Ireland and in the Nordic countries. The relative commitment by business in Ireland is less than Sweden's but greater
than that in Denmark, Finland and Norway. The gross expenditure on R&D in Ireland is, however, lower than any of the Nordic
countries. Three further trends in the Irish BERD profile are significant:[26,27]

- Expenditure by foreign-owned companies is about double that of indigenous enterprise.

- Only 14 per cent of the manufacturing companies spend more than £100,000 annually on R&D.

- There has been a notable shift in the division of expenditure between the five dominant sectors — electronics, software, chemicals and pharmaceuticals, engineering and food — which account for the bulk of the spend on R&D by business (Table 6.12). Note the exceptional growth in software R&D, from 7 per cent of total BERD in 1988 to 21 per cent in 1993 which, according to Breathnach,[26] is due to the emergence of new research-orientated software houses, both Irish and foreign-owned, and a shift from hardware to software development, reflecting the parallel decline in electronics R&D. This situation has been partially redressed in the recent burgeoning growth in inward investment into Ireland.

FIGURE 6.4: BUSINESS EXPENDITURE ON R&D PERFORMED IN-HOUSE (1988–95)[25]

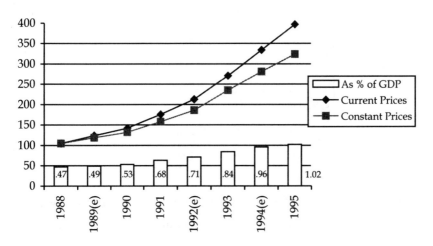

TABLE 6.11: GROSS EXPENDITURE ON R&D (GERD) AND THE RATIO
OF THE SPEND BY BUSINESS (BERD) AND THE PUBLIC ON R&D IN
IRELAND AND THE NORDIC COUNTRIES (OECD DATA, 1995)

|  | GERD (% of GDP) | BERD : Public |
|---|---|---|
| Denmark | 1.83 | 59 : 41 |
| Sweden | 3.04 | 71 : 29 |
| Finland | 2.30 | 63 : 37 |
| Norway | 1.59 | 54 : 46 |
| Ireland | 1.54 | 68 : 32 |

TABLE 6.12: SECTORAL ANALYSIS OF BUSINESS R&D
EXPENDITURE[26,27]

|  | 1988 | | 1993 | | 1995 | |
|---|---|---|---|---|---|---|
|  | Spend | As % of Total | Spend | As % of Total | Spend | As % of Total |
| Total BERD | £105 m | 100% | £271 m | 100% | £397 m | 100% |
| Electronics & software | £38 m | 37% | £101 m | 38% | £135 m | 34% |
| Electronics | £31 m | 30% | £45 m | 17% | £71 m | 18% |
| Software | £7 m | 7% | £56 m | 21% | £64 m | 16% |
| Chemicals & pharmaceut. | £13 m | 12% | £59 m | 22% | £71 m | 18% |
| Engineering | £20 m | 19% | £41 m | 15% | £83 m | 21% |
| Food | £12 m | 11% | £29 m | 11% | £48 m | 12% |
| All others | £22 m | 21% | £41 m | 14% | £60 m | 15% |

The combined expenditure on electronics/software R&D as a percentage of total BERD has, in fact, changed little between 1988
and 1993 but fell somewhat in 1995. Chemicals and pharmaceuticals, which are dominated by large foreign-owned companies,
increased its share of BERD from 12 per cent to 22 per cent be-

tween 1988 and 1993: this share also decreased in 1995 even though net expenditure increased by 20 per cent between 1993 and 1995, due in part to greater legal patent protection for new drugs (*c.f.* Section 3.8).

Table 6.13 indicates the way in which expenditure divides between different types of research. Pertinent indicators of R&D in Irish business are furnished in Table 6.14.[25-27]

TABLE 6.13: INTRA-MURAL R&D BUSINESS EXPENDITURE BY TYPE OF RESEARCH (1993)[26]

| Basic Research (£m) | Applied Research (£m) | Experimental Development (£m) | Total (£m) |
|---|---|---|---|
| 17.7 | 74.2 | 179.3 | 271.2 |
| (6.5%) | (27.4%) | (66.1%) | (100%) |

TABLE 6.14: SOME RECENT INDICATORS OF R&D IN IRISH BUSINESSES (1993) (LATEST AVAILABLE DATA)[26]

|  | Indigenous | Foreign | Total |
|---|---|---|---|
| Personnel (FTEs) | 1,939 | 2,560 | 4,499 |
| Total Spend (£m) | 91.3 | 179.9 | 271.2 |
| Spend as % of Sales in R&D performing companies | 0.8 | 2.5 | 1.5 |
| No. involved in R&D consortia with Irish HE sector | 81 | 50 | 131 |
| Number of R&D performers | 595 | 225 | 820 |
| No. with formal R&D depts. | 191 (57.5%) | 141 (42.5%) | 332 (100%) |

## 6.3.2 R&D Expenditure in the HE Sector

The pattern of total sectoral spending on R&D in the HE institutions (HERD) (Table 6.15) shows that growth has been quite dramatic over the 1982-94 period in the natural sciences, engineering, economics and the social sciences; the arts, humanities, the medical sciences have fared only about half as well, whereas the agricultural sciences suffered quite badly.[26]

TABLE 6.15: R&D EXPENDITURE IN THE HE SECTOR BY DISCIPLINE[26]

|                    | 1982 (£m) | 1992 (£m) | 1994 (£m) | % Real Increase 1982-1992 |
|--------------------|-----------|-----------|-----------|---------------------------|
| Natural Science    | 5.4       | 30.8      | 41.6      | 261%                      |
| Engineering        | 2.8       | 17.6      | 21.1      | 298%                      |
| Medical Sciences   | 2.1       | 7.1       | 10.0      | 114%                      |
| Agricultural       | 1.4       | 2.0       | 2.3       | -9%                       |
| Sciences           | 1.5       | 8.8       | 9.7       | 271%                      |
| Social/Economics   | 2.2       | 6.7       | 10.6      | 93%                       |
| Arts/Humanities    | *         | *         | *         | *                         |
| Total              | 15.4      | 73.0      | 95.4      | 200%                      |

Funding for research in the HE sector should be clarified. Firstly, over 40 per cent of the total expenditure on R&D in the universities (1994 data) is, in fact, an apportionment of academic salaries, based on an estimate of the amount of time that academics spend on scientific research. Secondly, about 20.0 per cent, or *c.a.*£20 million, has been directed to Programmes for Advanced Technology (PATs) operating at the cutting edge of current technology (Table 6.6). As indicated earlier, these programmes are prescriptive rather than competitive in the sense that they cannot be accessed by the research community at large under the usual norms of peer review. Non-prescriptive research includes basic research, strategic research and student support programmes for which the level of funding is small (Table 6.16).

TABLE 6.16: TREND IN DIRECT GOVERNMENT (OFFICE OF SCIENCE
AND TECHNOLOGY) FUNDING OF HE RESEARCH SINCE 1990 (£'000S)[27]

|  | 1990 | 1992 | 1994 | 1996 | 1997** |
|---|---|---|---|---|---|
| Basic Research Grants Scheme | 532 | 854 | 833 | 1,990 | 2,250 |
| Strategic Research Grants Scheme | 975 | 798 | 1,001 | 1,217 | 1,470 |
| Applied Res. Grants Scheme-RTCs | 972 | 1,303 | 991 | 746 | 1,000 |
| Applied Res. Grants Scheme-Univs | 1,202 | 728 | 152 | 1,326 | 1,700 |
| Industry Scholarships* | 343 | 401 | 399 | 294 | 260 |
| Research Scholarship Awards | 483 | 552 | 507 | 1,175 | 1,180 |
| Drugs Scheme |  |  |  | 525 | 294 |
| Total | 4,507 | 4,636 | 3,883 | 7,273 | 8,154 |

* 50 per cent of scholarships funded by sponsoring company which is not reflected in the figures

** Budgeted amounts

Expansion of the research effort and, less directly, the teaching
effort in the HE sector has been funded substantially by the EU
and an increased reliance on the private sector. While not denying
the competing claims on the education budget as a whole, the
level of funding from the private sector, important though it is,
has in large measure concealed the inadequate exchequer funding
of R&D in the HE sector by successive governments.

The recent allocation of £250 million, for the first time, has recognised the deleterious consequences for the economy of a poorly
funded national R&D capability. The evidence is now so compelling both in regard to the economic rate of return on such R&D
expenditure and to the significance of R&D as an attractor for direct foreign investment, that the case for realistic and sustained
funding of the HE sector cannot be gainsaid. The reality is that
unless the exchequer makes the necessary on-going investment in
R&D, the capacity of the economy to generate wealth to support

the broader social economy, including the earlier stages of education itself, will be compromised.

One practical consequence of this analysis is the need to increase expenditure on capital equipment: the allocation of £30 million is a significant first step in reducing the level of obsolescence in the national research equipment base (*c.f.* Section 6.4 below). Equally crucial is the development of an adequate postgraduate funding environment that can attract and retain creative young graduate researchers. The situation in Ireland is rapidly approaching crisis proportions as competing forces from the labour market are becoming stronger by the day with the sustained growth of inward investment. Only then can the national research capability be adequately nourished and the necessary bridgehead to emerging technologies and their future commercialisation be sustained. To contemplate less than a competitive stipend for postgraduates in science and technology is unrealistic.

### 6.3.3 The PATs Initiative

The Programmes for Advanced Technology (PATs) were designed to strengthen Ireland's indigenous capability in S&T and to increase competitiveness and innovation in Irish industry. A number of niche areas were selected where international competitiveness was feasible and where the technology developed could be readily transferred into the industrial sector. These included electronics, biotechnology, advanced manufacturing technology, opto-electronics, advanced materials, power electronics, software, telecommunications, sensor technology and analog devices.

The PATs are driven by excellence and relevance and are mission-orientated with well-defined technical goals and an overall requirement to achieve a significant measure of self-sufficiency within a specified period of time. They constitute an important policy initiative which is now operating well, following correction of a number of initial operational difficulties concerning the relationship between Research Directors and Programme Managers, unnecessary layers of bureaucracy with concomitant high administration costs, and the need for a flexible approach to intellectual property rights (Section 4.5). Nonetheless, the initial growth period of the PATs was a valuable learning experience.

### 6.4 RESEARCH EQUIPMENT

Just as experimental research and development is becoming ever more sophisticated with the march of science, so too is the equipment required to carry out that research. Researchers can only achieve their full potential through access to state-of-the-art facilities

An inadequate equipment base is impeding good research in many European countries as well as in the US (Section 4.3). A recent survey in the UK, for example, was particularly revealing as illustrated in Table 6.17, and offers some insight into deficiencies in current equipment and the steps proposed to rectify the situation in the UK universities.[28] An estimated expenditure in excess of £300 million is required to meet priority equipment needs.

The survey noted that the equipment actually provided tended to be project-orientated and located in a relatively small number of centres. This is an inevitable consequence of current research support schemes throughout Europe, including the European Structural Funds. Recall that EU funding is intended to augment rather than replace national indigenous R&D infrastructures that are presumed already to be in place.

The UK government's response by way of a cut in capital funding to English universities of £170 million in 1995-96 was less than encouraging. UK industry for its part did not intend to make up the shortfall, nor would it be attracted to "tired-looking departments with pensioned equipment". The Report based on the survey concluded that "a poorly equipped science base could have a negative effect on inward investment in the UK".

TABLE 6.17: EQUIPMENT NEEDS IN UK UNIVERSITIES IN THE NEXT
FIVE YEARS[28]

| Department | Current Equipment | | Priority Equipment Needed | | |
|---|---|---|---|---|---|
| | State-of- the-Art (%) | No longer adequate (%) | Items | Cost (£m) | No. of academics |
| Physics | 26 | 31 | 249 | 31.9 | 1,432 |
| Chemistry | 19 | 36 | 322 | 45.4 | 1,422 |
| Biosciences | 15 | 34 | 505 | 40.0 | 2,765 |
| Mechanical Engineering | 17 | 37 | 230 | 25.1 | 923 |
| All dept's | n/a | n/a | 3,372 | 307.2 | 16,338 |

Ireland can learn from this experience to correct a situation that is
significantly worse than in the UK. The level of obsolescence is
high and recurrent funding for equipment is low: it has been estimated that an immediate injection of £50 million is required to
bring the nation's research equipment up to an acceptable level.[4]
As discussed above, academic researchers have relied heavily on
contract research as opposed to public funding to maintain an
adequate equipment base by ear-marking 15-20 per cent of their
annual £50 million contract research earnings for this purpose.

### 6.5 MANPOWER NEEDS

In 1991, an IRDAC report comprehensively reviewed the skills
shortage in Europe and reasserted the importance of education
and training as a strategic instrument in Europe's competitiveness.[29] At that time, the report drew a number of important conclusions:

- Young people are a key factor in innovation and technological
  renewal, provided they have the right knowledge base and
  attitude.

- Industry expects graduates to have a solid foundation coupled with a capacity for adaptation, flexibility, creativity, mobility, teamwork, communication and language.

- The inevitable retraining required by the extant workforce (in 1991) — 80 per cent of which will still be operational 10 years on — affords a major opportunity for the HE sector to play a full part in the area of continuing in-service education which should be a *mainstream* rather than an *ancillary* activity.

- Non-technical people both in industry and throughout society at large should be aware of the newer developments in S&T which are an integral part of modern society's culture.

These recommendations were made against a backdrop of pervasive disillusionment with science and science-based careers throughout Europe, despite the continuous stream of exciting and challenging developments in science and technology. Between 1976 and 1986, for example, the number of accountants trebled and the number of lawyers doubled whereas the number of engineers increased by only 50 per cent. This can be traced to a number of factors: (a) the deepening ambivalence in the public's attitude towards science and technology discussed in Section 1.1; (b) diverse and well-rewarded professions ·compete with ever-increasing success for the diminishing pool of appropriately qualified entrants, a phenomenon which is more and more prevalent today; and (c) many trained scientists and engineers diffuse subsequently throughout the wider community into areas such as management, business, insurance and finance, with little or no comparable flow in the opposite direction.

This disillusionment is still prevalent although recent initiatives have been taken to counter the projected shortfall of skilled people in key growth areas. Cooley, in 1997, advanced a view on at least some of the underlying reasons:

> In many industrial nations, Science and Technology, with
> their perceived disregard of the environment and in some
> cases "the human spirit" are experiencing growing shortages
> of suitable recruits. . . . In the UK, to even maintain the present
> pace of growth requires 30,000 new engineers each year. In
> fact only 24,000 young people began studying engineering at
> all levels in 1995 and because of the high levels of drop-outs in
> these subjects it is anticipated that only around 15,500 will
> qualify in 1998.[30]

The problem has taken on a new dimension with the reintroduction of fees in the UK. Recent, though preliminary, figures suggest that new intake in 1998 will fall by 16 per cent following a stable intake over the last four years. This is in spite of an increasing number of 18-21 year olds in the overall UK population.[31] The European Commission's White Paper, *Teaching and Learning: Towards the Learning Society*, provided an overview of Europe's current and future manpower needs, wherein current inadequacies are summed up as follows:

> If ten million jobs were instantly created, employers would
> have considerable difficulty in finding suitably qualified peo-
> ple to fill them, even though there are 18 million unemployed
> people in Europe.[32]

The following key points of the White Paper reflect current thinking on the subject:

- The link between employment and education and training is reaffirmed.

- There is still a mismatch between the more traditional skills and knowledge available and the skills and knowledge required to cope with new developments in Science and Technology. As pointed out in Section 1.2, mental skills must replace purely manual skills in many areas of work. Canny and co-workers contend that increased employment in the five categories shown in Figure 6.5 may well account for more than

25 per cent of new jobs over the period indicated.[33] By the same token, new technology has created a section of the workforce that will remain essentially unemployable unless concerted retraining policy initiatives are implemented.

FIGURE 6.5: FASTEST GROWING OCCUPATIONAL GROUPS IN IRELAND (1991–98)[33]

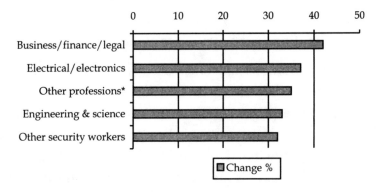

* Other professions include health and welfare services

• The White Paper noted that "what education and training systems all too often achieve is to map out an occupational pathway on a once-and-for-all basis; there is too little flexibility and too much compartmentalisation between these systems, too few bridges and too few opportunities for taking on board new patterns of lifelong learning".[34] This poses a clear challenge for the education sector and policy-makers alike who must review current trends towards ever-increasing specialisation and seriously consider a return to more broad-based education and training which focuses on generic skills, exploiting where possible new multimedia capabilities and student mobility throughout Europe and beyond. This will re-shape educational priorities and go some way towards equipping students to think flexibly, to be equipped with appropriate linguistic skills to enter the global arena, and to embark on life-long learning through in-service and continuing education

in what the White Paper terms *a Learning Society*. The philosophy *to educate for life*, not jobs, is reasserted.

- A preoccupation with university education as the only route
  to a fulfilling career takes no account of the disparate talents
  and predilections of people. The importance of vocational
  education in some advanced economies has been downgraded
  as a result. Germany is a notable exception. Vocational training plays a comparably critical role, in parallel with professional education, in the workplace of the future.

- Paper qualifications are often used as a convenient sifting
  mechanism to reduce large numbers of applications for a
  given post irrespective of the skills level required for the post
  in question. This has often led to the practice of "trading
  down" or "grade inflation" whereby over-qualified people fill
  the available jobs with inevitable frustration and lack of job
  satisfaction in later years.

- The pattern of employment in EU nations will be increasingly
  influenced by worker (and student) mobility throughout a
  borderless Europe. This, in turn, has implications for the nature and parity of paper qualifications from one country to
  another.

- Mobility on a global scale is also a feature of modern society,
  especially for the most highly qualified cohort. Brain drain
  from Europe to the US, for example, has been a notable feature
  in the past. The more highly educated people tend to be the
  most mobile, often as emigrants in the first instance, and subsequently as immigrants.[35]

- By the same token, the concept of "runaway" service jobs into
  and out of a country is gaining credence with the decision of
  companies such as British Airways in the UK and insurance
  companies and printing houses in the US to relocate a major
  part of their clerical and data entry work to India and Ireland,

respectively. This is facilitated by the rampant progress in computer and telecommunications technology. The notion of borderless nations clearly exerts a major influence on man-power requirements from one nation to another.[36] The distribution of manpower requirements is also influenced by "virtual companies" whose factory floors are accessed by national or global computer networks.[30]

## 6.5.1. Manpower in Ireland

In 1990, a regional study on competitiveness in Ireland identified four out of the five most positive factors as "people-orientated", namely, the availability of labour, access to quality education and training, a favourable social climate and access to skilled people.[37] This identified the relatively strong skills base that underpinned Ireland's current performance as the fastest growing economy in the EU in the 1990s. In the most recent World Economic Forum Report, Ireland was ranked 16th in the league table of the most competitive countries in the world, ahead of Germany and France, spurred on, no doubt, by the entry criteria for participation in European Monetary Union.[38-41] Future predictions are equally bright with an anticipated economic growth of 5.5 per cent per annum up to the year 2000.[42,43]

The enhanced competitiveness of Ireland and the UK contrasts with other continental EU countries which slipped in their rankings. Overall, the report suggests that the EU is experiencing "a chronic crisis of declining competitiveness" not because of a lack of good technology, management and manufacturing, but because of fiscal and labour policy driven by an extensive social welfare state.

Ireland's competitiveness continues to be linked to the availability of a well-educated young labour force which, interestingly, was specifically cited as one of the key attributes of the two leading Asian Tigers, Singapore and Hong Kong, ranked first and second, respectively. Currently, 80 per cent of students in Ireland have completed second-level education and 40-50 per cent have been exposed to some form of higher education. Regarding supply and demand, future projections portrayed in Figure 6.6 resonate with the expanding jobs market for the well-qualified (Table 6.18).[39,44,45] The current participation rate in higher education exceeds that of the UK and is comparable to many of the more developed economies.

Clearly, this augurs well for the future, providing, of course, that the type of skills created match the requirements of industry in a continuing period of seismic change. But it is again stressed that industry's gain is the universities' loss in the sense that the number of well-qualified graduates who wish to proceed to postgraduate research is diminishing with consequent implications for the sustainability of the overall national research effort.

The data further show that the cohort of young people is diminishing with time (Figure 6.6), that the shift away from agriculture appears to have reached a plateau (Table 6.18), and that there is a gradual convergence in the growth rates of the Business/Financial/Legal and the Engineering/Science occupations (Table 6.19).

### 6.5.2 R&D Manpower in Ireland

A sustained supply of graduates is crucial to developing R&D programmes. The CIRCA report, while recognising that well-qualified researchers were available, showed that the support they were given was wholly inadequate relative to that provided by other countries (Figure 6.7).[12]

FIGURES 6.6: PROJECTED EDUCATIONAL ATTAINMENT OF THE IRISH
LABOUR FORCE AGED 20 TO 65

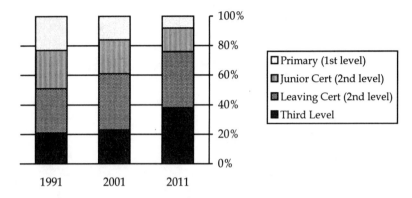

FIGURE 6.7: INTERNATIONAL COMPARISON OF EXPENDITURE ON
HERD (1991 OR NEAREST AVAILABLE YEAR)[1]

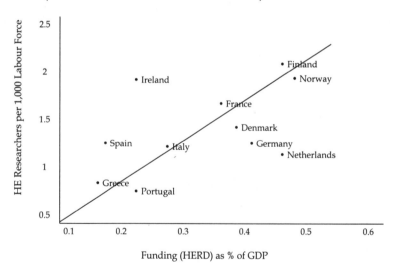

*Ireland and the Knowledge Economy*

TABLE 6.18: EMPLOYMENT IN IRELAND BY OCCUPATION (ADAPTED FROM TABLE 2.1, 2.2, IN REF. 32)

|  | 1971 | | 1981 | | 1991 | | 1998 | |
| --- | --- | --- | --- | --- | --- | --- | --- | --- |
|  | No. | (%) | No. | (%) | No. | (%) | No. | (%) |
| Agricultural | 276,848 | (26.2) | 191,093 | (16.8) | 156,300 | (13.8) | 127,100 | (10.2) |
| Managers/Proprietors | 66,650 | (6.3) | 94,282 | (8.3) | 114,600 | (10.1) | 141,500 | (11.3) |
| Professional | 74,243 | (7.0) | 105,462 | (9.3) | 128,600 | (11.3) | 154,700 | (12.4) |
| • Education | 26,043 | (2.5) | 41,822 | (3.7) | 50,100 | (4.4) | 55,800 | (4.5) |
| • Engineering/Science | 8,054 | (0.8) | 12,782 | (1.1) | 15,900 | (1.4) | 21,300 | (1.7) |
| • Business/finance/legal | 6,469 | (0.6) | 17,071 | (1.5) | 26,300 | (2.3) | 37,300 | (3.0) |
| • Others | 33,677 | (3.2) | 33,787 | (3.0) | 36,400 | (3.2) | 40,300 | (3.2) |
| Associate Professional | 28,862 | (2.7) | 46,903 | (4.1) | 55,100 | (4.9) | 67,800 | (5.4) |

TABLE 6.19: PERCENTAGE CHANGE IN EMPLOYMENT IN IRELAND
FOR SELECTED OCCUPATIONS

|  | Change 1971–81 | | Change 1981–91 | | Change 1991–98 | |
|---|---|---|---|---|---|---|
|  | No. | (%) | No. | (%) | No. | (%) |
| Agricultural | -85,755 | (-31.0) | -34,793 | (-18.2) | -29,100 | (-18.7) |
| Education | 15,779 | (60.6) | 8,278 | (19.8) | 57,000 | (11.4) |
| Engineering/ Science | 10,602 | (163.9) | 9,229 | (54.1) | 11,000 | (41.8) |
| Business/ Finance/Legal | 4,728 | (58.7) | 3,118 | (24.4) | 5,400 | (34.0) |

Table 6.20 lists the personnel engaged in R&D by sector of employment and occupation in Ireland in 1989, 1992 and 1995.[27] The totals are made up of the numbers of actual researchers (listed separately) plus support staff such as technicians. The Business and HE sectors account for the lion's share. The large growth in the number of researchers in the business sector between 1989 and 1995 (120 per cent) is a direct consequence of the strengthening relationship between education and jobs, the continuing success in attracting foreign multinationals to Ireland, and the burgeoning indigenous research base. The growth of 130 per cent in the HE sector over the same period parallels these trends because of the accelerated demand for higher education with greater numbers seeking higher degrees. This growth, in some measure, resulted from the depressed jobs market at the time, a situation that has now reversed quite dramatically. It also reflected the overall increase in research activity. Postgraduates account for about one-third of the academic research cohort and one of the challenges for the future is to maintain the supply of well qualified and motivated Science & Technology-based research students.

The failure to nurture a future researcher cohort strikes at the very heart of regional policies within the EU. At best, it would create a deficit which would be filled by subsidised foreign nationals: at worst, it risks marginalising the needs of Foreign Direct Investment (FDI) as well as indigenous industry, thereby jeopardising the momentum of the last decade which was predicated on an ample source of skilled postgraduates.

TABLE 6.20: TOTAL R&D PERSONNEL BY SECTOR OF EMPLOYMENT AND OCCUPATION IN IRELAND (FULL TIME EQUIVALENTS)[27]

| | 1989 | | 1992 | |
|---|---|---|---|---|
| | *Researcher* | *Total* | *Researcher* | *Total* |
| Business Enterprise | 1,534 (37%) | 2,872 (45%) | 2,352 (42%) | 4,234 (49%) |
| Higher Education | 1,961 (48%) | 2,190 (35%) | 2,722 (48%) | 3,010 (35%) |
| Government | 443 (11%) | 1,038 (16%) | 315 (6%) | 1,016 (12%) |
| Private/Non Profit | 160 (4%) | 228 (4%) | 222 (4%) | 316 (4%) |
| National Total | 4,098 | 6,328 | 5,611 | 8,576 |

In practical terms, in the new and challenging environment created by the single currency regime within the EU, the failure of small open economies to pay its researchers even a basic minimum will fatally compromise their ability to achieve convergence through knowledge-driven competitive strategies.

## OBSERVATIONS AND RECOMMENDATIONS

- *Best practice procedures for managing and, where appropriate, commercialising HE research should be initiated.*

- *A rigorous appraisal of an institution's potential downstream liability is essential.*

- *There are formidable difficulties in extracting unambiguous measures of public expenditure on R&D: strictly quantitative estimates of returns on investment are difficult to make.*

- *A philosophy of investment must replace the more established notion of expenditure in the areas of education and R&D.*

- *Policy, as currently stated, is riddled with paradoxes. For example, the implication that the universities have no officially recognised role in the commercialisation of research is at odds with the innovation culture that has grown up in the universities.*

- *In recognising that funding is a major instrument of government, care must be taken that it does not lead to a "culture of compliance" which is anathema to the ethos of university education and research. Equally, compliance with the stated needs of industry to an extent that undermines the central pedagogical mission of the universities is equally undesirable.*

- *An enhanced R&D contribution by academics will affect the division of academic time between research and lecturing. The choice of appropriate areas of research in each institution will be guided by "critical mass" criteria, the development of essential support services, and the identification of acceptable performance indicators for research evaluation.*

- *Policy designed to maximise the benefits of the nation's R&D capabilities must ensure effective technology transfer from the knowledge generators to the knowledge users. There are several effective models for this.*

- *A twin-track approach involving more imaginative innovation transfer mechanisms specifically tailored to the micro-enterprises and large multinationals respectively is a priority.*

- *In light of the economic rate of return on R&D expenditure and the significance of R&D as an attractor for direct foreign investment, the case for realistic funding of the HE sector can no longer be gainsaid. The recent allocation of £250 million is a significant first step.*

- *The level of obsolescence of large research equipment is high and recurrent funding is low: an immediate injection of £50 million is re-*

*quired to bring the nation's research equipment up to a minimally acceptable level.*

- *The HE sector must play a full part in the area of continuing in-service education as a mainstream rather than an ancillary activity.*

- *The philosophy to educate for life, not jobs, is reasserted.*

- *The practice of "trading down" whereby over-qualified people fill available jobs will lead inevitably to frustration and lack of job satisfaction in later years.*

- *Inward investment depends critically on available well-qualified manpower at both professional and vocational levels in key growth areas. The expanding market of well paid jobs is having a deleterious affect on the numbers of graduates who wish to proceed to post-graduate training, due in part to the derisory level of funding for post-graduate education. The overall national research effort will suffer as a result. A stipend of at least £10,000 per annum for post-graduates is proposed.*

## References and Notes: Chapter 6

1.  *Growth, Competitiveness, Employment: the Challenges and Ways Forward into the 21st Century,* EU Commission White Paper, Bulletin of the European Communities, Supplement 6/93, 1993.

2.  EU Commission *Green Paper on Innovation,* Supplement 5/95, 1995.

3.  E.P. O'Neill, Innovation Services Office, Trinity College Dublin, private communication.

4.  *Making Knowledge Work for Us,* Report of the Science, Technology and Innovation Advisory Council, (D. Tierney, Chairperson), Stationery Office, Dublin 2, Ireland, 1995.

5.  *Science, Technology and Innovation,* Irish Government White Paper, Stationery Office, Dublin 2, Ireland, 1996.

6.  *Report on the National Education Convention,* J. Coolahan (ed.), Dublin Castle, 11-21 October, 1993, Stationery Office, Dublin 2, Ireland, 1994.

7.  *Charting our Education Future,* Irish Government White Paper on Education, Stationery Office, Dublin 2, Ireland, 1995.

8.  *The Universities Act, 1997,* Stationery Office, Dublin 2, Ireland, 1997.

9.  R.P. Kinsella and V.J. McBrierty, "Campus Companies and the Techno-Academic Paradigm: The Irish Experience", *Technovation,* 1997, 17, 245.

10. *Shaping our Future,* Forfás Report, 1996.

11. E. Geisler, "When Whales are Cast Ashore: the Conversion to Relevancy of American Universities and Basic Science", *IEEE Transactions on Engineering Management,* 2(1), February, 1995, pp. 3-8.

12. *A Comparative International Assessment of the Organisation, Management and Funding of University Research in Ireland and Europe,* The CIRCA Group Europe Ltd., Roebuck Castle, Dublin 4, Ireland. Report commissioned by the Higher Education Authority.

13. G. Walshe, L. Georghiou, H. Cameron, K. Barker and G. Butler, *Returns to Research and Development Spending,* The Office of Science and Technology (UK) and the Programme for Policy Research in Engineering Science and Technology at Manchester University, HMSO, UK, 1993. See also Forfás, Basic Research Support for Ireland, 1998, Dublin, pp. 7-10.

14. L.R.K. Paul, *Research Returns and Effectiveness,* Report to the Joint Research Centre, August, 1992, *cited in* ref. 9.

15. W. Happer, "Diversity Needed in Federal Support of Basic Science after SSC", *American Physical Society News,* March 1994, p.12.

16. *The European Report on Science and Technology Indicators,* EUR 15897 EN, European Commission, Luxembourg, 1994, p. 49.

17. Ref. 2, p. 97.

18. Z. Griliches, "Productivity, R&D and Basic Research at the Firm Level in the 1970s", *American Economic Review,* 76(1), 141-154 (1986): see also "R&D and Productivity: Measurement Issues and Econometric Results", *Science,* 237, 31-35 (1992).

19. V.J. McBrierty and R.P. Kinsella, "Intellectual Property: A Social Paradox" *Studies,* 87, 57-68 (1998).

20. Ref. 2. p. 98.

21. It is disconcerting to find that this view is a recurring theme, for example, in the Irish *White Paper on Science, Technology and Innovation,* Ref. 5.

22. V.J. McBrierty, "The Changing Face of Universities in the Innovation Age", *Physics World,* The Institute of Physics, January, 1997, pp.15-17.

23. *Science and Irish Economic Development,* Irish Survey Team/OECD (1996), Stationery Office, Dublin 2, Ireland, 1996.

24. *Reviews of National Science Policy – Ireland,* OECD, Paris, 1974.

25. *Irish S&T Indicators: an Up-date,* The 1996 Annual Report of FIOS: The Advisory Committee on S&T Indicators, Forfás, Dublin,2, Ireland, 1997.

26. M. Breathnach, *Research and Development in the Business Sector,* Forfás, Dublin 2, Ireland, 1995.

27. A. FitzGerald and K. Lydon,. *State Investment in Science and Technology, 1996,* Forfás, Wilton House, Dublin 2, Ireland.

28. M. Durrani, "Old Equipment Stifles Research", Report on the survey of 973 departments in 91 universities by policy researchers at Manchester University. *Physics World,* July 1996, pp. 6,7.

29. *Skills Shortages in Europe,* Report of IRDAC to the EU, 1991, p. 46.

30.  M. Cooley, *Tapping the Human Resource in Science and Technology,* Conference Proceedings, Dublin Castle, June 10, 1997. Organised by Women in Science and Technology (WITS), pp. 7-9.

31. A. Utley, *"Drastic Fall in Numbers",* THES, Oct. 17, 1977, pp. 1,15.

32. *Teaching and Learning: Towards the Learning Society,* European Commission White Paper, Office for Official Publications of the European Communities, Luxembourg, 1996, p. 2.

33. A. Canny, G. Hughes and J.J. Sexton, *Occupational Employment Forecasts,* FÁS/ESRI Manpower Forecasting Studies, Report No. 4, FÁS, the Training and Manpower Authority, Dublin 4, Ireland. March, 1995, p. 19.

34. Ref. 32, p.11.

35. J.J. Sexton, A. Canny and G. Hughes, *Changing Profiles in Occupations and Educational Attainment,* FÁS/ESRI Manpower Forecasting Studies, Report No. 5, FÁS, the Training and Manpower Authority, Dublin 4, Ireland, November, 1996.

36.  S. Mitter, *Tapping the Human Resource in Science and Technology,* Conference Proceedings, Dublin Castle, June 10, 1997. Organised by Women in Science and Technology (WITS), pp. 15-17.

37. *An Empirical Assessment of Factors Shaping Regional Competitiveness in Problem Regions, Vol. 5. The United Kingdom and Ireland,* IFO-Institut für Wirtschaftsforschung, Munich, May, 1990.

38. *World Economic Forum Report,* Davos, Switzerland, 1997.

39. M. Canniffe, *Irish Times,* 21 May, 1997, pp. 1, 18.

40. Morgan Stanley, *World Competitiveness Report*, London, 1996.

41. The WEF Report defines competitiveness as the ability of a country to achieve sustained high rates of growth in Gross Domestic Product (GDP) *per capita* over a 5 to 10 year period.

42. OECD, Paris, 1996.

43. *Medium Term Outlook*, ESRI, Dublin, 1997.

44. *Irish Labour Force Survey*, Stationery Office, Dublin, 1997.

45. Ref. 32, pp. 26,27.

*Chapter 7*

# CAMPUS COMPANIES IN THE HE SECTOR: SURVEY AND ANALYSIS

## 7.1. INTRODUCTION

Previous work by the authors (a) established the important role of campus companies, (b) helped catalyse subsequent policy interventions and (c) established an example of leverage between public and private sources in financing the knowledge economy as described in ensuing chapters.[1] The recent Campus Company Venture Capital Fund of £6 million, comprising £3 million private/university funding matched with £3 million public funding, is one tangible manifestation of this leverage.

This chapter updates and extends the earlier formative analysis. The growth of campus companies within the HE sector has spawned a new and developing component of Irish indigenous industry. The analysis presented in this chapter, in particular, builds upon the review of the campus company sector carried out in 1994, and the discussion on campus companies as an element of the Techno-Academic Paradigm in Chapter 5.[1] In addition, fieldwork in the form of questionnaire-based research was undertaken with a cross section of universities and National Institutes of Technology (NITs) as well as campus companies within their hinterland. The results, while not entirely comprehensive, do provide substantive and important insights into the dynamics of, constraints on, and scope for development of this important niche of knowledge-intensive Small-and-Medium-Sized Enterprises (SMEs).

There is a potentially high payback to the national economy of Fast Growth campus companies, working in highly specialised technologies with, by definition, little or no displacement effect.

The operational definition of a campus company used by Trinity College Dublin provides a useful template for discussion:

> A campus company is a private limited company with permission from the College authorities to trade in a range of goods and services for a limited period of time (three years, extended to five as mutually agreed).[2]

The company is normally promoted or organised by a staff member of the College. The process of its formation as authorised by the College is summarised in Figure 7.1 which lists the steps to be taken, the relevant College Officers involved in those steps, and the general considerations which arise during the approval process. Further details are furnished in Appendix III.

## 7.2 CAMPUS COMPANY SURVEY

As indicated above, the analysis draws upon a survey of campus companies within the university sector and the NITs. Two questionnaires were sent out to each institution. The first related to the institution itself; the second was relayed by the Institution to campus companies within their hinterland. The objective was to obtain as informed and rigorous a perspective on campus companies in Ireland, the sectors in which they are established, their governance, and the factors that currently inhibit their growth.

### 7.2.1 Methodology

Questionnaire-based research, particularly where it is not conducted face-to-face, is subject to well-recognised limitations. The design of the questionnaires and, where appropriate, follow-up questions to individual institutions attempted to minimise these constraints. Further limitations emerged from the responses received. In particular:

FIGURE 7.1: SUMMARY OF STAGES OF APPROVAL FOR FORMATION OF CAMPUS COMPANY IN TRINITY COLLEGE[1]

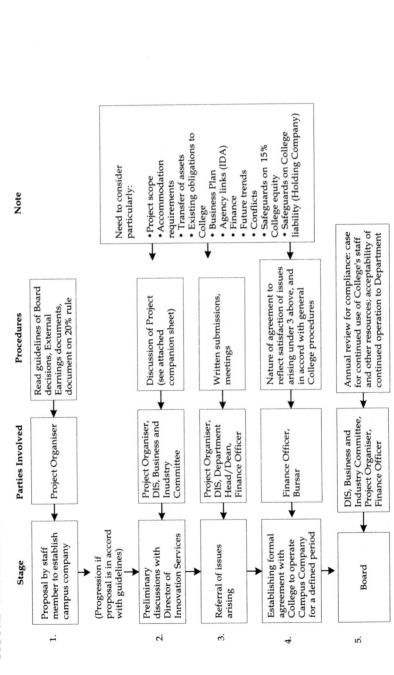

- One university's interpretation of "campus company" differed from that stipulated in the questionnaire and it provided adjusted figures in respect of its own broader definition.

- The definition of campus company excluded certain organisational forms — industrial laboratories are one example — which share at least one of the characteristics of campus companies.

- In the case of one institution, there were a number of campus companies which had recently spun-off but which, arguably, should be included in the institution's returns. In this regard, one of the NITs included within its definition of campus companies, enterprises located on campus but which had no employee contractual relationship within the institution.[3]

- Not all of the completed questionnaires provided all of the information requested.

In spite of these limitations, the survey still provided an informed analysis of the sector as a prototype of the Techno-Academic Paradigm. The strategy has therefore been to distil as much information as possible and where appropriate to make informed estimates of the overall contribution of the campus company sector to the economy as a whole.

### 7.2.2 Sectoral Participation

Institutions were asked to identify the sectors in which campus companies were established. Companies in the wider set of commercial activities including industrial laboratories are involved in a variety of knowledge-intensive activities, in particular, biotechnology, software, life sciences and microelectronics.

Each of the institutions identified a small number of sectoral activities in which they had particular involvement. A number of institutions reported "clusters" of campus companies in and around these sectors or activities. These clusters complement the

PATs in providing a platform for the commercialisation of leading-edge technologies within Ireland's industrial base.

### 7.2.3 Patents and Innovative Capability

Patents are a, albeit imperfect, measure of innovation and the latent scope for commercialisation of new knowledge *via* campus company activity (Chapters 3, 4). Patents may underpin the formation of a campus company in which case the host institution has a proprietary interest. On the other hand, the protected intellectual property may be created within the campus company, once established, and, as such, it is wholly owned by the company.

The survey revealed an estimated 60 patents held by responding institutions which generated significant financial returns. As pointed out in Section 4.4, they also provide scope for reinforcing linkages with industry and enhancing the credibility of the institutions concerned in the area of technology transfer.

An important finding to come out of the survey concerns the wide differences across HE institutions in respect of the management and commercialisation of patents and, more generally, intellectual property (IP). These differences include systems for remunerating inventors and arrangements in respect of the holding and licensing of patents. The main conclusion is that the patent portfolio of the HE sector as a whole is not being actively managed or optimised in a cohesive manner. This has obvious bearing on an institution's attitude to campus companies (*vide infra*, Section 7.2.6).

### 7.2.4 Support Facilities

The results of the survey indicated wide differences across institutions concerning the facilities provided to support academic entrepreneurs who wish to set up campus companies. These differences exist in respect of a number of important activities:

- *Leave of absence:* The key issue here is whether such leave of absence should be paid or unpaid.

- *Access to the institution's facilities:* From a national perspective, a major dynamic behind campus companies is their capacity to leverage the collective knowledge of the research community and the extant technological infrastructure. In this respect, a number of key points emerge from the survey. While most institutions provide access to facilities, usually in consultation with the head of department, there are differences as to whether an overhead is charged to the company or not and, if so, the level at which it is levied. The important point here is that these facilities, which are a key central and accessible facility for SMEs including campus companies, are already under severe pressure because of under-funding of capital equipment over the years (*c.f.* Section 6.4).

This again highlights the importance of systematic and substantial investment in up-grading and enhancing major capital facilities. It also underlines the importance of a speedy implementation of projects designed to improve the research infra-structure, envisaged as part of government's Educational Technology Investment Fund (ETIF) initiative. Such facilities can be leveraged, in the national economic interest, by campus companies who pay for access under a service contract between the company and the university.

It is again important to stress that good state-of-the-art research facilities preserve the basic research capability of the institution which is both an "attractor" of knowledge-intensive foreign investment and the seed bed for indigenous "frontier industries", including campus companies.

### 7.2.5 Management of Intellectual Capital

A recurring theme of this analysis is the role of intellectual capital as the cornerstone of the knowledge economy. In this regard the survey revealed a number of important features regarding the way in which intellectual property is viewed within the HE sector:

- All of the institutions have a strongly proactive approach to the exploitation of intellectual property, including patents.

- As pointed out in general terms in Chapter 4, there are wide differences in the way that IP is viewed and managed. The lack of a coherent, and coordinated, strategy across the HE sector as a whole directly militates against the interests of in- dividual institutions and the wider national economic interest. There is no formal policy on intellectual property at all in a number of institutions and, among those institutions that have such a policy, there is quite a diversity of approach.

- All institutions surveyed asserted ownership of intellectual property generated by staff in the course of their employment. Some institutions vest ownership in a holding company in or- der to facilitate the exploitation of IP and to maximise returns. Others license IP to campus companies.

- The basis on which the institutions sought remuneration dif- fered substantially: some favoured a royalty or an equity stake in a campus company which exploits the IP whereas others sought a mandatory stake together with a share of royalty earnings. The proportion of royalty earnings accruing to the institution was, in most cases, on a sliding scale, in the sense that the institution's share increased in proportion to the size of the royalty. There are, however, a number of institutions that opted for a 50-50 split.

From an overall perspective, there is a compelling case for devel- oping "best practice" in regard to the management of IP at na- tional and local level. From the national perspective, as the knowledge economy develops and the role of the HE sector within this knowledge economy increases, a proactive strategy for managing the IP portfolio of the HE sector as a whole is becoming increasingly necessary. This will require, *inter alia*, a strengthening of management systems for IP both within the institution itself and within the Department of Education and Science.

### 7.2.6 Governance of Campus Companies

The issue of best practice regarding the governance of campus companies is an important issue. On the one hand, a designated campus company carries the imprimatur of the host institution. There is, therefore, an added onus on the company to ensure good governance. Furthermore, public funds support the institutions within which campus companies are located which adds yet a further dimension to the need for meticulous accountability and transparency. On the other hand, campus companies are constituted with limited liability, and subject to the laws of the land including the Companies Acts that confers legal autonomy on them. It is in the interest of both the company and the host institution that this autonomy be recognised and respected. It is also an important element in its healthy growth.

Most, but not all, of the universities have a formal policy on campus company development: the majority have a specialist unit to facilitate their establishment and development in their formative years. In a number of instances, campus companies operate within, or are aligned with, more broadly-based industrial support and innovation programmes.

At a more detailed level, there are significant differences regarding the documentation and due diligence required prior to being designated a campus company. There are also differences in respect of compliance requirements. The legal status of contractual relationships between the host institution and campus companies differs across the sector. There are also differences in respect of internal controls. In general, institutions assert their right to inspect the accounts of a company and, where the company is substantial and/or where the institution has a major shareholding, to obtain a full set of audited accounts for consolidation with those of the institution.

What emerges from all this is the need for a robust and legally enforceable framework of governance based on existing best practice within the institutions themselves. Systems for screening, monitoring and managing relations with campus companies need to be standardised across institutions. Intending campus companies should be required to provide detailed documentation, including a development plan, on a common basis across every institution. It is also clear from the survey that designation should be contingent upon the completion of a management training programme (where necessary) in order to underpin the investment.

### 7.2.7 Constraints on Campus Companies

Institutions were asked to rank the main perceived constraints on the development of campus companies within their hinterland. The companies were themselves asked to identify the main constraints from their own perspective. There were differences, as might be expected, across institutions and among campus companies. The key points to emerge include the following:

- The lack of infrastructural facilities available within which to nurture campus companies during their initial period of development. Specifically, incubator units have an important role to play in addressing this weakness. This reinforces, once again, the importance of infrastructural enhancement within the HE sector, as envisaged by the government's recent funding initiatives. It also underlines the leverage that such enhancement will generate in relation to fostering knowledge intensive campus companies.

- Weaknesses in the internal management of campus companies. Such deficiencies are common in all start-up companies but there is no evidence that they are any greater in the case of campus companies than the general population of SMEs: indeed the evidence of Storey and coworkers suggests the contrary.[4] Nevertheless, the evidence in the survey clearly points to the need for high-level training for academic entrepreneurs as an integral part of the process of designation.

- The lack of venture capital, and also seed capital which would allow the institution to encourage potentially commercial enterprises, is a recurring theme of the responses to the survey. This is compounded by the fact that the banks located within the host institutions appear to play no role whatsoever in interfacing with campus companies. Given the investment in, and expertise of, the banks in small companies, this is a major deficiency. There is now a compelling case for the banks, having resolved the SME issue, to develop a corresponding expertise in new technology-based firms (TBFs) including campus companies and to deliver this through the network of banks already in place on the campuses of the HE institutions. This point is revisited in Chapter 9.

- There are also differences in respect to the appointment of College directors to the boards of campus companies. This raises important issues regarding the statutory responsibilities of such directors.

### 7.3 SUMMARY CONCLUSIONS

The survey points to two immediate recommendations:

- The creation of a *Campus Company Development Director* located within the Industrial Liaison Office. The purpose of this new post would be to promote and manage the interface between campus companies, once established, and potential commercial partners, including venture funds.

- The establishment of incubator units, preferably on campus or in close proximity, as a key element of a national campus company strategy. These facilities should be developed/ enhanced, as part of a coordinated upgrading of the HE infrastructure. The funding for this initiative should come from the public sector and the HE institutions, using, where appropriate, the taxation incentives in Section 25 of the Irish Finance Act.

- Provision for specialised training for campus company personnel, including managing/marketing/financing modules drawn from within the HE sector and capable of being delivered in a variety of modes. It is clear from the survey that a major deficiency relates to perceive management weakness within campus companies which this initiative would address. At present, practice varies widely across the HE sector and, it must be said, there are glaring gaps and deficiencies. As indicated above, the completion of such training should be a prerequisite for designation of a campus company and for access to campus-based seed and venture capital funds which, hopefully, will come on stream.

- As part of a wider strategic relationship between industry, Forbairt and the HE sector, all campus companies should have access to experienced non-executive directors/mentors.

- The campus company sector is already a significant subset of industry occupying a pivotal position at the cutting edge of technology-driven Irish industry and with important strategic linkages to the foreign multinational sector. There is, accordingly, a compelling case for *a National Campus Company Group* to represent the interests, needs and potentialities of these companies in policy and related fora.

- Similarly, and within this broader framework, an equivalent set of procedures and systems are needed in respect of the establishment and management of campus companies. These initiatives are essential (a) to ensure that all of the HE sector effectively mobilises its "knowledge equity" and (b) to avoid differences in contractual arrangements and incentives structures, which would both impede mobility and also create distortions and tensions across the sector as a whole.

It is important, finally, to restate the broader purpose of these initiatives. Firstly, to ensure that campus companies have access to infrastructural support including "soft services" in the key start-up stage. Secondly, there is the potentially high payback to the national economy of fast growth campus companies, working in highly specialised technologies with, by definition, little or no "displacement effect". Thirdly, there is the scope for encouraging "clusters of companies" within these incubator facilities, with associated positive externalities or "spill over" effects. Fourthly, there is the scope for leveraging such clusters and incubator facilities for research and teaching purposes within the host institutions.

## OBSERVATIONS AND RECOMMENDATIONS

- *A recent survey provided an informed analysis of the Campus Company sector as a prototype of the Techno-Academic Paradigm.*

- *All institutions asserted ownership of intellectual property generated by staff while in their employ.*

- *All institutions have a strongly proactive approach to the exploitation of intellectual property, including patents.*

- *There are wide differences in the way that intellectual property is viewed and managed. There is a total absence of a formal policy on intellectual property in a number of institutions and, among those institutions with such a policy, there is quite a diversity of approach.*

- *The lack of a cohesive strategy on intellectual property across the HE sector as a whole directly militates against the interests of individual institutions and the wider national economic interest.*

- *There is a compelling case for developing "best practice" in regard to the management of intellectual property at national and local level. This will require a strengthening of management systems for intellectual property both within the institution itself and, also, within the Department of Education and Science.*

- *An estimated 60 patents held by institutions in the HE sector generated significant financial returns.*

- *Most, but not all, of the universities have a formal policy on campus company development.*

- *There are wide differences regarding facilities provided to support academic entrepreneurs who wish to set up campus companies.*

- *Constraints on campus companies include the lack of infrastructural facilities available at the early stages of start-up, internal management weaknesses, lack of venture capital and seed capital, and the absence of bank support.*

- *Campus companies are involved in a broad range of the leading-edge technologies.*

- *There are differences in respect to the appointment of Directors to the Boards of campus companies which also raises important issues regarding the statutory responsibilities of such Directors.*

- *A robust and legally enforcible framework of governance based on existing best practice within the institutions themselves is required.*

- *Designation as a campus company should be contingent upon the completion of a management training programme in order to underpin the investment.*

- *There is a compelling case for the banks to develop expertise in new techology-based firms (TBFs) including campus companies.*

- *Incubator units, preferably on campus or in close proximity, should be established as a key element of a national campus company strategy with funding from the public sector and the HE institutions using the taxation incentives in Section 25 of the relevant Finance Act.*

- *There is scope for encouraging "clusters of companies" within these incubator facilities, with associated positive externalities or "spill-over" effects.*

- *There is scope for leveraging such clusters and incubator facilities for research and teaching purposes.*

- *Specialised training for campus company personnel, including managing/marketing/financing modules drawn from within the HE sector and capable of being delivered in a variety of modes is required.*

- *The completion of such training, in the absence of proven competence, should be a prerequisite for designation as a campus company and, therefore, for access to campus-based seed and venture capital funds (when available).*

- *As part of a wider strategic relationship between Irish industry (IBEC), Forbairt and the HE sector, all campus companies should have access to experienced non-executive directors/mentors.*

- *A National Campus Company Forum (NCCF) should be set up to represent the interests, needs and potentialities of these companies in policy and related fora.*

- *The creation of a Campus Company Development Director located within the Industrial Liaison Officer (ILO) function is recommended.*

- *Within this broader framework, an equivalent set of procedures and systems are needed in establishing and managing campus companies to ensure that all of the HE sector effectively mobilises its "knowledge equity" and to avoid differences in contractual arrangements and incentives structures, which would both impede mobility and create distortions and tensions across the sector as a whole.*

## References and Notes: Chapter 7

1.  R.P. Kinsella and V.J. McBrierty, *Economic Rationale for an Enhanced Science and Technology Capability*, Report to Forfás, the Irish Science Policy Agency, 1994.

2.  E.P. O'Neill, private communication.

3.  Employment in this context implies receipt of a salary: it does not include, for example, academics who make a major contribution but do not receive additional remuneration for the work.

4.  D.J. Storey (ed.), *New Technology-Based Firms in the EU*, Report for the EU Commission, University of Warwick, Centre for SMEs, 1996.

*Chapter 8*

# FINANCING THE KNOWLEDGE ECONOMY (1): A CONCEPTUAL FRAMEWORK

## 8.1 OVERVIEW

This chapter is the first of three that addresses the financing of innovation and the funding of the knowledge economy. A conceptual basis for the analysis is first established and then the distinction between market-based financing and state investment in Science and Technology is drawn, in Chapters 9 and 10 respectively. In each instance, developments in Ireland within the broader context of the wider EU are emphasised.

While this distinction between market-based and state financing is useful for expositional purposes, central to our argument is the need for a new, holistic approach to the funding of science and innovation. It is only within this framework that the inadequacies in the *volume* and *composition* of financing for innovation can be properly analysed and addressed.

The need for an integrated approach to the funding of innovation is based on a number of considerations:

- Firstly, it is implicit in the increasingly dynamic overlap between universities — which are primarily state-financed — and technology-based industry. This overlap is reinforced by trends such as the out-sourcing of R&D by large corporations to universities and other research institutions, as well as by the commercialisation of the knowledge base in the HE sector, typically through campus companies and science parks. The

key to this, in terms of maximising the future growth potential
of the economy, is to widen the "Corridor of Opportunity"
portrayed earlier in Figure 5.5.

- Secondly, it is clear that in order to maximise the leverage of
  market-based and state funding *operating in concert*, a perspective is required on the *total flow* of financing available to support innovation in its broadest form. In this regard, we believe
  that there are strong conceptual arguments, reinforced by the
  empirical data, for developing a *Technology Financing Foresight
  Model*, within which the volume and composition of funding
  for innovation can be aligned with national competitive objectives.

- Thirdly, economic efficiency requires that financial institutions and markets are allowed to operate in a manner that is
  informed by the risk/return profile specific to technology financing. At the same time, it is abundantly clear from the data
  presented later that market-based financing is constrained by
  informational and other forms of "market failure".

What are the implications? First and foremost, government must
identify such gaps and weaknesses and, second, develop market-
based mechanisms to overcome such constraints, where possible.
This provides a justification for government intervention, based
on securing positive return to the economy and to society from
investment in science and innovation, including interventions
aimed at overcoming these market failures. It also reinforces the
need for the proposed Technology Financing Foresight Model
(Figure 8.1) to match the volume and composition of funding to
national innovation objectives as suggested above.

Essentially, what the figure shows is that an integrated flow of
finance, encompassed within a financing technology foresight capability, would bring both a stability and increased leverage to
the financing of technology in Ireland. More specifically it is

shown that by bringing the present largely *ad hoc* and diverse streams of financing together, within a forecasting framework targeted towards national technological objectives including those within the HE sector, there would be a substantially increased volume and more targeted financing.

FIGURE 8.1: FINANCING TECHNOLOGY FORESIGHT MODEL

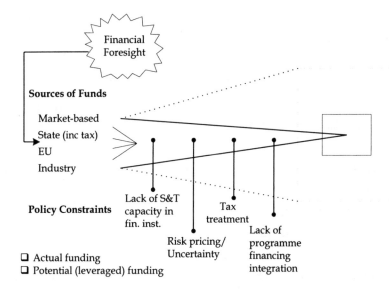

What is central is (a) the total *flow* of financing for innovation and the science base in which it subsists; (b) the efficiency of the financial markets which is predicated, *inter alia*, on the existence of a technological competence of middle and senior management; and (c) the *leverage* which is created between state- and market-based financing. Thus, to take one example, additional bank finance for knowledge-based companies including campus companies will accelerate the ability of such companies to gain access to equity funding. This, in turn, will facilitate the development of additional capital market instruments to finance innovation including Technology-based Firms (TBFs).

This is crucially dependent on the existence of a proactive technology capability within the banks which, in turn, impacts on their ability to price technology risk and their willingness to develop products and services to support innovative technology-based companies. The latter should take particular account of a disposition to provide funding which is secured, not necessarily on fixed assets or financial guarantees, but on Intellectual Property (IP) as a form of knowledge equity which is a primary asset of TBFs.

## 8.2 CONCEPTUAL FRAMEWORK

The ensuing development of a conceptual framework in the form of a set of building blocks relating to the financing of innovation draws upon empirical data as well as recent research.

The concept of "knowledge equity" as the counterpoint to, and equivalent of, financial equity is the starting point.[1] It is at the heart of the Techno-Academic Paradigm (Chapter 5).[2] In Figure 8.2 the conversion of knowledge equity into jobs is further developed and deficiencies in financial engineering (including the pricing of technology risk and low S&T capability of financial institutions) are identified as one reason for the low conversion rate of knowledge equity into jobs. It is argued that this reflects, in part, the nature of TBFs, as well as an "information gap" regarding the *perceived* relative riskiness of TBFs compared with the wider set of SMEs. The important distinction between *risk* (with which banks are comfortable) and *uncertainty* (to which they are strongly averse) is underlined and examined further.

On the basis of recent authoritative evidence regarding survival and growth rates of TBFs compared with SMEs,[3] we set out a different, idealised approach to technology-based lending which is secured on intellectual property — or knowledge equity — as opposed to the traditional model which, it is argued, constrains the availability of market-based financing. Finally, against this background, we set out, in conceptual terms, the case for a holistic approach to technology financing, encompassing market-based finance and state funding, as an alternative to the present inadequate and flawed structure. This new approach should be based on technology financing foresight, matching the total prospective funding to national strategic objectives and providing an innovative and robust platform for public/private sector partnership.

FIGURE 8.2: CONVERSION OF KNOWLEDGE EQUITY INTO JOBS: LEAKAGES AND POLICY RESPONSES

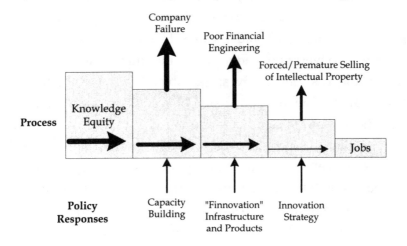

### 8.3 KNOWLEDGE EQUITY REVISITED

The term "knowledge equity" is further interpreted here to reinforce the embedded *financial* value of intellectual property and, more generally, the "human capital" in which this knowledge equity is encompassed. In this sense, knowledge equity can be regarded as the creative capability of Ireland — or indeed the wider EU — which could be commercialised to generate employment and wealth with suitable systems/policy engineering.

It is important to look briefly at the practicality of such a concept. To take the example in Section 3.1, leading-edge multinational companies are increasingly seeking to reshape traditional accounting systems to take account of the fact that what they deal in is intellectual property which creates shareholder value. This reinforces the financial value of IP and it broadens the basis around which the companies' systems, including accountancy and planning, should be shaped. It is the 21st century equivalent of equity. In reality, knowledge equity is a more appropriate collateral for secured lending/financing than are fixed assets. The evidence suggests that banks are not as yet in tune with this viewpoint.

In terms of *process*, the challenge for government and market-based institutions is to convert knowledge equity into high-quality jobs and shareholder value. In terms of *policy*, the challenge is to convert knowledge equity into high quality jobs as efficiently and cost effectively as possible. The nature of the challenge, namely, the low conversion of knowledge equity into jobs, is predicated on leakages from the present system which include, in particular, the mortality rate of TBFs – and, more generally, SMEs – as well as the failure to exploit its knowledge equity. This also points up the importance of policy responses, in this instance, the need for building a capability within TBFs and robust national and EU innovation systems, respectively.

Leakages from the system arising out of deficiencies and weaknesses in national and EU financial systems, specifically the banks, are of primary concern. These deficiencies in the banking infrastructure, which are clearly evident in the data generated in this analysis, are a major cause of the low conversion of national and EU knowledge equity into jobs and wealth.

## 8.4 TECHNOLOGY-BASED FINANCING

The most recent authoritative evidence regarding the performance of technology-based firms in the EU is provided by Storey and co-workers who suggests that:

> Small technology-based firms have higher growth rates and survival rates that are at least as high as that of small businesses in non-technology sectors. On these grounds, investments in technology-based enterprises should be equally, if not more, attractive than investments elsewhere.[4]

The implications for national competitiveness are compelling:

> . . . among high technology small firms, those with the most sophisticated technologies are the most likely to report continual financial constraints on the development of their business. Given that these firms are also the most likely to make a major economic contribution, it provides support for the view that market imperfections characterise the supply of finance in the market place.

There is robust evidence that market-based financial institutions systematically under-invest in innovation, including technology-based firms. The evidence that is adduced later reinforces the results of earlier studies in the field. Before discussing the data in detail, it will be helpful to develop some of the underlying issues.

## 8.5 MEASURING RISK AND UNCERTAINTY

The measurement and pricing of risk is the key to asset and maturity transformation which is at the heart of financial intermediation. What is of immediate interest here, however, is whether there may be conceptual or practical difficulties in the measurement of risk attached to lending to TBFs. This may relate, in turn, to a reluctance on the part of financial institutions to accept intellectual property as collateral.

In this context, it is important to distinguish between *risk* as opposed to *uncertainty*. For the purposes of this analysis, Knight's definition goes to the heart of the matter:

> If you don't know for sure what will happen, but you know the odds, that's risk; if you don't know the odds, that's uncertainty.[5]

Banks are, to a greater or lesser extent, comfortable with risk. Pricing risk and managing this risk both on and off the balance sheet is central to their core business of intermediation. They do know the odds in respect of SME mortality rates and the expected values of losses associated with these loans. Structural change including deregulation and a technology-induced increase in the contestability of the banking franchise has made this a little more difficult. But, as against this, banks have become more sophisticated in their approach to risk. Greater use is made of statistical methods, including probability and computer-based credit scoring systems. Moreover, systematic investment by banks across the EU in recent years in enterprise/SME support units has enhanced their screening/monitoring capabilities, thereby reducing default risk.

Uncertainty is altogether a different matter. It is a pervasive feature of the new and emerging technologies, including the TBFs that exploit these technologies. It impacts directly on the applicability for newer methodologies, such as Option Price Theory, to the valuation of technology investment. It may be helpful, therefore, to identify some of the key areas in which this uncertainty resides.

The distinguishing characteristic of the balance sheet of TBFs is the intangibility of their primary asset, namely, intellectual property. Equally, the human resources of these firms in which much of the IP is subsumed are highly mobile. Both contribute to uncertainty as perceived by banks. A second characteristic relates to the fact that many TBFs are R&D-intensive which, as indicated earlier, may result in negative balance sheets for considerable periods after start-up. These two features alone stand in sharp contrast to the banks' preferred approach of short-term lending secured on physical assets and/or predictable cash flows.

TBFs operate in a highly unpredictable environment with the continual threat of technological obsolescence and/or product emulation by larger, better capitalised, firms. Biotech companies, to take one example, are highly vulnerable to the results of successive regulatory tests: negative results can obviate the latent value of years of R&D, wiping out the value of the underpinning financial investment. This relatively high degree of uncertainty is mirrored in volatility in the aggregate share price index of biotech companies. Furthermore, as alluded to above, the indications are that the "economic value" embedded in the IP of such companies may be relatively more liable to litigation of one kind or another than is the case with the generality of firms. In short, in the biotech sector, returns are high but the risks are also high (*c.f.* Chapter 3).

From the banks' perspective, the latent uncertainty associated with TBFs is compounded by the lack of their preferred collateral, namely, physical and/or financial assets. Financing what they *perceive* as the unknown or the uncertain (knowledge equity) will as a matter of sound banking practice require the setting aside of additional capital to cover the prospective volatility of returns including not just the *expected* but also the *uncertain* loan loss rates. In the present environment of lending opportunities and robust share price performance, banks have an incentive to minimise such costs by minimising their exposure to what they perceive as the small, or the uncertain.

## 8.6 RISK PRICING AND TBFS: PERCEPTION VERSUS REALITY

In principle, the pricing of a financial instrument incorporates three elements: (a) the cost of funds to the institution, (b) administration and (c) an appropriate risk premium.

The cost of funds can, for present purposes, be taken as given. Administrative charges subsume search costs in originating the loan (or other instruments) as well as verification, monitoring and enforcement. These, in aggregate, will be a function of the efficiency of the financial institution. Originating and servicing a large number of small loans increases overheads. The majority of TBFs are, and remain, small (in EU terms) which increases monitoring costs. This is especially the case where the bank does not have informed procedures for assessing the technological parameters of a loan from a TBF including the valuation of the underlying IP.

The risk premium comprises interest (the time value of money) margin over the risk-free rate of return or, more generally, the margin above that paid by Blue Chip companies. The size of the premium will reflect the perceived risk/return profile associated with the investment. It will be shaped by the methodology, or absence of it, for assessing technology as opposed to credit risk. These factors are of major importance since they act as a rationing device leading to increasing costs of, and/or restricting access to, funding for innovation including technology-based firms.

The risk premium will also vary systematically with the availability of collateral, since this provides protection for the bank and reduces "moral hazard". This, once again, is germane to the financing of TBFs whose main balance sheet asset is intellectual property. Banks may prefer a charge over fixed assets, notwithstanding the inappropriate nature of this approach when dealing with knowledge-based firms.

This would suggest, *inter alia*, that the nature of the business seeking funding is important. Other things being equal, TBFs built around new and/or rapidly emerging technologies — and which offer limited scope for risk diversification — are likely to be perceived by the bank as inherently more risky than the funds in established businesses. The point at issue is not whether the perception is well grounded in the banks' own experience and/or in robust empirical evidence: what is at issue is the purported reasons for this perception.

Some start-ups have relatively high failure rates. The "risk premium" attaching to TBFs might be expected to be at least, and probably greater than, those applying to SMEs in general; greater because of the perceived greater uncertainty associated with technological change (*vide infra*) and hence greater possible variance of loan losses, compared with the general population of SMEs.

Another way of looking at this is that banks may not differentiate sufficiently between SMEs in general and TBFs in particular. Even in cases where banks do draw an operational distinction, they may lack the systematic data on the characteristics and performance of TBFs necessary to estimate an appropriate risk premium. They may not, for example, generate separate data on bad loans for TBFs. Most banks do not do so (*c.f.* Section 9.3) which might, in turn, lead them to transpose failure rates for the general population of SMEs to a set of TBFs with distinct characteristics, including mortality and performance.

At issue, therefore, is a perceptual problem rooted in a lack of pertinent management capabilities and an "information gap" which leads the banks to adopt the attitude that lending to TBFs is inherently more risky compared with SMEs in general. Importantly, a reluctance to accept intellectual property as collateral against financing of TBFs would tend to reinforce a reluctance to develop financial products and services to facilitate innovation, thereby servicing the needs of TBFs.

What, in essence, underlies the banks' approach to technology financing is a perceived greater uncertainty which may be linked to the valuation of IP as collateral, rather than risk *per se*. This perceived greater uncertainty would generate the possibility of unacceptable loan losses, at an increased variance in loan losses, requiring banks to provide costly additional capital against such a contingency.

## 8.7 Nature of Technology-based Firms (TBFs)

At any price (level of interest rates), there are likely to be companies that, because of their perceived risk/return profile, will be "crowded out" from the financial markets. They will not have access to funds or alternatively, the risk premium will be prohibi-

tively costly. This, from the bank's perspective, is because the prospective rate of return may not compensate for the *perceived* risk.
This is of direct and immediate relevance to the financing of innovation including TBFs.

In an increasingly knowledge-driven economy, risk becomes
more pervasive and more difficult to measure despite advances in
credit analysis. There are many reasons for this which include the
following:

- Many technology-based firms must spend large amounts of
  money up-front — on R&D for example — without necessarily
  having a marketable product.

- Prior to recent advances in the application of Option Price
  Theory (OPT) to the valuation of R&D,[6] the valuation of IP
  created major difficulties for financial institutions. As a result,
  TBFs can face an indefinite period with significant negative
  cash flow that sits uncomfortably with the provision of
  short/medium debt finance secured by existing and prospective cash flows preferred by banks.

- The process of developing a market product, in biotechnology
  for example, is fraught with regulatory hurdles which, if not
  met in every particular, can obviate massive investment in
  R&D.

- Even where a product is developed and marketed, it is vulnerable to two hazards which are a pervasive feature of the
  new knowledge economy, namely, technological obsoles-
  cence/emulation and litigation.

- At the end of all this, the core assets of the company are intangible: they subsist in intellectual property, both in an explicit
  form (patents) and in the even less tangible form of human
  capital and the "culture" of a company in which people work.

Banks generally have an established view of the odds when lending to the general population of SMEs: they have the historical data as well as familiar balance sheets, including fixed assets and positive net cash flow. This is not the case with S&T or technology-based companies: hence banks either screen out such uncertainty by minimising their lending to TBFs and/or transpose onto technology-based firms mortality/growth rates based on the generality of SMEs which may be wholly inappropriate.

Where investment in certain kinds of assets or instruments become either more risky or less profitable because of tax distortions (two sides of the same coin), there will be a tendency systematically to under-invest in S&T-based companies and activities. In Ireland, in recent years, there have been a number of measures that provided support for indigenous industry and, even at the cost of creating further distortions, they facilitate investment that would otherwise not take place. This supports the case for proactive taxation policies to underpin investment in science and technology, especially by market-based financing, as recommended by STIAC.[6]

## 8.8 A NEW APPROACH TO RISK PRICING FOR TBFs

Figure 8.3 illustrates the existing, traditional model of risk pricing where lending is secured on fixed (or financial) assets (Model 1). The willingness of banks to acquire the assets of TBFs is determined by the Risk/Reward profile attaching to such assets. This will be influenced, in particular, by the Risk Premium that will, in turn, embody expected losses on such lending and, also, uncertainty in regard to unexpected losses. This provides a robust basis on which to construct what may be termed the traditional approach to technology financing which results in a "Risk Capital Gap" (Model 2) (Figure 8.4). Model 2, in turn, is the genesis of a new model which conceptually sets out the way in which inherent inadequacies might be addressed and tackled (Figure 8.5).

FIGURE 8.3: RISK PRICING FOR TECHNOLOGY-BASED FIRMS (MODEL 1)

Traditional Model (1):
Financing Secured on Physical Asset

FIGURE 8.4: RISK PRICING FOR TECHNOLOGY-BASED FIRMS (MODEL 2)

Traditional Model (2):

- "Risk Capital Gap"
- Impact on High Tech Companies

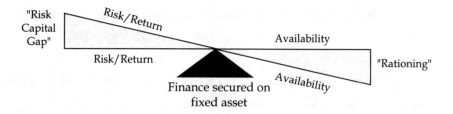

In essence, the higher risk premium attaching to TBFs tilts the Risk/Return axis upwards because of prospective losses and *uncertainty* (Figure 8.4). This opens up a "Risk Capital" gap, leading to a rationing of finance for TBF's. Note that here, as in Figure 8.1, lending is secured on fixed assets since banks are reluctant to accept intellectual property as collateral for financing TBFs, as indeed the empirical data shows.

Figure 8.5 shows, conceptually, how the traditional Model 2 might be transformed. The key points are, firstly, that financing is now secured on IP and, secondly, it is assumed that banks price risk in line with the evidence which, as noted earlier, suggests that TBFs are, if anything, a more attractive investment opportunity compared with the generality of SMEs.

This will require a change in the management's mind set within banks, in the area of technological capability, and a parallel investment in systems development. This should lead to a change in expectations on the part of banks, namely, an adaptation, in terms of risk pricing, to the prospect of superior returns with un-changed levels of risks. This eliminates the "Risk Capital Gap" and, *pari passu*, rationing of funding of TBFs. Indeed, it would be reasonable to expect, over the medium-term, an *enhanced* supply of finance to TBFs associated with a broadening of the range of financial instruments available to them.

FIGURE 8.5: NEW MODEL FOR RISK PRICING TECHNOLOGY-BASED FIRMS

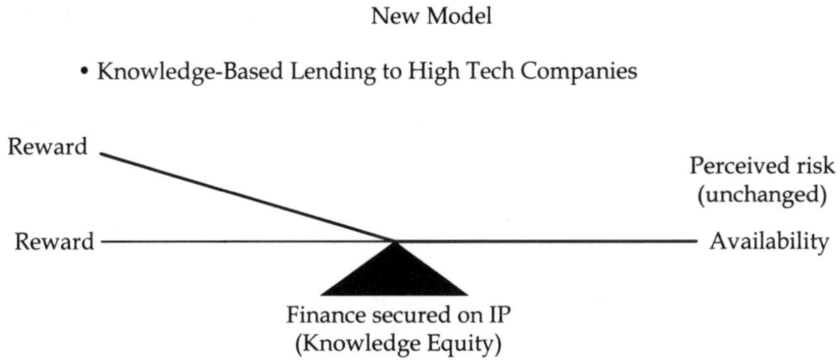

New Model

• Knowledge-Based Lending to High Tech Companies

Reward

Reward

Perceived risk (unchanged)

Availability

Finance secured on IP (Knowledge Equity)

## OBSERVATIONS AND RECOMMENDATIONS

- *Policy in relation to funding S&T and innovation depends critically on the total flow of financing for innovation and the science base in which it subsists, the efficiency of the financial markets which is predicated, inter alia, on the existence of a technological competence of middle and senior bank management, and the leverage that is created between state and market-based financing.*

- *There is a need for an integrated and flexible approach when funding TBFs.*

- *Funding criteria for TBFs should not only be predicated on fixed assets or financial guarantees, but also on intellectual property as a form of knowledge equity which is the primary asset of TBFs.*

- *Government has an interventionist role to play in creating a support infrastructure for TBFs.*

- *There is need for an integrated Technology Financing Foresight Model to match the volume and composition of funding to national objectives.*

- *Deficiencies in financial engineering, including the pricing of technology risk and low S&T capability of financial institutions, are identified as a reason for the low conversion rate of new technology into jobs.*

- *This also reflects, in part, the nature of TBFs, as well as an "information gap" regarding the perceived relative riskiness of TBFs compared with the wider set of SMEs.*

- *Knowledge equity is a more appropriate collateral for secured lending/financing than are fixed assets. Banks are not as yet in tune with this growing reality.*

- *The perceptual problem rooted in a lack of pertinent management capabilities and an "information gap" is responsible for the banks adopting the attitude that lending to TBFs is inherently more risky, compared with SMEs in general. This undermines confidence in TBFs throughout the financial sector as a whole.*

- *The measurement and pricing of risk is the key to asset and maturity transformation which is at the heart of financial inter-mediation.*

- *Banks do not differentiate between TBFs, with their special characteristics, and the general population of SMEs.*

- *The distinction between risk (with which banks are comfortable) and uncertainty (to which they are strongly averse) is emphasised.*

- *Of crucial importance is this distinction between "risk" and "uncertainty" and the different structure of the balance sheet and cash flow of TBFs compared with the wider population of SMEs. A new model of risk pricing which takes these special characteristics into account is proposed.*

## References and Notes: Chapter 8

1. V.J. McBrierty, *Making Sense of Science Policy*, Administration, 42(2), 143-158 (1994).

2. R.P. Kinsella and V.J. McBrierty, "Campus Companies and the Techno-Academic Paradigm: the Irish Experience", *Technovation*, 17, 245 (1997).

3. D.J. Storey (ed.), *New technology-Based Firms in the EU*, SME Centre, University of Warwick, 1996.

4. D.J. Storey, *ibid.*

5. F. Knight, *Risk, Uncertainty and Profit*, University of Chicago Press, 1985.

6. *Making Knowledge Work for Us*, Report of the Science, Technology and Innovation Advisory (STIAC), D. Tierney, Chairman, Stationery Office, Dublin 2, Ireland, 1995.

*Chapter 9*

# FINANCING THE KNOWLEDGE ECONOMY (2): THE ROLE OF MARKET-BASED FINANCE

## 9.1 INTRODUCTION

Technology-Based Firms (TBFs) by their nature require access to a wide range of financial instruments in order to accommodate their quite uniquely rapid development cycle from R&D through to start-up and beyond. The function of market-based finance, encompassing the credit and capital markets, is to provide finance in a form, and on terms, that reflect the risk/return characteristics of TBFs at specific points of their development cycle.

In principle, projects with a positive Net Present Value (NPV), whether technology-based or otherwise, should be able to attract appropriate financing for their needs. In reality, the financial markets may not operate efficiently or, as they should, in a complementary and seamless manner. There are a number of reasons why this might be the case:

- Perceived difficulties on the part of banks and/or other financial institutions in pricing technology risk, as discussed in Section 8.5.

- The search and monitoring costs associated with a large number of relatively small technology-based investments.

- The lack of leverage which a more fully integrated public/market-based system would bring to the funding of technology.

- The nature of technology-based firms and, more specifically, their balance sheet which presumably centres as much on intellectual property (IP) as on fixed assets.

- The availability of alternative (frequently tax-driven) investment opportunities, characterised by lower perceived uncertainty.

- The small size of the domestic capital markets with an attendant lack of liquidity, which may deter potential investors.

- A "technology-averse" mind-set or culture within major financial institutions in Ireland and the wider EU.

What these and related factors amount to is a market failure in the provision of financing for innovation and, by implication, TBFs. There are information gaps and asymmetries as between those seeking and those able to provide the finance which undermines the efficiency of market-based financing of TBFs. There is, in other words, a "technology financing gap". The cost of this in terms of its impact on future growth, competitiveness and the strengthening of the national knowledge base is incalculable.

This "market failure" justifies intervention by the public authorities at both national and EU levels. There is an obvious price to pay to the extent that such intervention may, at least temporarily, "crowd out" market-based financing (*c.f.* Section 8.7). But these interventions are nonetheless necessary and are additional to the public funding required to maintain the S&T infrastructure, research and essential support services. In short, they are justified on "public good" grounds because of the positive externalities that flow to the wider economy and society.

The role of market-based financing can be approached in three ways:

- By summarising recent evidence regarding the extent to which the availability of market-based finance constrains the growth of technology-based firms within Ireland and the EU.

- By setting out the findings of recent research regarding the role of EU banks in financing technology-based firms.

- By assessing the perspective of banks and institutional investors towards the funding of TBFs including campus companies.

## 9.2 OVERVIEW OF MARKET-BASED FINANCING

Consider the evidence generated by recent studies. In its *Green Paper on Innovation*, the EU makes the point that

> the Communities' ability to innovate depends largely on the effectiveness of its innovation financing systems: [the lack of] financing is the obstacle to innovation most often quoted by firms, whatever their size, in all member states of the EU and in virtually all sectors. (see also Table 1.2).[1]

This is echoed in the findings of the Forfás Innovation Survey (1994) which pointed out, on the basis of extensive survey evidence, that

> financial and risk factors, including lack of the appropriate sources of finance, are judged to be the most significant impediments to innovation by both innovators and non-innovators alike.[2]

Mindful of our earlier analysis, it is important to underline the resultant impact of this technology financing gap on national growth and competitiveness. This is especially the case in an economy such as Ireland's which has sought to position its growth and development strategy on a high technology trajectory. The findings of a recent study of UK high technology firms — which are broadly comparable with those in the Irish indigenous sector — are relevant:

> Among high technology small firms, those with the most so-
> phisticated techniques are the most likely to report continual
> financial constraints on the development of their business.
> Given that these firms are also the most likely to make a major
> economic contribution, it provides support for the view that
> market imperfections characterise the supply of finance in the
> [high technology] sector.[3]

Consider the nature and extent of these imperfections and whether they are grounded in reality or, alternatively, are due to information gaps. In this context, it is convenient to differentiate between the credit (banks) and capital (institutional investors and venture capital) markets. Regarding credit markets, the EU reported that

> the major commercial banks in most countries are reluctant to
> get involved in innovative financing. Their ability to assess
> the technical risks of innovation and their relationship with
> organisations specialising in technology or innovation are still
> largely under-developed. [This would include the HE sector].[1]

This is borne out in recent academic studies:

> In general, European financial institutions have either been
> consistently reluctant to finance business [in high technology
> sectors] or have retreated from these sectors following unfa-
> vourable experiences.[4]

Turning to the capital markets (*c.f.* Section 9.4 below), the EU Green Paper refers to

> a neglect of innovation on the part of institutional investors
> holding long-term savings . . . linked in many cases to an ab-
> sence of information, a lack of market transparency and li-
> quidity and, in many countries, excessive prudence in the
> choice of placement.[1]

This encapsulates the current situation within Irish capital markets, notwithstanding a number of recent initiatives.[5] In this regard, too, Forfás (1996) has taken note of a lack of expertise and resulting caution in assessing the potential of companies operating in certain sectors, particularly high tech sectors. Such companies often have to seek equity from the UK or US where investors appear to be more informed.[6]

The key issue underlying the theme of market-based technology financing is whether or not TBFs are inherently more vulnerable to failure or less likely to grow compared with SMEs in general. If the reality were that TBFs are more risky, then this would be reflected in the risk premium attached to the financing of such firms.

This point is important at different levels. If it were the case that the banks perceived TBFs to be inherently more risky (whether correctly or not is an issue to which we shall return), then this would impact upon the price and availability as well as the terms and conditions attaching to bank financing. Banks provide a multiplicity of payments and other services, in addition to their role as lenders, without which TBFs cannot function.

But, equally, banks play a special role as intermediaries. Their "inside information" and accumulated experience means that they assume a screening role. The provision of bank finance signals the credit worthiness of a firm to other potential providers of finance. It is this unique role that makes banks so important in the whole process of innovation financing, including its interface with state funding.

The most recent authoritative evidence is provided by Storey and co-workers. On the basis of a pan-EU study of TBFs, they suggest that:

> small technology-based firms have higher growth rates and survival rates that are at least as high as those of small business in non-technology sectors. On these grounds, investment in technology-based enterprises should be equally, if not more, attractive than investments elsewhere.[7]

### 9.3 EU BANKS' SUPPORT FOR INNOVATION

Consider the evidence set out in a recent detailed analysis of the nature and extent of financing for innovation by the EU banks.[8] Five of the leading banks in each of the 15 EU Member States were requested to provide data in a detailed questionnaire on the financing of TBFs. Usable responses were received from 31 banks in 12 EU nations, giving an acceptable response rate of over 40 per cent. The responses expand upon the studies reported in Section 9.2.

Tables 9.1 and 9.2 show the range of bank products and services available to TBFs and, perhaps even more strikingly, those that are not currently available from EU banks. Despite the fact that TBFs require access to a wide spectrum of finance, Table 9.2 shows that, beyond the core bank products, over 80 per cent of the banks do not operate an informal capital network, nor did 40 per cent provide venture capital. The tables confirm that the major financing gaps arise in regard to equity and longer-term funds, both of which are central to the development cycle of TBFs.

The vital issue of collateral/security for lending for small firms and especially for TBFs was also explored. As repeatedly emphasised, intellectual property is the core asset of innovative firms and TBFs in particular. The evidence in the report cited above indicates that a charge against physical assets and/or financial guarantees is cited by the overwhelming majority of respondent banks as the basis for lending to TBFs. Only a minority of banks (27 per cent) accepted IP as collateral whereas some two-thirds of banks responding to this question indicated that they positively did not accept IP as collateral for loans to TBFs.

The preceding data highlight and quantify deficiencies in the key dimensions of financing innovation: the lack of adequate and diverse financial instruments and the unwillingness of banks to accept IP as collateral. The evidence regarding some possible causes and consequences of this are worthy of further examination.

TABLE 9.1 FINANCIAL PRODUCTS AND SERVICES FOR TBFS PROVIDED BY EU BANKS[8]

| Product | % of Banks Offering Product |
|---|---|
| 1–3 Year Fixed Loans | 87 |
| Overdraft Facility | 87 |
| Working Capital | 84 |
| Invoice Discounting | 81 |
| Leasing of S & T Equipment | 77 |
| 3–5 Year Fixed Loans | 74 |
| Risk Management Products | 68 |
| Venture Capital | 58 |
| 5 Year + Loans | 52 |
| Equity/Equity-Type Products | 39 |
| Preference Share Financing | 29 |
| Informal Venture Capital Network | 16 |
| Advise "Angels" of TBF's | 16 |
| Informal V.C. as part of "Package" | 7 |

TABLE 9.2 BANK SERVICES *NOT* AVAILABLE TO TBFS

| Service | Number of Banks *Not* Providing Service | Number of Banks Responding to Question |
|---|---|---|
| Informal Capital Network | 25 (83%) | 30 (97%) |
| Preference Share Financing | 21 (70%) | 31 (100%) |
| Equity/Equity-type Products | 18 (60%) | 30 (97%) |
| 5 Year + Loans | 15 (48%) | 31 (97%) |
| Venture Capital | 11 (38%) | 29 (93%) |

| | | |
|---|---|---|
| Risk Management Products | 10 (32%) | 31 (100%) |
| 3–5 Year Loans | 8 (26%) | 31 (100%) |
| Leasing of S 7 T Equipment | 7 (23%) | 31 (100%) |
| Invoice Discounting | 6 (19%) | 31 (100%) |
| Advise to "Angels" re. TPF | 6 (55%) | 11 (35%) |
| Working Capital | 5 (16%) | 31 (100%) |
| Overdraft | 4 (13%) | 31 (100%) |
| 1–3 Fixed Term Loans | 4 (13%) | 31 (100%) |

Regarding causes, one of the most striking findings of the survey relates to the fact that, notwithstanding the increasingly knowledge-based nature of the corporate banking sector, scientists and technologists are significantly under-represented in key management functions. Only a small cohort of EU bank chief executives have science/technology based qualifications. More striking still, in not one instance does the Head of Small Business Lending Divisions have science/technology-based qualifications. An S&T culture is therefore almost totally absent in EU banks which denies even a basic understanding of the ethos and needs of technology-based firms.

As indicated earlier, TBFs differ in a number of important respects from the general population of SMEs. Given the rapid and pervasive growth of technology applications, it was important to identify whether, and to what extent, banks differentiate TBFs as a subset of SMEs requiring a customised service.

The data suggest that two-thirds of banks do not differentiate one from the other. Building on this distinction, banks were also asked if they specifically monitored bad loans to TBFs. The result was that only one bank out of the total sample did so which, perhaps, is surprising and also indicative of a general antipathy to opportunities in the TBF sector. It would, of course, be routine to modify and apply existing techniques and procedures to identify bad loans as an input to risk pricing.

Building on this distinction, banks were asked if they provided a "focused and customised" service to TBFs. It is, of course, possible to provide such a customised service without necessarily drawing a sharp distinction between TBFs and other businesses. That said, just over half of the total sample of EU banks indicated that they did not provide such a service to TBFs: less than one bank in three saw themselves as providing a customised and focused service to TBFs. Perhaps more significantly, just over half of the sample indicated that the provision of such services to TBFs was not part of their forward strategic planning.

Why then are banks reluctant to provide customised service to TBFs? The reasons cited by the banks themselves fall into three categories:

1. The perceived small size of the market.

2. The view that the banks already provide a full range of services which encompass the needs of TBFs.

3. A view that technology-based funding fell outside the bank's core commercial area of activity.

The EU also observed that:

> the major commercial banks in most countries are reluctant to get involved in innovation financing. Their ability to access the technical risks of innovation . . . are still largely under developed.[1]

## 9.4 EVALUATION

The reality that major banks throughout the EU, by and large, do not systematically support TBFs is clear from these findings. It might be inferred from the lack of technology capability within the banks' own management structure that skills relevant to technology lending are underdeveloped. In this regard, the analysis of bank support for technology provides strong evidence on a number of key points:

- As indicated above, in assessing a request by a firm for funding, some 56 per cent of EU banks do not differentiate between TBFs and other SMEs. This is important. But it is also significant that a substantial minority of banks do take this into account since it highlights an apparent contradiction in their approach. It makes little sense for such banks to single out TBFs in assessing credit applications if, at the same time, this is not reflected in their approach to risk pricing (see below) or in tracking loan losses attributable to TBFs.

- Returning to the EU's criticism that the ability of EU banks to assess the technical risk of innovation is underdeveloped, the survey data indicate that the overwhelming majority of the banks do not use specific criteria or methodology for pricing technology as opposed to credit risk. Over half of the sample responded to this question and, of these, only one bank indicated that it used such a mechanism.

- In response to the question: "Does your bank view the pricing of technology risk as posing special difficulties for the bank in developing more innovative financial products and services for TBFs", some 55 per cent saw no particular difficulty. But a significant percentage of respondents (11 out of 25) reported that they did see technical and/or other difficulties in pricing technology risk. Notwithstanding this, only one bank indicated that it used specific criteria for pricing technological as opposed to credit risk.

## 9.5 USE OF UNIVERSITIES FOR TECHNOLOGY ASSESSMENT BY EU BANKS

The provision by banks, directly or through a third party, of a Technology Advisory/Assessment Service bears directly on the support for, and financing of, TBFs. Where such a service is provided, it brings together the technological and financial dimensions of support that jointly determine its commercial viability. In effect, it provides a vital commercial/financial interface between the generation and the commercialisation of technology. Given the lack of a technological culture and capability among bank management, a Technology Advisory Service for screening potentially commercial, leading-edge technologies would provide a valuable risk service for banks as well as the individual TBF. In addition, it also plays a *foresight* or *signalling* role for the wider financial sector, including the venture capital sector.

The data indicate that 80 per cent of EU banks do not provide such a service. It should be said that banks in virtually all nations have, in recent years, developed robust and important support mechanisms for the broad base of SMEs. There is compelling evidence that these contributions have played a major role in supporting national and EU initiatives for the SME sector. The data also indicate that Technology Advisory Services for TBFs, a pivotally important sub-set of SMEs are, by comparison, greatly underdeveloped.

Banks were also asked whether, in practice, they used the services of universities/HE institutions to assist them in assessing requests for funding by TBFs. One bank out of the total sample did, the remainder did not. EU banks do not have formal linkages with universities in respect of technology assessment and, as a corollary, do not use them for such purposes. This points to a gulf between banks which, ostensibly, should be in the business of financing technology, and universities which are in the business of generating and developing technology.

The extent of this gulf is even more evident when account is taken of the level of support (or lack of it) provided by the banks to campus companies (*c.f.* Chapter 7). As indicated earlier, such companies are, by their nature, highly innovative: they are the bedrock of Silicon Valley and the Route 128 technology clusters in the US. For countries like Ireland, campus companies are the nuclei of prospective "growth clusters". Of the seven banks that responded to the question relating to the financing/support for campus companies, four do not provide informal venture capital or brokerage services. Equity products and financial guarantees are not provided to campus companies by three of the seven banks.

### 9.6 BANK PARTICIPATION IN EU AND NATIONAL TECHNOLOGY DEVELOPMENT PROGRAMMES

The participation or non-participation of banks in EU and national technology programmes, including technology financing and support, is an issue of pivotal importance for policy. It also, underlines the argument for a more holistic approach to technology financing (*c.f.* Figure 8.2) Indeed, this is so central an issue that it can be safely considered a necessary condition for the effectiveness of technology programmes.

When asked if they monitored EU programmes relevant to the R&D capability of small firms including TBFs, some 60 per cent of the total set of EU banks cited in the survey indicated that they did not do so. Perhaps, more strikingly, 75 per cent of respondents, comprising more than 20 of the EU's major banks within their respective national markets, indicated that they have not participated in the EU technology financing initiatives. A similar picture emerges in relation to national programmes where some 70 per cent of banks did not enter or participate in national technology programmes.

## 9.7 EU BANKS AND TECHNOLOGY FINANCING: EVALUATION

The reality is that TBFs have to use banks and if banks are un-willing to participate in EU/national technology financing pro-grammes, or perhaps in some cases are unaware of such pro-grammes, then the total financing needs of TBFs will not be met. Quite simply, banks as yet cannot or do not wish to meet their needs. Therefore what may be at issue here is the following:

- A *culture gap* in respect of the technology capability of bank management.

- An *information gap* in regard to the *real*, as opposed to the *perceived*, commercial potential of TBFs.

- A *financing gap* in relation to the availability of a diversity of bank financing for TBFs, with the consequent impact on the willingness of the wider financial markets, including capital markets, to support TBFs.

During the 1990s the Irish government, in collaboration with the banks and in some instances backed by the EU, created a suppor-tive environment for SMEs, much of which was attributable to the Report of the *Taskforce on Small Business*.[9] More recently, there has been some strengthening of the venture capital sector, notably through Advanced Capital Trust (ACT), the largest of the venture capital providers. These initiatives have been developed against the background of a more stable macroeconomic climate, includ-ing low inflation and declining interest rates that, disproportion-ately, benefit small business.

These initiatives have greatly enhanced the supply of finance available to SMEs which include technology-based companies for whom some of the specific tax reliefs — for example, those relat-ing to R&D — are of considerable importance. Moreover, exper-tise developed by the banks has facilitated more effective risk pricing for SMEs.

However, what the banks and government have done for SMEs, individually and collectively, is largely beside the point. The SME battle has been fought and substantially won. The issue of bank and equity-based funding for TBFs, a sub-set that is more important for domestic and foreign investment strategy, has not begun to be addressed.

There is persuasive evidence that TBFs, including campus companies, are different at a number of levels from the generality of SMEs. Banks do not sufficiently differentiate between SMEs and TBFs in assessing credit and in pricing risk. Banks across the EU are not investing in developing a capability in innovation financing, including support for TBFs. It can be argued that the banks' perception, predicated essentially on a view that TBFs are a somewhat more risky form of investment, is flawed. The real issue is one of *uncertainty* rather than of *risk* and that the substantive evidence points to the relative strength of TBFs compared to the general population of SMEs. Mis-pricing the risk attaching to TBFs and a failure to channel adequate amounts of funding and a sufficient range of services to TBFs is an inevitable consequence. This strikes directly at the heart of Ireland's innovation strategy and that of the universities.

The consequences for industrial policy and the wider community are the following:

- Lack of access by individual TBFs to bank financing initiatives which partly explains, and certainly compounds, the lack of access to domestic capital market facilities.

- The consequent squandering of one of the most valuable assets of TBFs, namely, senior management time and the lost opportunity in terms of market development.

This vicious circle generates extensive market failure based primarily on a lack of S&T assessment capability within financial institutions, including banks. Such market failures are diminished through initiatives by government, supported by the EU. But these initiatives or partnerships are "second best" solutions. Partnerships between banks and governments (especially where these are channels for EU support) are to be welcomed when they lead to "additionality" in terms of innovation funding. In this instance, it substantially compensates for what the financial markets should in any event be doing if the principle of additionality were working efficiently.

## 9.8 CAPITAL MARKETS

The weakness of capital markets in relation to technology financing, as argued by the EU, is mirrored in Ireland. The availability of equity funding is, in itself, essential for the development of knowledge-based firms, firms that are subject to uncertainty, technology risk, and that require, *inter alia*, resources for R&D before positive cash flow is generated. This is all the more so where banks are reluctant to become involved directly in the provision of equity capital.

Irish capital markets are attenuated: the Stock Exchange is dominated by a small number of large companies, with the top ten accounting for 60 per cent of market capitalisation. The relative illiquidity of the Stock Exchange is compounded by two factors: firstly, the reluctance of institutional investors to invest in companies with a market value much below £100 million. Secondly, the abolition of the "localisation of investment" requirement which gives institutional investors the freedom to invest throughout the EU unconstrained by the previous requirement to invest a specified proportion of their assets in Ireland. This means, in practice, that the Stock Exchange is a negligible source of equity for TBFs. The recent attempt by the Exchange to establish a Developing Companies Market (DCM) has not been as successful as initially hoped: to date, only one company has sought a listing.

Within the framework of a capital market where the Stock Exchange is, *de facto*, marginal to the ability of the technology-based firms to raise equity, the availability of venture capital becomes of central importance.

As noted earlier, there has been a strengthening of venture capital, supported by government through Forbairt as well as the banks. It is in these circumstances that the role of the banks as facilitators becomes important. The branch network and the "in-house information" available to the banks regarding potential investors is a major resource for developing informal venture capital (Business Angels). For the most part, this resource remains under-developed and under-utilised. Experience in the US strongly indicates that informal venture capital is of particular relevance to the growth of TBFs.

The portfolio of one of the large venture capital institutions (Advanced Capital Trust) highlights the strengths and limitations of formal venture capital availability for TBFs. ACT has invested in a number of knowledge-based companies but, all in all, the need for adequate risk diversification means that the absolute number of such investments is marginal to the national challenge of developing a strong continual stream of TBFs which would qualify for listing on the Technology-Based Exchanges such as NASDAQ or EASDAQ.

Institutional investors, including pension funds, are central to the savings/investment process in Ireland, no less than in other countries. The evidence, from a European perspective, is that such institutions tend to be averse to risk, and especially to technology, even taking into account their fiduciary responsibilities. In Ireland, these institutions manage assets in excess of £16 billion, with an annual cash flow of £1 billion. One report suggested that pension funds were indeed reluctant to invest in indigenous industry.[10]

There has been a number of specific initiatives agreed with government by the pension funds, including a commitment to invest up to 0.8 per cent in indigenous companies. However, the initiatives taken to date have not impacted upon the new indigenous technology-based sector in a manner that reflects either the strength of the investors or the urgency, from a national development perspective, of providing support to TBFs.

While individual firms can avail of a range of state aids including tax expenditures as well as funding from market-based institutions, the reality is that (a) there are major "gaps" regarding the availability of equity and (b) the volume of bank financing and ancillary services (for example, technology assessment) are less than those required for companies that characteristically grow in a rapid and "stepped" manner. They require both a range of financial instruments and greater flexibility. Consequently, companies are constrained to seek external equity funding which is particularly costly for the typically over-stretched management of TBFs. A further consequence may be the enforced sale of intellectual property in order to retain the financial integrity of the company.

The recent introduction of seed capital funds amounting to £10 million (a banks/state joint venture) by both the major Irish clearing banks and the joint Forbairt/university/private sector initiative alluded to earlier, are welcome developments. But they do not go far enough.

In summary, there is a need for fresh thinking in relation to re-engineering capital markets in order to provide the necessary support for the technology-based sector. Specifically,

- A new mind-set is needed within the institutions themselves to be responsive to the needs, and growth pote,ntial of technology-based firms.

- As the breadth of the TBF sector expands, the scope for developing new instruments expands.[11]

- As was argued elsewhere, there is a compelling need to set up a dedicated *Campus Venture Capital Company* to meet the specific needs of one growing subset of TBFs (*c.f.* Chapter 7).[12] Given the implicit risk-sharing provided by the host institutions, in the form of "screening" of investments as well as access to facilities, we believe that the funding of such an initiative by institutional investors — of the order of £10 million on a revolving basis — would do much to fill the financing void currently experienced by campus companies.

## OBSERVATIONS AND RECOMMENDATIONS

- *TBFs require access to a wide range of financial instruments in order to accommodate their quite uniquely rapid development cycle, from R&D through to start-up and beyond.*

- *Regarding the financing of TBFs, there is a "technology financing gap", the cost of which, in terms of its impact on future growth, competitiveness and the strengthening of the national knowledge base, is incalculable.*

- *This "market failure" justifies government intervention on "public good" grounds.*

- *The key issue underlying market-based technology financing is whether or not TBFs are inherently more vulnerable to failure or less likely to grow compared with SMEs in general.*

- *Banks play a special role as intermediaries where their "inside information" and accumulated experience confers on them a "screening" role which can signal the credit worthiness (or otherwise) of a firm to other potential providers of finance. It is this unique role that makes banks so important in innovation financing.*

- *Recent evidence confirmed the singular preference for physical assets and/or financial guarantees as opposed to IP-based collateral as the basis for lending to TBFs.*

- *There is no S&T "culture" in Irish and EU banks, which denies even a basic understanding of the ethos and needs of technology-based firms. This compromises their ability to assess the technical risk of innovation. Nor did they consult the universities who are at the leading edge of knowledge generation.*

- *There are culture, information and financing gaps between the banks and the TBFs.*

- *Few banks distinguish TBFs from the general population of SMEs.*

- *The provision by some banks, directly or through a third party, of a Technology Advisory/Assessment Service bears directly on the support for, and financing of, TBFs. It provides a vital commercial/financial interface between the generation and the commercialisation of technology.*

- *About two-thirds of the banks in the EU did not monitor, nor participate in, EU or National Technology Programmes.*

- *Overall, the lack of access to banks by TBFs leads to a major "market failure.*

- *In the EU, EASDAQ, as well as national technology-based exchanges, are emerging as an important part of the financing infrastructure. This has to be encouraged, especially in regional economies where capital markets are likely to become more attenuated in the face of EMU.*

- *The branch network and the "inside information" available to the banks regarding potential investors is a major resource for developing "informal" venture capital (Business Angels); this resource remains under-developed and under-utilised.*

- *Overall, the reality is that there are major "gaps" regarding the availability of equity and that the volume of bank financing and ancillary services such as technology assessment are inadequate for TBFs which require both a range of tailored financial instruments and greater flexibility.*

- *These arguments apply equally to campus companies which are a subset of TBFs.*

## References and Notes: Chapter 9

1.  EU Commission, *Green Paper on Innovation*, Supplement, 5/95, 1995.

2.  *Innovation Survey*, Forfás, The Irish Science Policy Agency, 1997.

3.  D.J. Storey, *New Technology-Based Firms in the EU*, University of Warwick, 1996.

4.  D.J. Storey, *ibid.*

5.  Recent initiatives in Irish capital markets include the establishment of a new Smaller Companies Market by the Stock Exchange (mirroring the establishment of Secondary Markets for high technology companies in a number of other EU countries). See also Forbairt, Annual Report, 1996 and Advanced Capital Trust's Annual report, Dublin, 1996.

6.  *Shaping Our Future*, Forfás, The Irish Science Policy Agency, May, 1996.

7.  D.J. Storey (ed.), *New Technology-Based Firms in the EU*, Report for the EU Commission, University of Warwick, Centre for SMEs, 1996.

8.  R.P. Kinsella, *An Evaluation of EU Banks' Support for Technology*, EU Commission, Luxembourg, 1997.

9.  *Taskforce on Small Business*, Stationery Office, Dublin 2, Ireland, March, 1994.

10. P. Bacon and M. Walsh, *Pension Fund Report*, IAPF, Dublin, 1993.

11. R.P. Kinsella, "Banks and the Role of Equity", *Irish Banking Review*, pp. 21-38, 1995.

12. R.P. Kinsella and V.J. McBrierty, "Campus Companies and the Techno-Academic Paradigm: The Irish Experience", *Technovation*, 17, 245-258, 1997.

*Chapter 10*

# FINANCING THE KNOWLEDGE ECONOMY (3): STATE FUNDING OF S&T

## 10.1 INTRODUCTION

The decision by government in November 1997 to establish an Education, Technology Investment Fund (ETIF), involving the allocation of an additional £250 million, represents a watershed in the development of S&T policy in Ireland and an acknowledgement — amounting to a vindication — of the pivotal role of the HE sector in creating and sustaining a national knowledge base. It validates the Techno-Academic Paradigm which is the central spine of our whole analysis. The importance of the government initiative can be assessed at three levels:

1.  The rationale for the initiative is predicated on a recognition by government that economic growth in the knowledge economy of the third millennium will be driven by skills and competencies (human capital) and by advanced research and development (knowledge equity), which help to sustain innovation. It acknowledges that the HE sector is at the heart of this process.

2.  It articulates the interdependence — long advocated by the HE sector — between, on the one hand, a vibrant HE knowledge base and, on the other, the capacity of the development agencies to attract and retain foreign direct investment and to grow indigenous industry. In terms of our own analysis, it can be seen as corresponding to the role of the knowledge base as

both an attractor of Foreign Direct Investment (FDI) and a generator of domestically-based knowledge industries.

3.  It gives practical effect to these approaches to economic growth through the allocation, for the first time in the history of the state, of substantial resources directed, *inter alia*, at specific deficiencies which have been identified in the existing support for Science and Technology, particularly within the HE sector. They include infra-structural facilities, support for advanced research, support for postgraduate students, technology transfer mechanisms and a renewal and upgrading of capital research equipment. These deficiencies, long masked by the creativity and commitment of the HE sector, including its ability to attract research funding, would, if unaddressed, fatally erode the Irish economy's capacity to adapt to and to exploit the emerging Techno-Academic Paradigm. That they are now being addressed represents a welcome and overdue sea change in government policy (*vide infra*).

Consider first some methodological considerations concerning the rationale for national investment in science and technology to be followed by an examination of the economic rationale, taking account of stated government policy and the conceptual basis for all our analysis, that is, the Techno-Academic Paradigm set out in Chapter 5. The issue of national S&T funding has been exhaustively reviewed in a number of recent studies and, rather than revisit these, attention is directed specifically to a number of key measures, drawing on the most recent data.

## 10.2 SOME METHODOLOGICAL ISSUES

State financing of the knowledge economy from the national perspective is based on fundamentally different criteria to those pertaining to market-based financing. As indicated in Chapter 9, the two are conceptually distinct. Nevertheless, the potential leverage at the interface of market-based financing and state investment is of critical importance to the effectiveness of S&T policy over the medium term.

By the same token, a distinction can be drawn between the *economic rationale* for such investment and what can be termed the *constitutional rationale* for adequate and appropriate funding of national S&T policy.

The constitutional reasons have to do with the pervasive importance of scientific and technological literacy for the exercise of fundamental freedoms within the new prevailing culture across the developed world.[1] They carry with them a corresponding responsibility for government in regard, *inter alia*, to financing. These constitutional considerations can, as argued by Cooney, be summarised under three stylised headings.

1. *The need for critical independence*: This encompasses not just specific freedoms such as free speech under the constitution, it must also encompass equipping the individual to develop those critical faculties in relation to the prevailing culture, which is largely technological.

2. *The right to participate*: Universities are, by their nature, committed to fostering a critical and scientific ethos. Individuals have a right to participate to a degree that is appropriate to the economic status of a country or community. This freedom can only properly be exercised if government fosters such participation. In the context of our present analysis, this requires a commensurate investment in the technological capability of the higher education and commercial sectors.

3. *Individuals as stakeholders in society*: The competitive success of the economy within the global trading system impacts directly upon the individual's present and prospective living standards. Such success depends, in particular, upon the technological skills and competencies rooted, in turn, in the national knowledge base. Inadequate funding by government

diminishes the value of the stake of individuals in a knowledge-based economy.

In short, these freedoms are compromised by the failure of government to implement a coherent S&T policy, encompassing an appropriately funded HE sector.

In *realpolitik*, these arguments, though compelling, are unlikely to carry weight with programme managers or with those charged with curbing public expenditure. The current constraints imposed by reducing government expenditure so as to achieve sustainable convergence within the context of Ireland's participation in EMU add weight to this. However, there are other important, more tangible, economic arguments in support of an appropriate level of investment in Ireland's present and prospective knowledge-economy.

- The economic returns to higher education are not fully captured by the individual alone: there are positive externalities or "spill-overs" that justify government investment.[2]

- The empirical literature points to increasing returns to scale from investment in R&D (*c.f.* Section 6.2.2). This presupposes adequate funding of the HE Sector, efficient technology transfer between the HE sector and industry, and the sustained promotion of an entrepreneurial and technological culture throughout industry (capacity building).

- The instruments of policy should, as a matter of principle, be appropriate to policy goals or objectives. The government's stated industrial policy is predicated upon investment in education including, in particular, technology and innovation. This oft-repeated policy goal implies that investment in the science base is an essential element of national policy. In practice, all of the evidence points to a level of expenditure on S&T that is wholly inadequate to sustain a knowledge-driven high skills pattern of industrial development.[3,4]

## 10.3 FINANCING THE HE SECTOR: ECONOMIC RATIONALE

The discussion in Section 5.3 highlights the two-fold importance of incentives for developing and exploiting national knowledge equity. First, it provides the essential technological input into indigenous industry in the form of R&D, notably to innovative firms.[4] Forbairt, for example, cites an R&D/Sales multiplier of 3.5.[5] Secondly, the HE sector is a central generator of national knowledge equity (*c.f.* Figure 5.1) which, in turn, plays an important role as an attractor of foreign investment. This is now accepted government policy.

It is important to see how, in practice, the two goals relate to each other. The Committee of Vice Chancellors and Principals (CVCP) in the UK provides an insightful critique of the role of incentives in fostering R&D, one which applies even more so to Ireland because of the size structure of Irish industry and the resultant narrower research capability.

> Universities do most of the UK's long-term strategic and basic research in science and technology (including medicine and the environment). . . . They are also responsible for a great deal of shorter-term applied and near-market research, in collaboration with, or commissioned by industry and government. Universities also have the key role of training the researchers recruited by industry and commerce, government research organisations and the universities themselves.[6]

Consistent with this view of universities as central to the innovation process (at the heart of which is R&D), Ireland's Industrial Development Authority (IDA) has argued that Ireland is on an irreversible course to being a high skills economy and, as such, has become a focal point for investment by many of the world's leading companies in high technology and high value products and services. These companies are the driving force for much of the current growth in employment, accounting for up to 40 per cent of this growth. This will require a coordinated and sustained

focus on education. The policy implications of this are compelling.
The chief executive of Intel, for example, has argued that

> Intel was located in Ireland because we felt that there was an
> education system that was producing a larger number of
> technical people than there were job opportunities for. . . .
> Consequently, we had a superb start-up. So we are just
> building on exactly the same strengths that attracted us here
> in the first place.[7]

The rapidity of technological change and the systemic nature of
uncertainty as part of the process of science have been stressed in
previous discussion. This requires appropriate levels of planned
investment in education: above all, a robust science base, the capacity to engage in meaningful R&D, an adequate technological
infrastructure commensurate with the requirements of the most
advanced technologies and, most importantly, a strong cadre of
intelligent, well-supported and well-motivated postgraduate students. These are necessary conditions for effective technology
generation and transfer along with capability building within individual firms. In terms of policy consistency, all of this implies
commensurate levels of investment by government.

There has been extensive discussion of the whole issue of investment in science and technology in recent years. The arguments are set out in official reports, notably the STIAC report,[8] the
CIRCA report commissioned by the HEA,[9] the White Paper on
Science, Technology and Innovation[10] and authoritative critiques,
notably by the Royal Irish Academy[11] and others.[12] These studies
provide up-to-date assessments of the governance, management
and institutional arrangements relating to S&T. Much of this is
taken as read.

Importantly, it is accepted that there have been significant institutional changes; the recent decision by government to fold
S&T into what is now the Department of Education and Science is
one example. Others include initiatives launched by Forbairt, un-

derpinned by EU support. The success of the university and the HE sector itself in reshaping its capabilities to play a dynamic role at a regional and national level is also noted.

### 10.4 CENTRAL IMPORTANCE OF FINANCING S&T: KEY COMPONENTS

Funding, however, still remains the issue of key importance, in particular the adequacy, or otherwise, of government investment in the knowledge economy. It has already been noted that there are major market failures and deficiencies in the market-based financing of S&T (Chapter 9). In this respect, four main issues are considered:

1. Funding of basic research

2. Financing capital equipment

3. Funding R&D in the HE sector which is central to the innovation process.

4. The adequacy or otherwise of support for postgraduates as key contributors to the national S&T effort.

Pertinent data contextualise the extent of deficiencies in state funding of S&T, particularly in light of the objectives and aspirations of industrial policy. They also serve to highlight the scale of the government's recent initiative which, of course, was designed to address these deficiencies. As we saw earlier in Tables 6.7–6.9, for example, which list government funding of science and technology, the data encompass broadly defined S&T expenditure spread over 10 government departments and some 30 agencies. Tables 6.7 and 6.8, in particular, highlight the crucial impact of increasing EU funding of S&T in Ireland.

The focus here is much narrower, consonant with our theme enshrined in the Techno-Academic Paradigm. It will develop primarily in terms of the capacity of academics to respond in new and innovative ways to the rapidly evolving needs of globally knowledge-intensive companies.

At the outset, the data confirm that the scale of government funding is wholly inadequate by any objective comparator in light of the scale of the technological challenge facing Irish industrial policy and the rate of expansion of the HE sector. What is equally significant is the growth in contract research, income, particularly in the HE sector, all of which is returned as expenditure by government on S&T.[13] Typically, contract research earnings in Trinity College Dublin have grown from £1 million in 1981 to their current level of £14 million which currently represents about 20 per cent of its operational budget.

What in effect has happened is that the EU and industry have provided both the catalyst for a reassessment of S&T policy as well as a significant proportion of the funding to implement this policy, a policy which is aimed at setting the foundations for Ireland's prospective economic performance through the early part of the 21st century.

This is not to argue that EU funding, predominantly from Community Structural Funds (CSF) and EU Framework Programmes is, in itself, inappropriate. Nor that co-funding by is undesirable. The issue is one of additionality, given the government's own policy objective and the need for policy consistency and credibility. There has been until quite recently a conspicuous reluctance by government to act, notably in relation to funding, on the implications of its own analysis. In short, the EU and industry should complement, but not be a substitute for, government funding for S&T.

## 10.5 EXPENDITURE ON R&D

The logical starting point for a review of the most recent data on R&D expenditures is the government's own premise, reiterated by the development agencies, that R&D is central to the innovation process.[5,14] We do not propose to replicate the data on Ireland's comparative R&D performance.[13] Instead, a number of key themes are identified, the details of which are embodied in data presented in Chapter 6.

- Total gross expenditure on R&D (GERD) in Ireland as a percentage of GDP is 1.40 compared with an EU and OECD average of 1.84 per cent and 2.16 per cent, respectively (Table 6.9).

- 23 per cent of GERD is financed by government in Ireland, which compares with an EU/OECD average of some 36 per cent.

- There has been a significant improvement in R&D spending by industry, supported by a range of Forbairt initiatives. It is still, however below the EU average (Figure 6.4).

- Government spending on R&D per head of population in Ireland is £29.7 compared with an average of £115 for EU countries and, to take one example, £127 for Denmark (Table 10.1).

- Expenditure on R&D in higher education (HERD) as a percentage of GDP in Ireland is well below the EU and OECD average and also below the corresponding figures for small comparable countries (Table 10.2).

## 10.6 RESEARCH FUNDING IN THE HE SECTOR

Table 10.3 sets out trends in public funding of university research expenditures prior to the government's recent expenditure commitments. The data largely speak for themselves in highlighting the difficulties confronting the sector for years. Funding for basic research amounted to some £2 million per year. There was less for strategic research and less again for applied research in the RTCs (redesignated National Institutes of Technology). In commenting on the provision for 1997, Forfas noted:

Monies provided in this way, while facilitating a minimum level of S&T research actively by academic staff, do not provide sufficient resources to establish a strong on-going research base within the colleges.[15]

The CIRCA report, reviewing the data in an international context, noted simply that "there is virtually no financial support for basic science".[9] The RIA, in its critique of the White Paper on Science Technology and Innovation, noted that "funding for basic research in Ireland is about 10 per cent of the OECD average".[11]

In short, (a) the scale of the funding is wholly inappropriate to domestic industrial, let alone educational policy objectives and (b) Irish researchers are compelled to seek funding from other sources that are not necessarily relevant to Ireland's policy objectives.

TABLE 10.1: GOVERNMENT FINANCING OF R&D PER HEAD OF POPULATION (IR£)[15]

| France | 185.4 |
|---|---|
| Sweden | 181.5 |
| Germany | 155.9 |
| Finland | 132.3 |
| Denmark | 127.0 |
| EU-15 | 112.1 |
| Netherlands | 115.5 |
| Austria | 115.2 |
| Belgium | 92.7 |
| UK | 90.7 |
| Italy | 73.0 |
| Spain | 40.2 |
| Ireland | 29.7 |
| Portugal | 27.8 |
| Greece | 13.5 |

TABLE 10.2: EXPENDITURE ON R&D IN THE HE SECTOR (HERD)[15]

|  | % GDP |
|---|---|
| Netherlands | 60 |
| Norway | 45 |
| Finland | 44 |
| Denmark | 41 |
| EU Average | 39 |
| OECD Average | 38 |
| New Zealand | 30 |
| Portugal | 27 |
| Ireland | 27 |

TABLE 10.3: GOVERNMENT FUNDING OF HE RESEARCH (IR£M)[15]

|  | 1990 | 1992 | 1994 | 1996 | 1997 |
|---|---|---|---|---|---|
| Basic Research Grants | .532 | .854 | .833 | 1.996 | 2.250 |
| Strategic Research | .975 | .798 | 1.001 | 1.217 | 1.470 |
| Applied Research – RTC | .972 | 1.303 | .991 | .746 | 1.000 |
| Applied Research – Universities | 1.202 | .728 | .152 | 1.326 | 1.700 |
| Industry Scholarship | .343 | .401 | .399 | .294 | .260 |
| Research Scholarship | .483 | .552 | .507 | 1.175 | 1.180 |
| Drugs |  |  |  | .525 | .294 |
| TOTAL | 4.507 | 4.636 | 3.883 | 7.279 | 8.154 |

## 10.6.1 Comparison with the UK

An interesting perspective on the level of funding in Irish universities can be gleaned from a comparison of funding in TCD and in the Queen's University of Belfast (QUB). Data for 1994/5 show that the total income (state and non-state) of the university per student in TCD was about two-thirds that of QUB (Figure 10.1). The breakdown of TCD's grant is equally revealing. The total grant including funding under the EU Advanced Technical Skills Programme (ATS), minor works and supplementary grants amounted to £31,602,000. Of this, 57 per cent £17.99 million (57 per cent) was deducted in taxes leaving a net contribution of £13.6 million. The tax breakdown was as follows: PAYE/PRSI, £15.02 million; VAT/Levies on energy, telephone and insurance, £0.24 million; VAT on purchases not reclaimable, £2.25 million; Rates, £0.48 million.

FIGURE 10.1: COMPARISON OF STATE SUPPORT IN TCD AND QUB
TAKING INTO ACCOUNT DIFFERENCES IN STUDENT NUMBERS (£M)

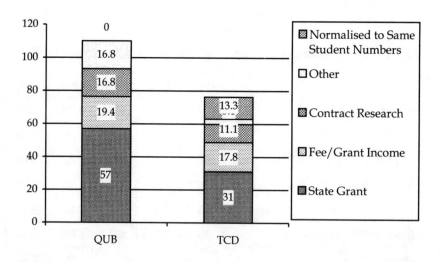

Regarding the wider impact of TCD's overall contribution, the value to the economy as a whole arising directly from the College's conference activities was of the order of £21 million in 1992: on the state Tourist Board's own estimate, the per capita spend/value of the 21,000 overseas conference delegates in that year was £1,000. In addition, the value to the economy of the extra 400 jobs created on foot of College's contract research earnings (one job per

£27,500 contract monies earned). These figures begin to put into perspective the degree of leverage generated by state investment in the universities in only two areas of the universities' additional contribution to the community.

## 10.7 CAPITAL EXPENDITURE: RESEARCH INFRASTRUCTURE

The HE sector provides a wide range of services to industry (*c.f.* Figure 5.1), requiring an adequate infrastructure of facilities and equipment that are relevant to leading-edge science and technology in specified niches. However, persistent and chronic underfunding for capital equipment has resulted in ageing/obsolete equipment, as signalled in Section 6.4. Equipment relevant to current and emerging niches frequently cannot be purchased, even in cases where they are demonstrably of value to individual policy objectives.

The impact of this on national competitiveness from the perspective of research capabilities in knowledge-intensive areas has not been quantified. But it can be inferred from the discussion in Section 6.4 where, in the UK, the CVCP Report[6] found that, in the case of pharmaceuticals research, some 80 per cent of university departments were unable to conduct critical experiments because of inadequate funding. More than 20 per cent of equipment in research intensive universities was over 15 years old and nearly two-thirds had a useful life of less than 5 years. Commenting on the Report, the Association of British Pharmaceutical Industries stated that "one of the factors in our success has been access to well trained graduates and the depth of the UK science base, which the Report shows is seriously eroded".

More recently, the chief executive of Glaxo Wellcome, one of the largest UK science-based companies, has argued that funding for research in British universities is "creaking at the seams":

> Recognising the need for a strong science base is critical to Britain's future competitive position.[16]

He goes on to say that the UK must get its research infra-structure "back to internationally competitive standards".

Similarly, the head of R&D at SmithKline Beecham Pharmaceuticals, in a critical analysis of the CVCP Report, has pointed out that the decay in the science infra-structure:

> As well as undermining the quality of science education . . . also threatens the capacity of university's to engage in collaborative research. We have established strategic collaborations with the top-ranked research universities and make considerable intellectual as well as financial contributions to these liaisons. We also funded the provision of the state-of-the-art equipment in specific research collaborations when it is appropriate that the costs and benefits are shared by industry and academics [echoing the relevance of the Techno-Academic Paradigm]. However, it is not the function of industry, or the charities, to finance normal, generic academic infrastructure.[17]

There are obvious lessons of central importance to the issue of the funding of the science base in Ireland and, indeed, all smaller regional economies. Compelling research evidence indicates that deficiencies in the funding of long-term basic research constrains the scope for generating intellectual property and, thereby, ultimately limits innovation in industry, which is the key determinant of national/regional competitiveness.[18]

### 10.8 ROLE OF THE HEA

The Higher Education Authority has statutory responsibility for funding capital equipment for universities. It is widely acknowledged that its distribution of scarce funds is objective and informed. The reality confronting the HEA is well summarised by the CIRCA report:

> The equipment position appears to be particularly bad . . . the sector as a whole receives about £2 million from the HEA for replacing and enhancing equipment . . . for institutions attempting to maintain a world presence in leading research ar-

eas as well as accommodating a growing number of students,
the position would seem to us to be quite untenable.[9]

Even the CIRCA proposal to increase funding from £2 million to
£5 million is inadequate. What is required is a capital equipment
audit which is likely to identify the need for a once-off injection of
some £20 million to bring capital equipment into line with stated
policy objectives, together with an annual equipment budget of
£10 million. These are not large sums when set against the
"growth dividend" generated by Ireland's national knowledge
base and the overriding need to preserve and enhance this base.

The thrust of the CIRCA report in regard to the consequences
of the under-funding of capital equipment is reiterated and underlined:

> Unless this is done, the credibility of an industrial policy
> which is predicated upon a knowledge — intensive develop-
> ment will be seen internationally as an aspiration without any
> substance. It requires no analysis to appreciate that knowl-
> edge-based economic development cannot occur in the ab-
> sence of leading research-based universities . . . it is evident
> that the "platform building" role of basic research is an intrin-
> sic component of university-industry interaction and not a
> separate kind of activity.[9]

## 10.9 NEW GOVERNMENT INITIATIVE

As indicated earlier, in November 1997 the government announced the establishment of a £250 million Education Technology Investment Fund (ETIF). This is intended to create a "medium-term" framework for financing the development of scientific and technological education in Ireland. The main objectives of
the Fund are as follows:

- To renew and modernise the infrastructure of HE institutions,
  particularly in the technological sector

- To develop new areas of activity where emerging skills short-ages have been identified and, in this regard, to facilitate the forecasting of skills requirements

- To invest in promoting innovation to maintain and foster eco-nomic growth. It is envisaged that this will include support for "advanced research and, also, for technology transfer". More specifically, the aim here is to "grow our knowledge base, through supporting research development and innovation".

The Fund is managed by the National Treasury Management Agency (NTMA) within seven broad areas that include skills needs, infra-structural renewal and development, R&D, and HE research equipment. The initiative is unequivocally linked to sup-porting present and prospective economic growth. In announcing the initiative, the Minister for Education and Science stated that

> the ETIF [will] address present and future needs of much of our education system. This will protect and promote job crea-tion in international and indigenous companies . . .

The announcement, however, leaves a number of key issues to be addressed. These include (a) the importance of attracting private investment to the fund, (b) the basis for assigning priorities given that resources will remain constrained and (c) the role of the HEA in administering additional funding. It also leaves unaddressed the key issue identified earlier, namely, the need for a holistic ap-proach as between state funding and the availability of market-based finance. In this regard, we reiterate that an integrated ap-proach to S&T funding involving the financial institutions as well as the state can provide major leverage.

Equally, it is important to assert that an expansion of infra-structural facilities must provide adequate support services for students within the HE sector. The reality is that such services have been seriously eroded in recent years and this has occurred against a background of a massive increase in numbers within an already over-stretched system. Even on economic grounds, we believe that there is a compelling case for appropriate provisions for student facilities such as counselling, recreation and student societies.

## 10.10 SUMMARY EVALUATION

Ireland has positioned itself, in terms of growth strategy, as a highly skilled, knowledge-intensive economy: in this, it has little option. Human capital is the necessary prerequisite for facilitating the spectacular growth of the Irish economy in recent years.

Government funding of S&T is demonstrably inadequate to support this strategy and to sustain such growth. In addition to the pervasive nature of scientific uncertainty, and in the face of highly mobile global knowledge intensive industries which are science-based, commensurate investment in education and technology is not an option: it is an economic and, arguably, a cultural imperative.

Government policy has, to date, been characterised by an emphasis on institutional structures and systems of governance. Necessary as these are, they only partly disguise the continued low level of funding by government of science, technology and innovation. This has been alleviated by a wholly disproportionate reliance on EU funding. Such reliance is not consistent with the spirit of additionality that underpins Community Structural Funds. In any event, it cannot be relied upon indefinitely against a background of enlargement and the prospective loss by Ireland of its preferential Objective I status. Equally, the government has not fully acknowledged, through investment in infrastructure, the scope for leveraging the Techno-Academic Paradigm through campus companies and strategically located science parks analogous to the Irish Financial Services Centre (IFSC).

At the heart of Ireland's development strategy has been an extraordinary dichotomy highlighted in this and the previous chapter, namely, an indifference by successive governments to fund adequately the human and physical capital necessary to sustain the industrial strategy on which jobs, wealth and living standards ostensibly depend. There is a comparable disinclination by market-based financial institutions right across the wider EU to provide the necessary financing on appropriate terms and conditions. The two are related. The recent investment by government should act as a catalyst for inducing increasing innovation in technology funding by market-based institutions. Equally, a capacity on the part of financial institutions, and particularly banks, realistically to appraise technology risk and to respond to the latent demand for funding by TBFs, including campus companies, would, no doubt, highlight the deficiency in complementary additional investment on the part of government.

A re-engineering of policy at both levels, based on an appropriate technology foresight model drawing upon the key features of the Techno-Academic Paradigm, would help resolve this dichotomy with the ensuing benefit of enormous leverage of the Irish knowledge-based economy.

## OBSERVATIONS AND RECOMMENDATIONS

- *Ireland has positioned itself, in terms of its growth strategy, as a high skills, knowledge-intensive economy.*

- *Universities do a significant part of the nation's long-term strategic and basic research in science and are also responsible for a great deal of shorter-term applied and near-market research in collaboration with or commissioned by industry and government.*

- *Universities and other HE institutions have a key role in training the researchers recruited by industry and commerce, government research organisations and the universities themselves.*

- *Investment in education and technology is not an option: it is an economic and arguably a cultural imperative.*

- *Policy instruments should be appropriate to policy goals or objectives.*

- *The government's stated industrial policy is predicated upon investment in education including, in particular, technology and innovation.*

- *A distinction can be drawn between the economic rationale for such investment and what can be termed the constitutional rationale for adequate and appropriate funding of national S&T policy. The constitutional reasons have to do with the pervasive importance of scientific and technological literacy for the exercise of fundamental freedoms within the new prevailing S&T-based knowledge culture across the developed world.*

- *Until quite recently, government funding of S&T is demonstrably inadequate to support this strategy and to sustain such growth.*

- *There is a comparable disinclination by market-based financial institutions to provide the necessary financing on appropriate terms and conditions for exploiting S&T.*

- *The leverage that arises at the interface of market-based financing and state investment is of critical importance to the effectiveness of S&T policy over the medium term. There are now signs that the private sector is responding to the government's recent initiative.*

- *A re-engineering of policy at both levels, through the financing of a Technology Foresight Model, would facilitate such leverage to benefit of the Irish knowledge-based economy.*

- *Government policy to date has emphasised institutional structures and systems of governance that partly disguises the continued low level of state funding of science, technology and innovation.*

- *Development of a vibrant R&D base has only been made possible by a wholly disproportionate reliance on EU funding. Such reliance is not consistent with the spirit of additionality that underpins Community Structural and Framework Funds.*

- *Funding from the EU and industry should complement, not be a substitute for, government funding for S&T.*

- *The economic returns to higher education are not fully captured by the individual alone: there are possible externalities or "spill-overs" that justify government investment.*

- *The empirical literature points to increasing returns to scale from investment in R&D.*

- *There is minimal financial support for basic science: it is currently about 10 per cent of the OECD average.*

## References and Notes: Chapter 10

1.   We are grateful to Mr. Thomas Cooney, BCL Statutory Lecturer in law, UCD for suggestions on these points.

2.   Special Symposium on the Deering Report, *Economic Journal*, 1997.

3.   See, for example, R&D, Northern Ireland Economic Council (NIEC), Belfast, 1993.

4.   *Second European Report on S&T Indicators*, EUR17639EN, European Commission, Luxembourg, 1997.

5.   Forbairt, *Annual Report*, 1996.

6.   *Research in Universities*, CVCP, Briefing Note, October, 1995.

7.   "Intel Reforms its Business when the Chips are Down", *Irish Times*, April, 1997, p. 3.

8.   *Making Knowledge Work for Us*, Report of the Science, Technology and Innovation Advisory Council (STIAC), (D. Tierney, Chairman), 1995.

9.   *The Organisation, Management and Funding of University Research in Ireland and Europe*, the CIRCA Group Europe Ltd, Roebuck Castle, Dublin 4, Ireland, 1996.

10.  *White Paper on S&T*, Stationery Office, Dublin, Ireland, 1996.

11. RIA: Response to White Paper on Science, Technology and Innovation. Dublin, 1997.

12. V.J. McBrierty, "The Changing Face of Universities in the Innovation Age" *Physics World*, Jan. 1997, pp. 18-21.

13. R.P. Kinsella and V.J. McBrierty, *Economic Rationale for an Enhanced Science and technology Capability*, Report to Forfás, Ireland's Science and Technology Agency, 1994.

14. *Shaping our Future; A Strategy for Enterprise in Ireland in the 21st Century*, Forfás Report, May, 1996.

15. A. Fitzgerald and K. Lydon, *State Investment in Science and Technology*, 1996. Forfas, Wilton House, Dublin 2, Ireland.

16. "Glaxo Chief Urges Better Funding for Research", *Financial Times* (London), Sept. 9, 1997, p. 12.

17. G. Poste, "An Acid Test for Excellence", *Financial Times*, June 7, 1996.

18. P.A. Geroski, J. van Reenen and C. Walters, *Innovation, Patents and Cash Flow*, CEPR (London), Discussion paper No. 1432, July, 1996 (IO).

*Chapter 11*

# OVERALL OBSERVATIONS AND RECOMMENDATIONS

## 11.1: S&T AND THE ECONOMY

- There is no unique model for exploiting the benefits of new technology: each country must find its own methodology for exploiting the central element in all schemes, namely, the national knowledge base.

- The capacity for innovation can be stimulated or inhibited by the institutional and policy framework within nations.

- Innovative, proactive management of new discoveries based on informed judgement must replace effete policies and blind belief in the importance of science and technology.

- Policy formulation is best approached through an iterative process based on the knowledge gleaned from hands-on experience.

- Scientists should be integrated into the decision making process so that they can fully appreciate the complex network into which their advice has to fit. Procedures that separate those with knowledge of science, technology and industry from the political and decision making apparatus is counterproductive in regard to fostering sustainable economic growth.

- If effective and balanced relationships are to be established between the main participants in the generation and use of new technology, it is necessary first to understand their cultural dif-

ferences and perspectives, respect these differences, and then
bridge the barriers of language, attitudes, priorities and perspectives. Any process that attempts to impose one culture on
another is destined to fail.

- A strong basic as well as applied research capability is important in terms of facilitating the generation, absorption and exploitation of new technologies by companies. It is also necessarily at the heart of any effective strategy aimed at promoting
  sustained inward investment into Ireland.

- Continuing efforts to attract inward investment must be
  matched with comparable development of Ireland's indigenous
  industry that is heterogeneous in size, nature of activity and
  origin. This will lessen both its cyclical and structural vulnerability to change.

- A bimodal strategy that reflects the dual nature of the industrial
  base in Ireland (research-based large multinational versus developing small (SME) or very small (VSE) indigenous enterprises) is required to achieve effective technology transfer between the HE sector and industry. Policy formulation must
  therefore reflect the business sector profile and take into account, for example, the relative cost of generating and/or acquiring and exploiting knowledge which is often prohibitive for
  the small firm.

- Building up an R&D culture and capability is relatively more
  risky and costly for smaller companies which find it more difficult to absorb the costs, and fully capture the benefits, of R&D:
  they need special assistance, for example, through the tax system which is one of the very few policy instruments available to
  Ireland.

- Investment in S&T should not be based on an either/or policy
  (either applied or basic research): they are mutually reinforcing.

- Undue reliance on imported technology leaves a nation's industry over-dependent on technologies already approaching their sell-by date, thus risking the marginalisation of that industry.

- An effective national S&T policy must establish guidelines for prioritising the different fields of research but the actual fleshing out of research priorities into specific programmes should be left to the scientific community itself, or to private businesses that are willing to provide the necessary finance.

- The HE sector must continue to address the servicing and technology needs of smaller companies in particular and increase their awareness of the availability of such services.

- In the drive towards stronger links with industry, care must be exercised to ensure that the academic ethos of the institution does not become unduly distorted as entrepreneurial and more commercially-driven endeavours are increasingly successful and therefore more visible.

- Technology transfer depends as much on an academic institution's ethos as on formal technology transfer programmes.

## 11.2: S&T AND THE NATIONAL KNOWLEDGE BASE: ECONOMIC AND METHODOLOGICAL ISSUES

- Science and its transformation into technology, and thereby jobs, involves a continuum of activities ranging from the initial conceptual idea to its most applied commercial form. Policy must be holistic and not based on ad hoc interventions.

- Enhancement of the applied research capability in the HE sector should be seen in conjunction with additional support for, and not in any sense competing with, industry's R&D needs.

- Stronger Industry/HE technology transfer mechanisms and a more effective use of HE resources is required to strengthen the capacity of Irish companies, particularly in the indigenous VSE sector, to absorb and manage R&D.

- S&T is not static: the knowledge base which drives S&T must be constantly renewed with basic research as its seed corn. Extant knowledge is yesterday's knowledge; future markets will not be present markets.

- All stakeholders must be involved in the policy making process. Science is a driver of technology and care must be taken not to marginalise scientists in S&T policy formulation. Equally, social, cultural, environmental, and commercial considerations also drive technology and must similarly be integrated into the policy making process.

- Ireland's expenditures on R&D, in relative terms, fall significantly short of those of most other countries of comparable size within the EU. The fact that EU Structural Fund expenditures are, in effect, replacing rather than augmenting national expenditures suggest that Ireland's S&T policy is informed neither by the vision nor the rationale of Community policy.

- S&T expenditure must be on a scale that reflects the fundamental importance of knowledge — and the national knowledge base — in generating economic activity and sustaining high quality employment. It is self-evident that current resourcing of S&T in Ireland by this criterion is wholly inadequate.

- Co-ordinated funding arrangements, embracing both the public and private sectors, are a necessary condition for an effective S&T policy.

- Policy must be informed by an understanding of the nature of scientific and technological processes and, hence, of the management of process innovation.

- Categorising research into different "types" is often no more than an administrative convenience that belies the non-linear, interactive character and latent synergy of the overall research effort.

- Any analysis that addresses the economic rationale for S&T expenditure requires a standard research nomenclature such as the Frascati definitions.

- Policy should build on the critical mass of knowledge workers, facilities and networks within the HE sector, while maintaining the primacy of the central education and training role.

- Mechanisms and procedures are necessary to ensure the genuine pooling of the human resources available in the HE sector as the foundation for a national S&T programme. The development of a proactive entrepreneurial technology-based culture at national level is a major policy goal.

- The establishment of a system of regional science research parks drawing on the combined strengths of HE institutions in those regions is one important priority in any national S&T strategy.

## 11.3: IP in a Knowledge Society

- The technology that flows from new knowledge is a valuable and tradeable resource because of its direct link to economic growth.

- Intellectual property is a tradable commodity in its own right.

- This reflects a new perspective on knowledge, namely, *knowledge as equity* which, in turn, reinforces the importance of intellectual property rights (IPR) whose scale, scope and importance in national economic development and in global trade cannot be over-stressed.

- Inventors, including academic researchers, do not always appreciate the scale of the additional funding required and often have inflated expectations of the worth of their new discovery.

- Non-exclusivity clauses in publicly-funded research contracts can constitute a major disincentive to the successful commercialisation of the new idea because companies seek exclusive rights to the intellectual property in order to justify the necessary additional post-research expenditure.

- Major legal ambiguities in protecting new discoveries in the biotechnology area remain to be solved.

- Despite recent EU and WTO initiatives, patent infringement and piracy are rampant.

- Patent activity in Europe lags behind the US and it lacks the vibrancy and growth of Japan and the Developing Asian Economies.

- The commitment within the EU to a competitiveness strategy that is innovation-led is likely to reinforce the importance of intellectual property in trade and investment.

- The patent culture in Ireland is grossly under-developed.

- The challenge for Ireland mirrors that of the wider EU, namely, rectifying the systematic under-investment in R&D and aligning both policy and institutions (including the financial sector) to the central role of intellectual property as the bedrock of economic prosperity.

- Despite compelling arguments in support of strong legal protection of IP, there remain conflicting viewpoints on the permissible level of monopoly power which should attach to proprietary new knowledge. This has led to a social paradox that is at the heart of issue of intellectual property management.

- Initiatives to resolve this paradox that seek to diffuse the economic benefits of IP throughout society at large will, no doubt, act as an effective counterweight against the tendency of the very large corporations to shift the historic and equitable balance between public good and private profit towards the private sector. By the same token, procedures at the national level for protecting intellectual property need to be made accessible to, and cost effective for, smaller companies.

## 11.4: IP RIGHTS IN THE HE SECTOR

- The role of the university has changed radically in the new innovation age because of the heightened strategic importance of education in a society which is now truly knowledge-driven.

- The HE sector is a rich and diverse source of new knowledge that underpins the nation's overall innovative culture.

- With the growth in innovation in the universities and other HE research institutions, it is essential that the intellectual property generated by academics is properly protected and exploited to the benefit of the institution and the community at large.

- The creation and management of intellectual property in Irish HE research institutions has been sporadic and unstructured. Institutions differ widely in their approach to IP.

- The sustained development of a balanced patent culture in the university sector requires a change in traditional attitudes coupled with measurement of performance.

- There is a growing appreciation of the worth of new technology and the value of patents as "performance indicators " in the HE sector.

- Limiting the universities' role to basic research alone runs counter to the growth of a strong and vibrant innovative culture in the Irish HE sector over the past three decades.

- The essential base for academic IP development is being eroded by a obsolescence of research facilities in universities. Initiatives such as the ETIF are critical.

- Equally, the excessive shift of academic workloads towards formal teaching in meeting the increasing demand for university education, and the inordinate time required to successfully negotiate and manage research grants erode research time.

- Intellectual property generated in the universities is becoming more focused with time.

- Ireland like most of Europe lags well behind the US in the area of academic intellectual property protection.

- Innovative companies should be encouraged to see the value of nurturing IP by facilitating and funding new ideas generated by their staff. This proactive approach can leverage the in-built knowledge equity of the company.

- There is an increasing awareness by academic institutions of the value of intellectual property and a growing propensity of companies and investors to exploit its market potential. The knock-on effects of technology licensing for the economy as a whole are considerable.

- Only 10-20 per cent of licensing agreements yielded substantial revenue and it takes between three and fifteen years for a typical programme to reach maturity, that is, to generate income in excess of expenses on a regular basis: technology licensing strategies are long-term.

- A portfolio of patents adds considerable weight to the university's negotiating position when setting up research contracts and joint ventures with industry.

- Academics and industrialists involved in R&D projects should be formally trained in all aspects of managing intellectual property and the realities of its commercial exploitation.

- The proposals of the Science, Technology and Innovation Advisory Council (STIAC) to draw up and adhere to a charter defining the key parameters in university/industry interactions should be implimented.

- The establishment of mutual trust is a key factor in joint university/industry collaboration.

- The creation of intellectual property involves personal, institutional and external investment, all of which must be recognised and also rewarded.

- Although the number of patents granted to academic researchers in Ireland is small by global standards, some are of high international standing.

- The almost exponential increase in the numbers seeking admission to higher education has compelled the Irish university sector to develop new sources of income to counter inadequate public funding. It is important that initiatives such as these are not penalised by a concomitant reduction in state funding.

- At the national level, the demonstrated prowess of the universities as innovators continues to support the current unprecedented growth of inward investment and economic prosperity in Ireland. The scale and importance of this support should be explicitly recognised.

### 11.5: The Emerging Techno-academic Paradigm

- A new Techno-Academic Paradigm is proposed to account for current trends in S&T and the pivotal role of the HE institutions in economic growth.

- Current developments in S&T fall into a number of categories, namely, invention, commercialisation, dissemination, globalisation and leveraging (upgrading to maximise the life cycle). These, in turn, require networking, flexible processes to manage change, innovation and a holistic approach to technology change through agreement.

- The human capital dimension of technology development and diffusion throughout society requires considerably enhanced emphasis.

- The global economy now operates *via* information superhighways and networks whereby industry's research needs and product development can be sourced globally. This "virtual organisation" is now a reality.

- Innovation now occurs in what is an increasingly "borderless" economy.

- Most of all new industry is knowledge-driven: it is born out of new knowledge and it requires access to the sources of new knowledge to ensure its continued growth. It is precisely this fact that gives the HE knowledge base a pivotal role within the emerging knowledge industries.

- The direct and dynamic interface between the universities as academic institutions and continually emergent technological innovation is evident in the growth corridors in the US and in the rapid proliferation of science parks throughout developed and developing nations.

- The HE sector is now central to the process of economic growth and of consequential societal change because of its important contribution to knowledge generation: the universities are catalysts for research-driven economic growth.

- The university is a node in an increasingly seamless global knowledge base, one which has a progressively larger interface with the knowledge-driven economy.

- Academic entrepreneurship can no longer be viewed as a mere cosmetic appendage to the central teaching function of the higher education research institutions.

- The importance of *national knowledge equity* in achieving economic prosperity is central. It has direct bearing on job creation.

- Financial institutions in Ireland, as in most European countries, are averse to risk, in contrast, for example, to the situation in North America.

- This reflects a simple but profoundly important reality, namely, an inability to price technological risk and to adjust to a knowledge-driven market place in which financial needs must be secured, not alone on physical assets, but on knowledge as equity.

- Campus companies form a crucially important "core" of Ireland's rapidly evolving technology-based indigenous industry — the nuclei of "cluster" of emerging technologies.

- The universities participate in financial risk-sharing in the establishment and promotion of campus companies.

- Management costs of providing and monitoring venture capital are significantly lower for campus companies compared with other SMEs. The risks are also significantly lower.

- The main policy constraints include a paucity of funding for R&D and inadequate funding for the universities and other HE institutions. The unit cost mechanism for distributing funds between Irish universities is, albeit unintentionally, impeding effective technology transfer between the universities and society at large.

- The diminishing supply of research students undercuts the capacity of universities to foster knowledge-driven growth. The economic consequences are potentially very damaging to future economic growth.

- Policy research directions for the future include further examination of the nature of academic entrepreneurship; ongoing development of policy strategies for fostering cohesive entrepreneurship in the HE sector across the relevant disciplines; and

continuous and systematic surveys of progress and performance in the HE sector.

## 11.6: Developing Strategies for S&T

- "Best practice" procedures for managing and, where appropriate, commercialising HE research should be initiated.

- A rigorous appraisal of an institution's potential downstream
  liability is essential.

- There are formidable difficulties in extracting unambiguous
  measures of public expenditure on R&D: strictly quantitative
  estimates of returns on investment are difficult to make.

- A philosophy of *investment* must replace the more established
  notion of *expenditure* in the areas of education and R&D.

- Policy, as currently stated, is riddled with paradoxes. For example, the implication that the universities have no officially
  recognised role in the commercialisation of research is at odds
  with the innovation culture that has grown up in the universities.

- In recognising that funding is a major instrument of government, care must be taken that it does not lead to a "culture of
  compliance" which is anathema to the ethos of university education and research. Equally, compliance with the stated needs
  of industry to an extent that undermines the central pedagogical mission of the universities is equally undesirable.

- An enhanced R&D contribution by academics will affect the
  division of academic time between research and lecturing. The
  choice of appropriate areas of research in each institution will
  be guided by "critical mass" criteria, the development of essential support services, and the identification of acceptable performance indicators for research evaluation.

- Policy designed to maximise the benefits of the nation's R&D capabilities must ensure effective technology transfer from the knowledge generators to the knowledge users. There are several effective models for this.

- A twin-track approach involving more imaginative innovation transfer mechanisms specifically tailored to the micro-enterprises and large multinationals respectively is a priority.

- In light of the economic rate of return on R&D expenditure and the significance of R&D as an *attractor* for direct foreign investment, the case for realistic funding of the HE sector can no longer be gainsaid. The recent allocation of £250 million is a significant first step.

- The level of obsolescence of large research equipment is high and recurrent funding is low: an immediate injection of £50 million is required to bring the nation's research equipment up to a minimally acceptable level.

- The HE sector must play a full part in the area of continuing in-service education as a mainstream rather than an ancillary activity.

- The philosophy to educate for life, not jobs, is reasserted.

- The practice of "trading down" whereby over-qualified people fill available jobs will lead inevitably to frustration and lack of job satisfaction in later years.

- Inward investment depends critically on available well-qualified manpower at both professional and vocational levels in key growth areas. The expanding market of well-paid jobs is having a deleterious affect on the numbers of graduates who wish to proceed to postgraduate training, due in part to the derisory level of funding for postgraduate education. The overall national research effort will suffer as a result. A stipend of £10,000 per annum for postgraduates is proposed.

## 11.7: CAMPUS COMPANIES IN THE HE SECTOR:
### SURVEY AND ANALYSIS

- A recent survey provided informed analysis of the Campus Company sector as a prototype of the Techno-Academic Paradigm.

- All institutions asserted ownership of intellectual property generated by staff while in their employ.

- All institutions have a strongly proactive approach to the exploitation of intellectual property, including patents.

- There are wide differences in the way that intellectual property is viewed and managed. There is a total absence of a formal policy on intellectual property in a number of institutions and, among those institutions with such a policy, there is quite a diversity of approach.

- The lack of a cohesive strategy on intellectual property across the HE sector as a whole directly militates against the interests of individual institutions and the wider national economic interest.

- There is a compelling case for developing "best practice" in regard to the management of intellectual property at national and local level. This will require a strengthening of management systems for intellectual property both within the institution itself and, also, within the Department of Education and Science.

- An estimated 60 patents held by institutions in the HE sector generated significant financial returns.

- Most, but not all, of the universities have a formal policy on campus company development.

- There are wide differences regarding facilities provided to support academic entrepreneurs who wish to set up campus companies.

- Constraints on campus companies include the lack of infra-structural facilities available at the early stages of start-up, internal management weaknesses, lack of venture capital and seed capital, and the absence of bank support.

- Campus companies are involved in a broad range of the leading-edge technologies.

- There are differences in respect to the appointment of Directors to the boards of campus companies which also raises important issues regarding the statutory responsibilities of such Directors.

- There is an urgent need to address the issue of "best practice" in regard to the governance of campus companies.

- A robust and legally enforcible framework of governance based on existing best practice within the institutions themselves is required.

- Designation as a campus company should be contingent upon the completion of a management training programme in order to underpin the investment.

- There is a compelling case for the banks to develop expertise in new techology-based firms (TBFs) including campus companies.

- Incubator units, preferably on campus or in close proximity, should be established as a key element of a national campus company strategy with funding from the public sector and the HE institutions using the taxation incentives in Section 25 of the relevant Finance Act.

- There is scope for encouraging "clusters of companies" within these incubator facilities, with associated positive externalities or "spill-over effects".

- There is scope for leveraging such clusters and incubator facilities for research and teaching purposes.

- Specialised training for campus company personnel, including managing/marketing/financing modules drawn from within the HE sector and capable of being delivered in a variety of modes is required.

- The completion of such training, in the absence of proven competence, should be a prerequisite for designation as a campus company and, therefore, for access to campus-based seed and venture capital funds (when available).

- As part of a wider strategic relationship between industry (IBEC), Forbairt and the HE sector, all campus companies should have access to experienced non-executive directors/mentors.

- A National Campus Company Forum (NCCF) should be set up to represent the interests, needs and potentialities of these companies in policy and related fora.

- The creation of a Campus Company Development Director located within the Industrial Liaison Officer (ILO) function is recommended.

- Within this broader framework, an equivalent set of procedures and systems are needed in establishing and managing campus companies to ensure that all of the HE sector effectively mobilises its "knowledge equity" and to avoid differences in contractual arrangements and incentives structures, which would both impede mobility and create distortions and tensions across the sector as a whole.

- There is a potentially high payback to the national economy of fast growth campus companies, working in highly specialised technologies with, by definition, little or no displacement effect.

## 11.8: FINANCING THE KNOWLEDGE ECONOMY (1): A CONCEPTUAL FRAMEWORK

- Policy in relation to funding S&T and innovation depends critically on the total flow of financing for innovation and the science base in which it subsists, the efficiency of the financial markets which is predicated, *inter alia*, on the existence of a technological competence of middle and senior bank management, and the leverage that is created between state and market-based financing.

- There is a need for a holistic and flexible approach when funding TBFs.

- Funding criteria for TBFs should not only be predicated on fixed assets or financial guarantees, but also on intellectual property as a form of knowledge equity which is the primary asset of TBFs.

- Government has an interventionist role to play in creating a support infrastructure for TBFs.

- There is need for an integrated *Technology Financing Foresight Model* to match the volume and composition of funding to national objectives.

- Deficiencies in financial engineering, including the pricing of technology risk and low S&T capability of financial institutions, are identified as a reason for the low conversion rate of new technology into jobs.

- This also reflects, in part, the nature of TBFs as well as an "information gap" regarding the perceived relative riskiness of TBFs compared with the wider set of SMEs.

- Knowledge equity is a more appropriate collateral for secured lending/financing than are fixed assets. Banks are not as yet in tune with this growing reality.

- The perceptual problem rooted in a lack of pertinent management capabilities and an "information gap" is responsible for the banks adopting the attitude that lending to TBFs is inherently more risky, compared with SMEs in general. This undermines confidence in TBFs throughout the financial sector as a whole.

- The measurement and pricing of risk is the key to asset and maturity transformation which is at the heart of financial intermediation.

- Banks do not differentiate between TBFs, with their special characteristics, and the general population of SMEs.

- The distinction between *risk* (with which banks are comfortable) and *uncertainty* (to which they are strongly averse) is emphasised.

- Of crucial importance is this distinction between "risk" and "uncertainty" and the different structure of the balance sheet and cash flow of TBFs compared with the wider population of SMEs. A new model of risk pricing which takes these special characteristics into account is proposed.

## 11.9: Financing the Knowledge Economy (2): The Role of Market-based Finance

- TBFs require access to a wide range of financial instruments in order to accommodate their quite uniquely rapid development cycle, from R&D through to start-up and beyond.

- Regarding the financing of TBFs, there is a "technology financing gap", the cost of which, in terms of its impact on future growth, competitiveness and the strengthening of the national knowledge base is incalculable.

- This "market failure" justifies government intervention on grounds of "public good".

- The key issue underlying market-based technology financing is whether or not TBFs are inherently more vulnerable to failure or less likely to grow compared with SMEs in general.

- Banks play a special role as intermediaries where their "inside information" and accumulated experience confers on them a "screening" role which can signal the credit worthiness (or otherwise) of a firm to other potential providers of finance. It is this unique role that makes banks so important in innovation financing.

- Recent evidence confirmed the singular preference for physical assets and/or financial guarantees as opposed to IP-based collateral as the basis for lending to TBFs.

- There is no S&T "culture" in Irish and EU banks, which denies even a basic understanding of the ethos and needs of technology-based firms. This compromises their ability to assess the technical risk of innovation. Nor do they consult the universities who are at the leading edge of knowledge generation.

- There are culture, information and financing gaps between the banks and the TBFs.

- Few banks distinguish TBFs from the general population of SMEs.

- The provision by some banks, directly or through a third party, of a *Technology Advisory/Assessment Service* bears directly on the support for, and financing of, TBFs. It provides a vital commercial/financial interface between the generation and the commercialisation of technology.

- About two-thirds of the banks in the EU did not monitor, nor participate in, EU or National Technology Programmes.

- Overall, the lack of access to banks by TBFs leads to a major "market failure".

- In the EU, EASDAQ, as well as national technology-based exchanges are emerging as an important part of the financing infra-structure. This has to be encouraged, especially in regional economies, where capital markets are likely to become more attenuated in the face of EMU.

- The branch network and the "inside information" available to the banks regarding potential investors is a major resource for developing "informal" venture capital (Business Angels); this resource remains under-developed and under-utilised.

- Overall, the reality is that there are major "gaps" regarding the availability of equity and that the volume of bank financing and ancillary services such as technology assessment are inadequate for TBFs which require both a range of tailored financial instruments and greater flexibility.

- These arguments apply equally to campus companies which are a subset of TBFs.

### 11.10: FINANCING THE KNOWLEDGE ECONOMY (3): STATE FUNDING OF S&T

- Ireland has positioned itself, in terms of its growth strategy, as a high skills, knowledge-intensive economy.

- Universities do a significant part of the nation's long-term strategic and basic research in science and are also responsible for a great deal of shorter-term applied and near-market research in collaboration with or commissioned by industry and government.

- Universities and other HE institutions have a key role in training the researchers recruited by industry and commerce, government research organisations and the universities themselves.

- Investment in education and technology is not an option: it is an economic and arguably a cultural imperative.

- Policy instruments should be appropriate to policy goals or objectives.

- The government's stated industrial policy is predicated upon investment in education including, in particular, technology and innovation.

- A distinction can be drawn between the *economic rationale* for such investment and what can be termed the *constitutional rationale* for adequate and appropriate funding of national S&T policy. The constitutional reasons have to do with the pervasive importance of scientific and technological literacy for the exercise of fundamental freedoms within the new prevailing culture across the developed world.

- Until quite recently, government funding of S&T is demonstrably inadequate to support this strategy and to sustain such growth.

- There is a comparable disinclination by market-based financial institutions to provide the necessary financing on appropriate terms and conditions for exploiting S&T.

- The leverage that arises at the interface of market-based financing and state investment is of critical importance to the effectiveness of S&T policy over the medium term. There are now signs that private sector is responding to the government's recent initiative.

- A re-engineering of policy at both levels, through the financing of a *Technology Foresight Model*, would facilitate such leverage to benefit of the Irish knowledge-based economy.

- Government policy to date has emphased institutional structures and systems of governance that partly disguises the continued low level of state funding of science, technology and innovation.

- Development of a vibrant R&D base has only been made possible by a wholly disproportionate reliance on EU funding. Such reliance is not consistent with the spirit of additionality that underpins Community Structural and Framework Funds.

- Funding from the EU and industry should complement, not be a substitute for, government funding for S&T.

- The economic returns to higher education are not fully captured by the individual alone: there are possible externalities or "spill-overs" that justify government investment.

- The empirical literature points to increasing returns to scale from investment in R&D.

- There is minimal financial support for basic science: it is currently about 10 per cent of the OECD average.

## *Appendix I*

## FRASCATI DEFINITIONS[A1]

- **R&D:** Research and development which is creative work undertaken on a systematic basis in order to increase the stock of knowledge and the use of this stock of knowledge to devise new applications.

- **Expenditure on R&D:** Measures the amount of money spent on the performance of R&D within the sector.

- **Funding of R&D:** Measures the amount of money spent by a sector on R&D which is not necessarily performed within the sector.

- **Intramural R&D:** Expenditure on R&D which is carried out inside the research department/company/academic department and so on.

- **Extramural R&D:** Expenditure on R&D which is carried out outside the research department/company/academic department and so on.

- **Pure Basic Research:** Research carried out for the advancement of knowledge without working for long-term economic or social benefits and with no positive efforts being made to apply the results to practical problems, or to transfer the results to sectors responsible for its application.

- **Oriented Basic Research:** Research carried out with the expectation that it will produce a broad base of knowledge likely to form the background to the solution of recognised or expected current or future problems or possibilities.

- **Applied Research:** Research undertaken in order to acquire new knowledge. It is, however, directed primarily towards a specific practical aim or objective.

- **Experimental Development:** Research drawing on existing knowledge gained from research and practical experience that is directed to producing new materials, products and devices, to installing new processes, systems and services, and to improving substantially those already produced or installed.

*Appendix II*

## Selected Academic Patents in the Irish Higher Education Sector

### The Nicotine Patch

Researchers working closely with the Elan Corporation have developed two patents in the area of transdermal drug delivery. The first[A2] is the basis for the successful nicotine transdermal patch manufactured by the Elan Corporation in Ireland and now licensed for sale in 22 countries world-wide. The second[A3] is used in a second-generation electrically assisted transdermal drug delivery device which is in clinical trial. The work, originally supported by Irish government funding as well as by Elan, has also led to the publication of almost 20 scientific papers in the international literature.

### New Magnetic Alloy

Permanent magnets are part and parcel of everyday life: they are essential components in computers, consumer electronics and transportation. The past few decades have witnessed unparalleled progress in the manufacture of better magnets, culminating in the development in 1983 of a high performance magnet based on iron, alloyed with boron and the rare-earth neodymium ($Nd_2Fe_{14}B$), independently in the US and Japan.[A4] A serious competitive disadvantage was created for Europe.

In a model example of European research collaboration, the Concerted European Action on Magnets (CEAM) was set up.[A5] Scientists from 13 countries now participate in the research programme co-ordinated by Professor Coey. A new high temperature magnet alloy comprising Samarium, Iron and Nitrogen ($Sm_2Fe_{17}N_3$) was discovered by Irish researchers for which a patent was granted in 1990.[A6] While not yet on a par with the US/Japanese alloy, the new material has distinctive advantages, particularly at high temperatures (Figure A.1).[A7] This discovery effectively re-established Europe's competitiveness in the field.

FIGURE A1: DIAGRAM SHOWING THE EXPONENTIAL INCREASE IN THE MAXIMUM ENERGY PRODUCT OF MAGNETS OVER THE PAST CENTURY, DOUBLING EVERY 12 YEARS[A7]

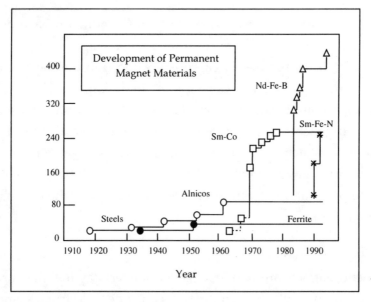

### The Electronic Eye

A working intelligent retina, or electronic "eye", was first demonstrated by an Irish scientist attached to the Hitachi Laboratory on the Trinity College campus:[A8,A9] Trinity College formed a joint venture with Hitachi in 1988. The approach was based on a combination of optical and computer neural network technologies. The electronic eye can respond to changing patterns, mimicking, albeit crudely, one of the functions of the brain. This is an example of world-class research carried out in an Irish university in cooperation with one of the world's largest high-tech multinationals. The research has important applications in areas such as robotic vision and intelligent human/machine interfaces.

## UV Curing of Monomers

One method for manufacturing contact lenses is to spin monomer liquid into the desired lens shape and then to polymerise it with UV light using a conventional UV sunray lamp as the light source (Figure A.2). A new and more efficient technology, using lasers instead of lamps, has been developed and patented by Irish scientists working in conjunction with the Bausch & Lomb Corporation.[A10] This is an example of an effective joint partnership between a long established subsidiary of a US multinational and an Irish university where, heretofore, all the technology was imported from the Company's Research Centre in the US. The generic nature of the patent is evident in the plethora of disparate applications that use UV light to cure monomers.

FIGURE A2: MANUFACTURE OF A POLYMER CONTACT LENS BY CURING MONOMER IN A ROTATING MOULD WITH UV LIGHT[A10]

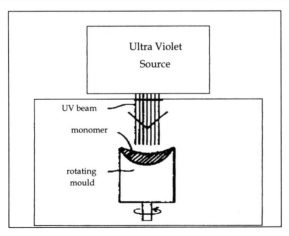

## Treatment of Neurodegenerative Disorders

Arising from a collaborative research agreement between UCD and American Biogenetic Sciences, Inc , Professor Ciaran Regan, Department of Pharmacology, and Heinz Nau, University of Hanover, have undertaken joint research on the development of a potential novel therapy for the treatment of neurodegenerative disorders. The success of the work has resulted in a world-wide patent being issued.

Ageing and neurodegeneration are associated with loss of nerve cell function and impaired memory and learning. Naturally occurring small proteins, termed neurotrophins, have the potential to alleviate these effects but their therapeutic use is restricted by poor penetration into the brain. Accordingly, a research programme was initiated to search for small organic molecules that would exhibit "neurotrophin-like" properties and readily penetrate the brain. This led to the successful indentification of a family of proprietary components based not only on their potency and safety profiles, but also on their ability to penetrate the brain and accumulate in regions known to be involved in memory and learning. In these regions compounds such as ABS205, one of the lead molecules, promotes the formation of nerve cell connections by influencing mechanisms that normally decay with ageing. Moreover, ABS205 greatly enhances cognitive ability in animal models of compromised learning.

## Diagnosis of BSE

Pharmapro Ltd is a joint company owned by UCD and UK-based Proteus International plc, which is a world leader in computer-aided molecular design. It was established to develop diagnosis tests an d vaccines for use in veterinary and human medicine. Pharmapro has developed a diagnosis test for the detection of BSE in the carcass of cattle, which has been licensed to an Irish-based diagnostic company, Enfer Scientific.

Enfer Scientific has reformatted the test for rapid and high throughput and is not testing carcasses for a national supermarket chain, SuperValu.

The test uses a small sample of tissue taken at the abattoir. This tissue is processed and the result returned before the carcass leaves the abattoir. The entire process takes less than 15 hours and provides confirmation that the animal did not have clinical BSE at slaughter.

The Enfer test has been validated by the Department of Agriculture, Food and Forestry and has been shown to be highly sensitive and specific in the detection of BSE.

*Appendix III*

# CAMPUS COMPANY FORMATION IN TRINITY COLLEGE DUBLIN

Procedures for the formation and approval of campus companies differ across the Irish Higher Education sector. Some institutions, such as the University of Limerick (Plassey Park) and University College Cork (NMRC) are structured in a way that facilitates the process. The Dublin Institute of Technology (DIT) has long experience of assisting start-ups and has rigorous procedures in place in regard to the designation of campus companies.

Enterprise formation is greatly facilitated by close interaction with industry, as is the case with Dublin City University (DCU) and, indeed, all of the HE institutions. University College Galway, Maynooth and University College Dublin (UCD), like other Irish universities, have research specialisations that provide underpinning for knowledge-intensive campus-based entrepreneurial activity.

In the case of UCD, this is facilitated by the University-Industry Programme, which encompasses a relatively large number of campus companies and which is to be augmented by a major investment in incubation facilities.

The National Institute of Technology has a specific remit to foster an enterprise culture through technology transfer and working with industry in their hinterland.

All of this applies equally to Northern Ireland. The University of Ulster has recently developed an innovative framework for commercialising its knowledge base and Queens University is long established in this field.

The reality is that there is no recognised standard applying to the formation and governance of campus companies in Ireland. While institutional autonomy and flexibility are essential, the absence of an agreed "bet practise" model is a major impediment in fostering the development of campus companies as a pivotally important subset of knowledge-intensified indigenous industry. It also makes it more difficult to secure financing, both state/EU and market-based, for the sector as a whole.

It would seem that — taking the EU as a whole — there is a role for the EU itself, through the Commission, in fostering cross-country best practise models in this field.

Trinity College Dublin has a wealth of experience, based on its world class research capabilities and industry programmes, which has been distilled into its procedures for campus company formation. These are set out below as a possible touchstone for further work, encompassing all of the Higher Education sector, through the HEA, in this field.

## A III.1. Rules for Campus Companies

1. A Campus Company is a private limited company with permission from the Board to trade in an agreed range of goods and services for a limited period of time (three years, extended to five as mutually agreed). The company is normally promoted or organized by a staff member of the College.

2. The process of formation of a campus company authorised by the College is summarised on the attached chart indicating the steps to be taken, the relevant College Officers involved in the steps, and the general considerations that will arise during the process: to obtain Board permission for a campus company, the outlined procedure must be followed.

3. The company may organise its internal operations as it sees fit, in accordance with its memorandum and articles of association.

4. The company will at all times ensure that those trading with it are aware of its limited liability status and that TCD is not in any way responsible for its operations.

5. Any employment agreement that a campus company has with any employee shall specifically state that the contract of employment is not with Trinity College. The company shall be solely responsible for the remuneration, tax, pensions and other obligations to employees.

6. The company shall be responsible for discharging all legal obligations under the Companies Acts.

7. The College shall have the right to nominate a director to the Board of any campus company, as it sees fit.

8. The College may inspect the accounts of any campus company by giving one month's notice.

9. The College may request details of any contract entered into by a campus company where a member of TCD staff is involved, but such information shall be kept confidential.

10. The College may request any information it deems requisite for a proper annual review of the company's activity in accordance with the declared purposes of the company.

11. If in the view of the College the review is unsatisfactory, or if the information or accounts requested have not been supplied, or if the company's activities are judged by the College to be prejudicial to the standing of Trinity College as an academic institution, the permission to use the designation campus company may be withdrawn on one month's notice, the company will cease active trading on the campus and will vacate any premises on the campus which have been loaned, leased, rented, or provided it by the College.

12. College staff authorised to engage in campus companies do so subject to the documents on external earnings.

13. College shall draw up operational rules for the conduct of business between campus companies and College departments.

14. Campus companies may begin operations on a basis authorised by the Business and Industry Committee, subject to satisfaction of all these regulations within a three month period.

15. All employees of campus companies shall accept the enforcement of any and all regulations made by the Board of TCD as a condition of employment insofar as such regulations govern any access the company or its employees has to TCD buildings, equipment, or personnel.

16. Trinity College will from time to time issue instructions as to the procedures to be adopted for the implementation of these rules.

17. The 15 per cent stake held by TCD shall not be diluted by the company through any share issue or sale or acquisition of capital except where the Board of TCD is satisfied that an arms length sale of the company to third parties is occurring and that no other arrangements exist which would have the effect of ranking TCD's stake in the company at a lower value per share than for those of the other owners. In no circumstances can the Board of TCD be forced to dispose of its stake in the company against its wishes. The Board of TCD may, however, with due notice to the company's board, dispose of any or all of its shares in the company, as it wishes.

## A III.2 Notes on Procedures

1. The object of procedures is to ensure compliance with College policy and to enable satisfactory monitoring of the growth and development of companies. It is also necessary to filter out unwelcome developments and to terminate activities that breach the regulations in some serious respect.

2.  A necessary tactic in enabling successful enterprise is to keep interference to a minimum and to position College to know what is happening while not getting involved in the business.

3.  The overall concept should be one of retaining substantial power in the hands of College, and rarely, if ever, using it.

4.  The right of appeal against administration should be exercisable very rapidly, and determinations should be decisive.

## A III.2.1 Procedures

1.  Applications made to the Director of Innovations Services specifying:

    - names of shareholders

    - object of company

    - financial arrangement

    - proposed location

    - startup date

    - agency support

    - accommodation requirements/leasing agreements

    - (Finance Officer, Treasurer).

2.  Approval in principle is given by Business and Industry Committee, to proceed to work out details.

3.  Detailed Negotiations.

    - Permission from Head of Department.

    - Inventory of Assets.

    - Company names, memorandum, articles of association.

    - Agreement with TCD on specifics.

    - Business Plan.

- Assessment by Director of Innovation Services for Business and Industry Committee.

- Reference to external advisors, if necessary.

- Programme for review and returns.

- Review by Finance Officer.

4. Issue of permission by Board on advice from Business and Industry Committee. Board may wish to delegate and simply wish to be informed.

5. Appeals are *via* the Bursar to Business and Industry Committee to Board.

## A III.3 Application to Form a Campus Company

1. Procedures

2. Statement of company objectives

3. Financial Arrangements: including statement or estimate of assets

4. Markets

5. Connection with TCD Research or Teaching

6. Employment generated

7. Relevant Assessments of Proposition

8. Describe status of Business Plan

9. Status of requests for Agency Support and executive responsible for projects

10. Approval of Head of Department

11. Acceptance of College Policy as enunciated in Board Documents. (Return signed copy of rules for campus companies):

12. Expected start-up date:

13. Accommodation required:

## A III.4 Regulations for the Conduct of Business Relations Between Campus Companies and College

1. The normal procedures for placing orders or contracts with any outside company are to be followed where campus companies are concerned, except where a College employee acts in a dual capacity, or has a dual interest in the business to be transacted.

2. A "dual" interest means that the person commissioning or authorising the work or payment for it on behalf of the College interest is also a member or associate of the company providing the service performed, either as a shareholder, executive, consultant or director, or close associate of such person.

3. It will be the responsibility of the College employee to declare his interest to his Head of Department, who will ask the Business and Industry Committee to provide for both technical or commercial audit of what is proposed and the Bursar to authorise financial procedures to be applied to the transaction.

4. The Finance Office will require registration of an authorised person to countersign orders and requests for payment on such contracts, as nominated by the Bursar.

5. The Business and Industry Committee may waive these requirements on once-off contracts for sums of less than £5,000. No waiver will be made where more than one transaction arises in any twelve-month period.

6. The existence of these regulations is intended to protect both the College's interest and those researchers who have a legitimate contribution to make through authorised campus companies. The regulations do not relieve individuals of their responsibility to the College which is to clear with the Business and

Industry Committee precise details of any transactions which could be interpreted as giving rise to a conflict of interest which would reflect on the College's good name.

## Appendices: References and Notes

A1. *Frascati Manual*, OECD, Paris.

A2. Y.B. Bannon, J. Corish, O.I. Corrigan, E.J. Geoghan and J.G. Masterson, *Methods for The Treatment of Withdrawal Symptoms Associated with Smoking Cessation and Preparations for Use in Said Method*, US Patent No. 4946853, 1990.

A3. Y.B. Bannon, J. Corish, O.I. Corrigan and J.G. Masterson, *Transdermal Drug Delivery Device*, US Patent No. 5135480, 1992.

A4. The discovery of a new iron-based high-performance permanent magnet based on the compound $Nd_2Fe_{14}B$ was announced in 1983. The breakthrough was made independently by Sumitomo Special Metals Company in Japan and the General Motors Corporation in the USA.

A5. J.M.D. Coey and I.V. Mitchell, "The Concerted European Action on Magnets (CEAM): A Prototype for International Scientific Cooperation?" in *International. J. Technol. Management*, V.J. McBrierty and E.P. O'Neill (eds.), 6(5/6), 1991, pp. 547-556.

A6. J.M.D. Coey and Sun Hong, *Improved Magnetic Materials*, European Patent, 0453270 A2, (1991).

A7. J.M.D. Coey (ed.), *Rare-earth Iron Permanent Magnets*, Clarendon Press, Oxford, 1996, p. x.

A8. P. Horan, A. Jennings, B. Kelly and J. Hegarty, *Applied Optics*, 32, 1311, 1993.

A9. G. O. Sullivan, J. Hegarty and P. Horan, *An Optoelectronic Integrated Circuit*, European Patent Application, No. 95650016.9, 1993.

A10 V.J. McBrierty, J. Magan and W Blau, *Laser Curing of Contact Lens*, US Patent 5,154,861 (1992); Irish Patent 65863 (1995); European Patent 0 447 169 (1995).

# INDEX